SWIFT JUSTICE:
The Story of John F. Morgan and the Last Public Hanging in West Virginia

SWIFT JUSTICE

The Story of John F. Morgan
and the Last Public Hanging in West Virginia

Merrilee Fisher Matheny

quarrier press

Charleston, West Virginia

Quarrier Press
Charleston, WV

Book and cover design: Mark S. Phillips

ISBN 10: 1-942294-12-3
ISBN 13: 978-1-942294-12-2

Library of Congress Control Number: 2019934512

10 9 8 7 6 5 4 3 2 1

Printed in the United States of America

Distributed by:

West Virginia Book Co.
1125 Central Ave.
Charleston, WV 25302
www.wvbookco.com

TABLE OF CONTENTS

ACKNOWLEDGMENTS

Several people have shared this journey with me and their unflagging support and encouragement kept me just guilt-ridden enough to see this project through. I want to thank my friends at the Jackson County Historical Society, particularly Mike Ruben, my first reader, who always celebrated my discoveries, Maxine Landfried, whose research tidbits proved invaluable, and Mike McGrew, who began pursuing John Morgan's story long before I did, and courteously shared his information and photograph collection.

Then there are the descendants of John Morgan and the men and women closely connected to his life and crimes: Stan Hall and Patricia Thaw, who have been extraordinarily generous with their family insights, memories, letters, and photographs; Bobbie Chancey who shared stories and scrapbooks over several delightful meals; Caroll Winter who graciously drove me from one cemetery to another pointing out the graves of those involved, as well as their homes and the original site of the murders; Jo Ann Jones; Joyce Boggess: Vicky King; Dallas Skeen; and also the late John Pfost, the last of Chloe's grandchildren. There are many others who simply wished me well and cheered me on. I am so very grateful to all of them.

I am also grateful for the vision of a young O. J. Morrison who decided there was money to be made writing about John Morgan and the Pfost-Greene murders. Sadly, that's no longer true, but that's not why I did it. And for those members of the Fourth Estate—hometown editor Henry Deem and the nameless journalists who doggedly followed John Morgan's story and refused to let it die until well after he did. Their words endure and more than a century later can be read again in these pages. There is one in particular—that anonymous special correspondent from the New York Sun—whose vibrant writing first fired my imagination when I was a kid and started my obsession to know more. This has all been his fault!

More than anyone I am indebted to my sister, Janice Nelson. Her merciless editing and ruthless reality checks were always painfully on target and her constancy moved me forward each time I stalled. Recalling everything I have to thank her for I am for once utterly speechless.

INTRODUCTION

This is the story of a young man who, despite his hardships, was viewed as having reasonably good character up until the day he went horribly, irrevocably wrong. In the fall of 1897 a series of dramatic events rocked the town of Ripley in Jackson County, West Virginia. A local farmhand named John Morgan murdered three members of the prominent Pfost-Greene family—Chloe Greene, her daughter Matilda Pfost, and her son Jimmy Greene—in a most grisly fashion and did his best to murder another daughter, Alice Pfost. In the speediest execution of justice ever witnessed in the state, he was captured, indicted, tried, and sentenced to hang, all within three days of the murders, despite the frantic efforts of his attorney to mount an insanity defense. Morgan made one confession after the other, each more outrageous than the last, all the while swearing he would never hang. Just weeks before he was to be executed he made a dramatic escape, humiliating local law enforcement officials and leading them on a merry chase, while the citizens of Ripley and the surrounding communities locked their doors in terror.

Jackson County was a hitherto rowdy, backwoods place just starting to gain a toehold in the twentieth century. Its citizens prided themselves on their general decency, industry, budding prosperity, and civilized aspirations. The ill-conceived actions of a young handyman with a hatchet caught them all unaware one fine autumn morning, and though they did their best to assign motive and meaning to the killings and the events that followed, they were largely unsuccessful and were haunted by them for the rest of their lives.

The news coming out of Jackson County attracted the attention of a fascinated nation and held it for weeks. The communal response during the trial and hanging thrust Jackson County and West Virginia into a critical spotlight. At a time when Appalachian culture was being newly discovered and the stereotype of the West Virginia *"hillbilly"* was in the early stages of development, the national press showed the region as barbaric, ignorant, and uncouth, and its citizens were held up for ridicule. The tide of opinion had already begun to turn against public executions, and out-of-state descriptions of the carnival-like atmosphere of Morgan's hanging embarrassed West Virginia lawmakers who vowed it would be the last such spectacle in the state.

A surprising amount of drama took place within a few short weeks during the fall of 1897, but this is not just a story about murder and its aftermath. It is also a story about the deeds of the ancestral past that haunt a man's life, and the seeds of inheritance destined to bear fruit in the future. And it provides an absorbing study of the men and women whose active part in these affairs has been all but forgotten. Their stoicism and courage, their ambitions, flaws, and foibles—the characteristics that determined the course of their lives and the lives of others—are remembered here.

Though no one knows what drove John Morgan to commit murder, several clues remain. Whether he acted alone or, as he himself would later claim, at the instigation of another and with the help of an accomplice, can never be known. There are deep mysteries here—dark secrets and unanswered questions taken to the grave by those few who knew the truth about what happened that November morning. Here in these pages the voices from the past speak for themselves, documented evidence is given, and where it is absent, plausible assumptions are offered. While some of these are new, many were commonly held views at the time, lost as the years went by and newly discovered.

This is a dead man's tale and though it comes as close to the truth as possible, in the end each of us is left to draw his own conclusions.

PROLOGUE

Taking her time, the old woman made her way along the stone walkway toward the house, her apron filled with apples fresh from the new winter cache out in the barn. Shivering slightly, she pulled the apron corners around her bundle with one hand and clutched her woolen shawl tighter across her chest. She was a slight woman, barely five feet in height and rather stout, but she carried herself well for her years and took secret pride in the fact that people thought her to be younger than she was. She had turned 61 last spring. Reaching the hewn rock step-way onto the porch, and feeling anxious of a sudden, she turned and looked behind her.

A weak October sun struggled to burn its way through the morning fog, leaving layers of mist floating in the low places and creating islands of the surrounding knobs and hills. She could hear the baaing of sheep somewhere on the hillside and from the direction of the stable came a soft whicker from one of the horses. Just past the front yard shocks of corn fodder stood beyond the fence line. Still fog-shrouded were the fruit trees and the edges of the woodland with its fading fall brilliance of maple, oak, hickory and beech. She saw it all so clearly in her mind's eye—the yard, the fence rows, the corn fields, the orchard, the pastures and autumn's woodland magic, but in truth it had been some years since she had viewed it all as clearly with her own eyes. She was very nearly blind now—her one concession to the years that claimed their toll—but still she could see well enough to get by.

Standing in front of the porch, peering out with fogged vision onto a landscape where the colors all blurred and ran together, she allowed herself to be comforted by the familiar sounds coming from the hog pen, the soughing of the October wind through the dry corn husks, and the faint murmur of the nearby stream. The drought was past being just worrisome and the creek was nearly dry. She prayed it would rain soon.

Chloe Greene hailed from pioneer stock—her ancestors had made their way from the German Palatinate and across what had once been the further reaches of the western frontier. They had lived with their hands on the plow and their eyes on the forest's edge, alert for the signs that could bring sudden death to those who dropped their guard. She was a mother who had given birth to nine children—all of them in this house—all of whom had lived to adulthood, even her youngest who'd turned eighteen this summer. It was as a mother that Chloe now examined this present worry, for she had learned well enough that a foreboding was something best not ignored. After all, she had buried two husbands, her last one just two years ago (had it really been that long?), and her daughter Serah, lost in another autumn at only 28.

Fall was harder on Chloe these days. It seemed a harbinger for winter's uncertainty—a kind of in-between time that marked the winking out of a lifetime of summer's hopes and dreams in the face of the cold unrelenting onset of death-like sleep. Even now, Chloe felt the cold begin to settle in her bones. She pulled her shawl tighter still, and wondered, not for the first time, if she would ever feel truly warm again. Today was Halloween—All Soul's Eve—and the dead felt so close.

Moving purposefully now, she made to step up onto the porch and for the first time in memory misjudged the distance. Her boot caught the edge of the floorboard and stumbling forward, she grabbed frantically for the porch column. Apples tumbled from her apron's clasp and bounced along the stone step and onto the grass. Shaken, she managed to right herself, only to feel a violent tremor pass through her body.

She stared down at her feet where the apples lay spread out upon the frost as red as blood and whispered, "Someone just walked over my grave."

GRASSLICK, WEST VIRGINIA, FALL 1897

Grasslick, named for the stream that runs through it, is an old pioneer community in Jackson County. It lies between the cities of Parkersburg and Charleston, about eleven miles from the county seat of Ripley. It is here along the choice bottoms of the small tributaries of the Ohio River that the first settlers established their farms and homesteads in the early 1800s.

The pasture fields and ridges bordering the creek were once filled with sheep and cattle and its farmhouses were overflowing with large families, the oldest among them still retaining strong elements of their German culture. The rural settlement was far more populated than it is today—a lifelong resident remarked, "*this creek used to be a-swarmin' with people*",[1]— and neighbors often lived within hailing distance of one another. At one time hogs and sheep outnumbered the human population and the area produced over 15 tons of wool per year. Although there were still plenty of sheep and hogs to be found on Grasslick a half century later, many of the larger farms had turned to raising cattle and horses. As a concession to the changing times, barbed-wire fences had been erected to keep track of the growing herds.

Most of these families were subsistence farmers; they had their own work horses, milk cows, sheep, pigs, and poultry, and raised their own grain for milling. Farmers regularly attended the livestock sales in Ripley, drove flocks of turkeys and herds of cattle into town to the railroad cars or on to Ripley Landing to meet the steamboats, and hauled wagon loads of grain, fruits and vegetables over rough terrain and rutted road beds. It was often an all-day affair for a four-horse team to pull a load into town and then return.

Residents picked up their staples—coffee, sugar, flour, baking powder and spices, along with hard candy and tobacco—either in Ripley or at smaller local stores. Chloe Greene's son, George Pfost, had a mercantile in the nearby community of Fairplain. O. J. Morrison, who wrote the first account of the Pfost-Greene murders, owned another in Kenna. Trading or bartering was common—eggs for cough elixir or other patent remedies, honey for a paper of pins or needles, tobacco for a pistol and a little ammunition. Several young men, like Jimmy Greene, ran trap lines in the fall and winter, and sold mink, muskrat, beaver, fox, and raccoon pelts to local fur traders.

O. J. Morrison, who grew up in nearby Kenna and eventually became the wealthiest retailer in the state, penned the following description of Grasslick: *"…its people in good circumstances, sheltered by comfortable homes, practicing the cardinal virtues, fearing God, giving of their tithes to the church, at peace with each other and with the world."*[2]

This was a little exaggerated. The area had been left exhausted and embittered in the aftermath of the Civil War. The bloody confrontations barely brushed Jackson County, but the fabric of this rural society was ripped apart nonetheless, as neighbor turned against neighbor and hostile fractures appeared along family bloodlines and the fences separating neighboring farms. The surrender at Appomattox did not erase these rifts and while the area escaped wholesale destruction, the men returned home to deal with the ruin wrought by absence and neglect and ruptured friendships. Many communities suffered from the random predations of roving guerilla bands, like the notorious Moccasin Rangers, fragments of which continued as outlaw gangs after the war, and it fell to each property owner to defend his own livestock and family.

The echoes of cannon fire had not yet subsided when land agents, accompanied by a U.S. marshal, arrived on the scene to inform longtime residents of Jackson and neighboring Roane counties that their farms belonged not to them nor their fathers before them, but to the heirs of a long-dead New Yorker no one had ever heard of named Mathias Bruen. Families who had lived on the land for generations were told to get out, unleashing a feud that carried over into the turn of the century. They did not go gently. Vigilantes rode the backroads and there were gunshots in the night. Barns were burned. Murders on both sides of the conflict went unresolved, but not forgotten.

Violence still lay hidden beneath a thin veneer of civilized manners, along with festering resentments—an old argument over a property line, a thoughtless remark or implied criticism, a misunderstanding in a business deal, old battles lost and won—all waiting to erupt.

Chloe Greene's young neighbor, Mary Chancey, bore witness to the aftermath of the Pfost-Greene murders, and later remembered this part of her childhood—and how deeply ingrained were the instincts honed during the last war:

*They would have dances and all the men would all take their guns and stack them in the corner. They'd hear a racket outside and then everybody would take a dive for their gun.*₃

Even now it is not so hard to go back in time—to imagine Grasslick as it was on that cool, crisp fall morning. It is November 3rd, 1897. The stream meanders through eleven miles of rolling farmland, and the Pfost-Greene homestead, a substantial farm of nearly a thousand acres, sits along its mid-point. The creek, a favorite playground for generations of children, carves its banks as it snakes its way across the property, but it is nearly dry now. There has been no rain to speak of since the end of August, and though the woods still show a bit of fall color, their usual grandeur has been muted due to the drought. Distant wildfires have been burning for days, leaving a permanent smoky haze across the far ridgelines, and the Pfost-Greene family, like their neighbors, has been keeping a weather eye and praying for rain.

The twice-widowed 61-year-old Chloe Greene lives here with her three younger children, all of them grown, though the youngest—Jimmy—is barely 18. She raised eight children in this house by her first husband, Marion Pfost, and all but one of them are still living. Jimmy is the only child from her second marriage to Edward Greene, who has been dead nearly two years.

The oldest children are all married with homes and families of their own and Chloe has several grandchildren. Her

Chloe Koontz Pfost Greene

two older daughters, Lelia Jane and Maggie, live near Ripley. The oldest son, George, runs a store in Fairplain. Later on today, he will be part of the mob surrounding John Morgan when he's brought into Ripley, and afterwards people will claim George pulled his gun and threatened to kill him. The middle Pfost son, John, studied medicine at the prestigious College of Physicians and Surgeons in Baltimore. He is now a practicing physician in Spencer some fifty miles away. In a few weeks, he will be watching as a second lynch mob gathers in the streets of his own town after Morgan is taken there following his escape and recapture.

At 35-years-of-age, the youngest Pfost son, Floyd, is an up-and-

Floyd Pfost

coming business entrepreneur and one of the most prominent men in Ripley. He runs the drugstore and serves on West Virginia's State Board of Pharmacists. He is also a partner in the large firm that owns the Ripley Merchandise Company, a sprawling main street department store that is already considered one of the largest in the state with annual sales of over $100,000.[4] He is married to Flora Crow, the daughter of one of the wealthiest men in the county.

Recently, Floyd was elected president of the Bank of Ripley. He remains close to his mother and is in the habit of going home for a week at a time at least twice a year; he has, in fact, just returned to Ripley after his latest visit, and will soon learn that John Morgan had plans to add him to the family's body count.

Sketch of Alice Pfost made after the murders

The youngest Pfost girls—the lovely Alice, just shy of her 29th birthday, and the lively 26-year-old Matilda, are still living at home with their mother and half-brother Jimmy. The newspapers will sensationalize them as *"young girls,"* but they are not.

In an age when most women marry young, both Alice and *"Tillie,"* as she likes to be called, are still single, though popular among their peers. Thanks to industrialization and the prevalence of factory work, many women now have the means and opportunity to make their own way in the world, and a surprising number are deliberately choosing to remain unmarried. The press refers to this vanguard of independent misses as the *New Women,* and they are looked upon with a combination of admiration and disapproval.

Alice and Matilda, both well past the usual age of consent, are quite capable of supporting themselves with proceeds from the farm; Alice, for example, raises and sells her own horses. In many large families, however, there is an unspoken expectation that at least one daughter will remain at home to care for aging parents. Chloe Greene is nearly blind now, and may soon be unable to care for herself. Neither daughter is currently linked to any suitor, though everyone will be quick to point out that not so long ago Alice was courted by the man who will try to kill her. In fact, she and John Morgan had once planned to marry. It is common knowledge that Morgan had been *"infatuated"* with Alice early on, but something or someone, came between them.[5] *"[H]e had been so fully trusted that he became a suitor of Alice Pfost, but from some cause the courtship came to naught."*[6]

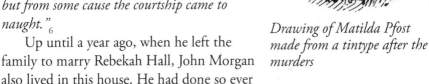

Drawing of Matilda Pfost made from a tintype after the murders

Up until a year ago, when he left the family to marry Rebekah Hall, John Morgan also lived in this house. He had done so ever since Edward and Chloe Greene took him in at the age of sixteen to help with the farm work. The orphaned John didn't like the arrangements at his new home, at least initially, and after three weeks, having stayed the course of the corn harvest and what he considered to be a probationary period, he made plans to move on. He will explain all this in a few weeks and claim that Alice, who is several years older, changed his mind by offering him certain inducements:[7]

When I first went there, went to help finishing shucking corn, I did not like to stay there very well. After the corn husking was completed I intended to leave and one Sunday morning, after I had been there three weeks she [Alice] came out to the well and asked me not to leave; begged of me not to leave, but to stay there for her sake. Naturally that set me to thinking, and she proposed for me to stay there under certain conditions and on those terms and conditions did I stay and none other.

These *"terms and conditions"* are never spelled out, but from comments Morgan made later, it can be speculated that he may have expected to end up with Alice and perhaps some of the Pfost-Greene property as part of a marriage agreement. It is not clear what happened to sever their relationship, though Chloe may well have intervened, as some people claimed. John would have us believe that he moved out of the house six months before his marriage to avoid further contact with Alice, which if accurate would mean that he left several months before Edward Greene died. But he didn't go very far—less than two miles up the road—and he hasn't abandoned the family who once fostered him. Even after his marriage to Rebekah, Morgan has continued to work off and on for the Pfost-Greene family and remains, or so it would seem, on friendly terms.

These days most of the daily work is handled by Jimmy and his half-sisters, with the occasional help of another local farm hand named Ben Anderson. Jimmy feeds the livestock and does most of the milking, while Tillie and Alice divide up the remaining chores: there are eggs to be gathered, butter to churn, meals to prepare, washing and cleaning, ironing and mending—the list goes on and on. Much of the farm work is seasonal—tilling and planting in the spring, hay-making and threshing in mid-summer followed by corn and fruit harvesting. The family finished molasses-making earlier this fall, and peach and apple butter have been put by. The last of the fruits and vegetables have been gathered in and the women are still in the midst of drying them, making preserves, or burying them in their root cellar which is lined with shelves bearing the heavy weight of brine crocks of sauerkraut and pickled beans. Hog-killing will soon commence with the first cold snap, and once the hams and sausage are added to the larder the Pfost-Greene family will be well-provisioned for the coming winter.

Drawing of James Greene made from a tintype after the murders

It is a Wednesday morning and Chloe and her children have awakened well before dawn. Jimmy puts on his jacket and heads out into the dark to put corn out for the hogs. While Chloe tidies up her bedroom, Alice and Tillie light the fire in the sitting room, add wood to the kitchen stove, and start the breakfast preparations. It is business as usual this morning in the Pfost-Greene household with one notable exception. John Morgan has spent the night with the family and has just followed Jimmy outside to the hog pen.

About 400 yards away, past the rows of shocked corn and across the stream, the nearest neighbors, John and Emily Chancey and their children, are waking up as well. The fifty-three-year old veteran of the Union army is in good health, although an old musket ball injury in his knee is aggravated by cold mornings like this. His 20-year-old son Billy has shouldered many of the farm chores and this morning will soon be heading to the barn to feed the livestock and start the milking. At the lower end of the Chancey acreage, John's oldest daughter Leanzia, her new husband Charlie Southall, and his brother Ed, are

Neighbor John Chancey

also beginning to stir. The Chancey's nine-year-old daughter Mary, whose memories of this morning's events will remain vivid even as she reaches centenarian status, has spent the night with her sister.

Mary's father is a handsome, gregarious man. A natural born storyteller, John Chancey has always entertained the neighborhood boys with his Civil War exploits. His run-in with legendary Confederate spy Nancy Hart has been one of their favorite tales. Chancey's 9th Regiment was holding the teenage spitfire prisoner at Summersville when she killed her guard and escaped, only to return with 200 Moccasin Rangers riding in her wake. His company was caught flat-footed and nearly all were taken prisoner in a raid led by Hart. Though no doubt humiliating at the time, this man knows how to entertain his audience and has transformed it all into a grand adventure. His young admirers, including the Pfost-Greene boys, John Morgan and the Southall brothers, have gathered on his front porch for years. John Chancey's warm acceptance and fatherly advice have been very important to these young men, many of whom have grown up without fathers of their own.

John Chancey, his son Billy, and the Southall brothers will be the first to find trouble at the Pfost-Greene farm this morning. In a few minutes the man who charged headlong into a hail of bullets at the Battle of Cloyd's Mountain will grab his Winchester and rush through the dark into yet another hell.

Less than two miles up the road, just above the little Ephesus Baptist Church, a woman has been tossing and turning throughout the night. Rebekah Hall Morgan is a worried woman. Her husband promised to be home by 9 o'clock last night, but like so many of his promises lately, this one has been broken. His side of the bed is cold and empty. She loves him. She knew when she married him that they would have little to start out with, but John was no stranger to hard work and she never doubted they would get along. Rebekah now worries about making ends meet and making meals out of next to nothing. Most of all she worries about this man who is increasingly becoming a stranger to her. Something terrible is happening and she has been helpless to change it.

Portrait of Rebekah Hall Morgan and son Albert courtesy of the family. This portrait was taken after the murders and given to John to keep in his cell.

Now nine-month-old Albert is beginning to fret. He is no doubt wet and probably hungry. And so his mother, exhausted from work and her own fretting, turns her attention toward her child and another lonely round of houschold tasks, hoping John will soon return. But there will be no relief when he comes home to her, for news of death and destruction will follow close behind.

Next door at the Jim Fisher residence the woman John Morgan calls "*Granny Fisher*" is still abed, unconscious of the nightmare that awaits her. Suzanna Koontz Fisher, Chloe Greene's 80-year-old mother, will not survive the coming winter or the darkness that is about to descend upon the lowlands this autumn morning. She will die just three months after the slaughter of her daughter and grandchildren. One month from now her son Jim will encounter the fugitive killer of his half-sister Chloe riding toward him out of the rain and darkness on the road to Walton.

The current sheriff of Jackson County lives on the left bank of Grasslick, just a few farms above the Pfost-Greene property. James Owen Shinn is the second son in a local political dynasty, one of the oldest and most influential families in the state. Owen shares his large cattle farm with his brother Reuben, known locally by his nickname "*Dug*" (often misspelled *Doug* in the press). Reuben also serves as his deputy.

The past few months have been difficult for the new sheriff and his brother. Their father, the Honorable George W., a large-scale cattleman and former member of the House of Delegates, lived just long enough to see his son pin on the badge. He died three months ago, leaving Owen and his brothers to shoulder the responsibilities of their father's business enterprises as well as their own. Little did Sheriff Shinn imagine on the day he buried his father that even darker days were in the offing. Within hours he will be dealing with the grisly deaths of his neighbors and facing an angry lynch mob.

Sheriff James Owen Shinn

Within weeks he will be riding night and day through sleet and torrential rain, heartsick and miserable and praying to pick up the trail of the triple killer who escaped on his watch. In a little over a month he will be required to ignore his own misgivings and follow duty up the steps of the gallows. And before an audience of thousands, he deliberately will put his neighbor to death.

But the sheriff isn't home this morning. Circuit court is in session in Ripley and Shinn has spent the night in town. When Billy Chancey gallops up to his door this morning to deliver the awful news it will be left to his brother Reuben to secure the crime scene and organize the initial manhunt.

Dr. John Bechtel, a local physician, lives near the Shinn brothers. He has been Chloe Greene's doctor for several decades, delivering her children, tending her family's illnesses and injuries, and succoring both husbands on their deathbeds. Soon now he will be called upon to make his final house call to the Pfost-Greene farm, this time in his role as the county medical examiner.

It is shortly after five in the morning—and for these next few moments the quiet darkness remains a comforting place. The inhabitants of Grasslick begin their day as they always do with murmured greetings, soft barn sounds, and the smell of hay, wood smoke and baking bread. Later on, in the weeks after Morgan's murderous rampage, O. J. Morrison will recall Grasslick as an *"ideal spot, an Acadia in its rural simplicity and innocent happiness."* [8]

But any innocence lingering here will be lost before the sun rises.

End Notes

[1] *Goldenseal Magazine,* Spring 1990.

[2] Morrison, O. J., *The Slaughter of the Pfost-Greene Family of Jackson County, W.Va. A History of the Tragedy*, 1897.

[3] *Jackson Star News,* Ripley, WV 27 February 1999. Interview with Mary Chancey.

[4] *Smith's Index,* Parkersburg, WV, 27 November, 1893.

[5] *Evening Bulletin,* Maysville, KY, 4 December, 1897.

[6] *Jackson Herald,* Ripley, WV, 17 December, 1897

[7] *Morgantown Post*, Morgantown, WV, 17 December, 1897.

[8] Morrison.

A MAN OF SENSE AND COOL-HEADEDNESS

Had there been no witness, John Morgan might never have been suspected of perpetrating the slaughter at the Pfost-Greene homestead. He had outgrown his hardscrabble youth and the stigma of his parentage had faded over time, though it was well known that his biological father had killed the man whose surname he carried. More than two decades after Clement Morgan, a self-styled preacher of the gospel, was cut down in cold blood by Andy Raines, Andy's son John had managed to garner respect from those who knew him.

He may have been gratified to read that a surprising number of local folks had good things to say about their homegrown ax-murderer. Many believed him to be conscientious in nature and scrupulously honest.[1] Even Wilson Slaughter, one of the deputies who served on Morgan's death watch, later said that he had known him all his life and always held him in high esteem.[2] Despite the prominence of the murdered Pfost-Greenes and the horrific nature of their demise, some people would stand by Morgan until the end, making last ditch efforts to sway the governor toward clemency. No one believed him to be innocent, but that didn't mean they wanted to see him hang.

Morgan was known to be an accomplished woodsman with *"splendid knowledge"* of the surrounding countryside in several counties, so much so that when he later made his remarkable escape from the jail no one really expected him to be found again.[3] He had a reputation as a daredevil with a temper to match, and could curse a blue streak at the drop of a hat. But he also had a keen sense of humor. Sadly, much of his *"playing the fool"* was recognized by those who knew him best as a rather desperate bid for attention.[4] He was, after all, a man of few successes, and eager to win approbation at any cost.

Physical descriptions penned by the press ran the gamut from the outright derogatory to the surprisingly complimentary. Although the pseudo science of phrenology had fallen out of favor in the legitimate medical community by the late 1800s, the head-reading craze remained a highly fashionable topic. Darwin's publication of *The Origin of the Species* gave the study of facial characteristics and the bumps and ridges of the skull a resurgence of popularity, and even in a provincial town like Ripley,

Portrait of John Morgan courtesy of his family. This was taken during his incarceration and he is wearing the new suit given to him by O. J. Morrison to wear to his hanging and an Elgin pocket watch, a gift from Rebekah, which remains in the Hall family today. O.J. Morrison sold a cropped version of this as souvenirs on the day of the hanging and used it in his murder pamphlet.

there was a well-attended phrenology society.[5] In those days any literate person understood the importance of a man's physiognomy since it was often used for a multitude of assessments—everything from his suitability for employment or marriage to his criminal propensities.

It was generally thought that the criminal element differed from the law-abiding public in that they were either smaller and lighter of build, or bigger and burlier. Alienists, the acknowledged experts on the subject, insisted that criminals had low sloping foreheads, large deep-set eyes, beaked or flat noses, pointed chins and high cheekbones. They also attested that, the *"perfect villain has a smooth face with absolutely calm and passionless features.*[6] All these attributes were ascribed to Morgan. A born criminal should look the part and it was the journalists' job to make it so.

[Morgan] is a small man, weighing not over 125 pounds, sharp featured, with a long hooked nose, large blue eyes and low forehead.[7]

The fact that Morgan's photograph shows us a man with a high forehead and a rather straight nose is beside the fact. Readers expected their *"arch fiends"* to conform and the press tried hard not to disappoint, though some found it more difficult than expected.

A reporter from the *Clarksburg Telegram* broke ranks and seemed particularly struck by this *"strong, healthy farmhand"* who was *"intelligent looking"* with a *"rugged appearance"* and *"rather handsome."* His *"large eyes were luminous"* and his voice was *"soft, emotional and tender... He looked not over twenty-two years of age and appeared not the low, depraved wretch, the butcherous murderer that he was."*[8]

And Henry Deem, the local editor, went out of his way to inform his readers that John simply didn't fit the mold:[9]

Those with an impression that John Morgan was of burly and brutal appearance and a dwarfish intellect have never known him, or having known him, judged him hastily. He was of a face not wholly unprepossessing, not of rude mien, he was deliberate in speech and possessed of a vice not in the least indicative of a criminal...Men who had been acquainted with him all his life were wholly unprepared for the news of the tragedies of Nov 3rd.

In his subsequent interviews with O. J. Morrison, Morgan recalled that after the death of his mother he had been left to wander *"from place to place, staying from three to twelve months at a place, until about the year 1891."* [10] Information passed down to Morgan's great grandson suggests that he was living rough during this time and on more than one occasion was completely homeless. His Raines' grandparents had already moved west, taking John's older siblings with them, and though his younger sisters found foster homes, John seems to have been either unwanted or prone to running away. He would not find a stable home environment until he moved in with the Pfost-Greene family at the age of 16. Even then, he said he would not have stayed had it not been for Alice Pfost.

Ultimately, he left the Pfost-Greene household, and on February 27, 1896, a little more than a year before the murders, he married Rebekah Catherine Hall. Their marriage took place at the home of the bride's parents on Poverty Ridge, just outside of Fairplain. On the marriage certificate John has listed his age as 23 and Rebekah's age is entered as 24. Rebecca's age is inaccurate, and John's may be as well. She was born in 1866, and was probably more than a decade older than John. Large-boned and above average height, she was also taller than her husband. While not conventionally pretty, she was a handsome olive-skinned woman who retained her striking looks well into old age. Family descendants report that she was also well educated for the time, having attended at least a year or two of college. Rebekah's role should not be underestimated in the story of John Morgan. She was an impressive woman, and by all accounts, someone to be reckoned with.

The day he sentenced John Morgan to hang, Reese Blizzard, the presiding judge, was so taken by Rebekah, and so moved by her plight and obvious devotion to her husband, that he directed these remarks to the defendant: [11]

In this moment you should be very grateful to that wife, who has clung to you, stayed by you through this trying ordeal; it would not have required more courage for that woman to have faced a lion's den than to have faced the public feeling caused in this matter; she has honorably done so, and it is one more monument to the character of noble womanhood...

The story goes that when Morgan left the family to marry Rebekah, Chloe helped the couple set up housekeeping not far from her farm in a little house belonging to one of her late husband's relations, John Washington Greene. It is likely that the newlyweds either rented outright or had a caretaking agreement in return for their use of the property. Just how much help Chloe gave them is a matter of conjecture, but it was widely acknowledged that she gave John a horse around the time of his marriage.

Rebekah's cousin would later write that when John took his leave of the Pfost-Greene family, *"he was given an old suit of clothing that belonged to the boy he was later accused of murdering and an old broken down horse."* [12] The old horse plodded into the limelight more than a year later when an overly optimistic Morgan decided to trade it for two younger horses and a promissory note. The mounting pressure associated with this financial obligation was believed by many to have contributed to Morgan's decision to destroy the family.

Rebekah was an older, nurturing woman and Morgan was, if nothing else, a man in need of mothering. She obviously found something in the unfortunate, ill-fated young man to love and admire, and there can be no doubt that Rebekah was cherished in return. The early days of their marriage seemed to go well. John worked hard at home and continued to hire himself out to the neighboring farms, including the Pfost-Greene's.

Photo of the Morgan home. The house still stands, although it has undergone considerable alteration.

He worked away most days, but always came home to Rebekah. For the first time in his life he was the center of someone's world. Rebekah was soon pregnant and Albert Thorn Morgan was born on February 5, 1897, just before their first anniversary.

One of John's teachers, George Thomas, spoke of his former pupil as, *"a boy of good behavior, excellent sense and not without promise."* [13] This does not sound like the same boy whose mother, as one relative claimed, lamented that, *"the hemp has grown to hang that boy."*[14] But while John Morgan was a hard worker, the truth was that he had little enough to show for his initial efforts in his role of breadwinner, and he'd recently become the subject of neighborhood gossip about his inability to adequately provide for his family. Supposedly he'd even overheard the Pfost-Greene women criticizing the way his wife and son were dressed, which further weakened his already fragile ego and self-esteem.

Inevitably, there were those eager to provide the news hounds with evidence of Morgan's depravity. There was an allegation of extreme cruelty to a hog as well as the story of a younger Morgan deliberately inflicting horrific injuries on another child.[15,16] This last assertion was resurrected a few decades ago in a hand-written account by an elderly woman who claimed to have heard the story when she was a young girl. She described an event very like the earlier newspaper account, although in her version the names of the injured child and her family, as well as the circumstances, are different. When the dates and ages of the children are compared, John Morgan would have been a mere toddler at the time.

The editor of the local paper described Morgan as *"a man of sense and cool-headedness,"* which does not sound like a man given to excess in the treatment of livestock, despite the fact that he was known to have a temper.[17] Only these two odd accounts of aggressive, unsettling behaviors, both offered by the same informant, were reported at the time. It is true, however, that in the months leading up to the murders, Morgan's behavior had become so erratic that Rebekah asked neighbors for help. John himself, in his interview with O. J. Morrison, admitted that he had not lived a life of Christian virtue. He referred to his wife's worries on his behalf, saying, *"she had talked to me time and time again about my soul's salvation."*[18] Still, it is a long stretch from cursing and cutting up rough, to cold-blooded murder.

It is doubtful that such stories of aberrant behaviors had been circulating in the community since Morgan's youth. Surely, if he had been labeled a devil-child early on, his neighbors would have had a lot more to say about it afterwards. Would the Greene family have brought a boy with this history into their midst to tend their valuable livestock and share a room with the impressionable Jimmy, who was only twelve at the time? Would John Morgan, as was widely reported, have been *"so fully trusted that he became a suitor of Alice Pfost?"* Would a level-headed man like

John Chancey have allowed a young degenerate to tend his own children and rock them to sleep? And would an intelligent, respectable woman like Rebekah Hall, a mature 30-year-old, have married him, even if she thought it was her last chance for a family?

Most of what was written about Morgan referenced his *"cool"* and *"careless"* demeanor during the trial, and his exceptional *"courage", "grit"* and *"nerve"* on the scaffold, and yet this same man completely unraveled just hours before his death, flinging himself weeping onto his cell cot when forced to take his final leave of his wife and child.

Baby Albert was barely nine months old when he first appeared in court at the murder trial, and he spoke his first word —*"Papa"*— just days before his father climbed the gallows.[19]

End Notes

[1] *Jackson Herald*, 17 December, 1897.

[2] *Ibid.*

[3] *Ibid.*

[4] *Ibid.*

[5] *Journal of Clinton Wolfe*, Jackson County Historical Society.

[6] Millon, Theodore; Eric Simonsen, Morten Birket-Smith, Roger Davis. Eds. "Historical Conceptions of Psychopathy in the United States and Europe," *Psychopathy: Antisocial, Criminal and Violent Behavior.* Guilford Press, 2003. p. 7.

[7] *Cincinnati Enquirer,* Cincinnati, OH, 6 November, 1897.

[8] *Clarksburg Telegram,* Clarksburg, WV, 24 December, 1897.

[9] *Jackson Herald,* 17 December, 1897.

[10] Morrison, O. J., *The Slaughter of the Pfost-Greene Family of Jackson County, W.Va. A History of the Tragedy,* 1897.

[11] Morrison.

[12] Letter written to John Morgan's granddaughter, Phyllis Hall Thaxton, on 21 October, 1986 by a cousin, Pearl Kessinger of Murrayville, WV.

[13] *Jackson Herald.*

[14] *Ibid.*

[15] Hand-written statement found in the Jackson County Historical Society records, signed by Delia Ernestine Casto Merical in 1993.

[16] *Jackson Herald.*

[17] *Ibid.*

[18] Morrison.

[19] *Jackson Herald.*

A FRACTURED FAMILY

During the jury selection, to help determine whether a particular Casto candidate might be directly related to him, John Morgan was asked where he was born. He responded by saying, *"I was born up there somewhere about Gay; I was small when my mother left me."*[1] In those days, blood relationship was determined, not only by surname, but by which part of the country a man was born in. By extension this helped identify his forebears in terms of the earliest pioneer settlements since entire family clans tended to migrate together, moving westward along the old wagon trails. John Morgan descended from solid pioneer stock whose roots ran deep, but a series of ill-fated and reckless decisions on the part of his parents loosened those foundations and set him adrift at an early age.

John's mother, Louisa Rollins, came from a large family of ten born to John and Mary Kauffman Rollins. Her grandfather, Elijah Rollins Jr, was one of the area's foremost Methodist preachers and his name appears on many of the early marriage certificates. Elijah's marriage to Lucretia Casto, who sprang from one of the prolific patriarchs heralding the great Casto invasion in those early days, united the two family trees and from that point on the branches of the Casto family tree and that of John Morgan frequently intertwined. Louisa Rollins was 18 years old when she married 17-year-old Andrew Mainard Raines on August 11, 1864, and the die was cast.

Andrew Raines was born to Abraham Raines and Lucinda Gandee in Roane County in 1847, in what was still western Virginia, and he grew up with his siblings on Flat Fork. His mother Lucinda was the offspring of one of the very earliest settlers in the area—Uriah Gandee, founder of Gandeeville. Lucinda's mother was Mercy *"Massie"* Hughes, the daughter of that infamous old Indian scout, Jesse Hughes, making Andrew Jesse's great-grandson.

Jesse Hughes remains a controversial figure in West Virginia history, but as the probable 2nd great-grandfather of John Morgan, his genetic legacy is intriguing and deserves further scrutiny. He was famously predatory and his psychological bent was a decidedly feral one.[2] Fortunately for him, he was born into a time and place where his unusual traits and savage predilections garnered him legendary notoriety as a border scout and protector of the settlements rather than as a cold-blooded sadistic serial killer. He was known to be *"profane and desperately wicked,"* and in a time when domestic violence was anything but rare, Jesse's harsh maltreatment of his family stood out.[3] As one of his acquaintances remarked, Jesse's temperament was *"not conducive to domestic happiness."*[4]

Hughes had no scruples about crossing the line between defense and preservation, and gratuitous brutality, torture, and atrocity. One 19th century historian gives Jesse his due, calling him one of the most successful Indian fighters of his day, yet he does not turn a blind eye to Jesse's more unsavory proclivities: *"Hughes was a noted border scout, but a man of fierce, unbridled passions, and so confirmed an Indian hater that no tribesman, however peaceful his record, was safe in his presence."*[5]

Still, it is perhaps naïve to remove a man like Jesse Hughes from his historical context and attempt to measure him by today's standards. To do so risks painting him as the sadistic sociopath some have labeled him. The truth is far more complicated. These were harsh times calling for harsh measures and while the methods employed might be arguable, without men the tenor of Hughes, most of our ancestors would have remained safely east of the Alleghenies or died at the hands of the original inhabitants.

Hughes lived to see old age and the end of border warfare, neither of which he welcomed. Restless and discontented, he moved his family from place to place in a vain attempt to outrun civilization before returning to what is now Jackson County. His daughter Massie also lived a long life, dying in 1883 just fifteen years before the Pfost-Greene murders. She may never have met her great-grandson, John Morgan, but she lived long enough to experience the shock waves of another murder closer to home— this one committed by his father, grandson Andy Raines, and perhaps even then she might have wondered if the sins of her father might live on in his descendants.

Louisa Rollins Raines had five children during her 13-year marriage to Andy Raines, and it is likely that most of them, even John Morgan, were fathered by him. In 1870, Louisa and Andrew Raines were living with their oldest children on a farm somewhere near Gay. Andy was working as a hired hand on neighboring farms until, as some accounts have it, the couple received an offer to move in with one of their neighbors—Clement Morgan, a local reverend, who went by the name of Clem. Some say that John Morgan was already born by this time, others say not until afterward, but either way it was after this association with Clem Morgan that all the trouble started, leading ultimately to murder and the destruction of two families, and setting the stage for later questions about John Morgan's paternity.

Clem Morgan hailed from a line of notable preachers of the gospel and in fact could trace his linage back to the famous founder of the state's first settlement, a Welshman by the name of Colonel Morgan ap Morgan (*"ap"* meaning *"son of."*) He was the son of a flour mill owner—the youngest of thirteen—and when Andrew and Louisa Raines first encountered him, he was in his early 30s, recently divorced, and caring for three young sons all on his own. It was later said that his wife left him because of his philandering ways.[6]

According to some accounts, Clem arranged for Louisa and her husband to move in with him to help with the chores and care for his children,[7,8] and there is some indication that either before or after the offer was made Louisa and Clem became romantically involved. Timelines, birthdates, and local gossip have become so entangled that it is impossible to determine when John was born in relation to this move or who his father was, although the evidence still points to Andy. A cousin claimed that Louisa knew him to be a Raines, despite her having told her husband that John was Clem's son.[9] What is certain is that Andy became increasingly jealous as his suspicions grew, and he threatened Clem Morgan on several occasions.

Yet there is more to this story than possible infidelity. Andy Raines was held in general contempt by his neighbors because of his cruel nature and his well-known abuse of his family and his animals.[10] A neighbor, Henry Evans, recalled that around the time John was born, Raines owned a pair of hunting hounds which he kept in a state of semi-starvation. According to Evans, Raines regularly choked them to the point of unconsciousness, *"Just so, as he expressed it, he could watch them come to."*[11] His neighbors disdainfully referred to him as a *"man of violent temper"*[12] and a *"wife beater"*[13], and it does not stretch the imagination to see how this type of behavior might have led Louisa to view the older Morgan as her protector.

Most of the information about this tragic triangle comes from newspaper reports at the time of Clem Morgan's murder, and the *like-father, like-son* references following the Pfost-Greene murders. The most credible account comes from the same Henry Evans, Clem Morgan's friend and neighbor. He provided a very different version of how Louisa ended up living in Morgan's home and affirmed that there was never any doubt about Andy Raines being the boy's father.[14]

Henry claimed that he and Clem Morgan, along with Henry's father Stephen, were out shocking oats one afternoon when the hotheaded Raines showed up and tried to shoot Morgan. The elder Evans got between the two to prevent further violence and Raines threatened him as well. The Reverend John Greenleaf, a local justice of the peace, was called in to settle the dispute and, according to Evans, Clem agreed that if Andy would stop trying to kill him, he wouldn't press charges. On the face of it this seems oddly magnanimous and one wonders if the Reverend Greenleaf felt that Andy had been unduly provoked. For his part, Andy is said to have reluctantly skulked off to Nicholas County where he worked for a time as a lumberjack, leaving his wife and children to fend for themselves.[15]

As Evans tells it, things were quiet until Raines unexpectedly resurfaced one day when the men were making molasses and asked to speak with Clem in private. *"He wants me to take his wife and care for her,"* Morgan informed Evans afterwards, to which Evans responded, *"Clem, for God's sake don't do that. Raines will kill you."*[16] According to Evans, Andy actually brought Louisa to Clem's house and handed her off, presumably with their children. Evans was certain that this event occurred sometime after the birth of their fourth child, Ida, in 1872 and that their son John had been born the year before that. While this coincides with Morgan's own statement about his birth year, it does not tally with his claim of being 22 years old at the time of the murders.[17] If he was, as was later claimed, 16 in 1891 when he first went to live with the Pfost-Greene family, his birth year would have most likely been 1873.

Raines left the area once again, but sometime before May 21, 1875, he returned home intent upon revenge. Most of the accounts written after the Pfost-Greene murders claimed that Clem Morgan was out cutting briars in his fields when he was ambushed and gunned down by Raines, but again Henry Evans recalled it differently.[18] He said that on May 21st, 25-year-old Andy borrowed a shot-gun from his mother, telling her he was going to ask a neighbor for work and promising that on the way home he would shoot some squirrels for their supper. Instead he loaded both barrels and headed straight for Clem Morgan's. He found Clem and Louisa busy sorting potatoes with the children playing nearby. Raines pointed the gun at Morgan and told him he'd come to kill him. Morgan supposedly retorted, *"You're too damned a coward!"* And Andy pulled the trigger.[19]

In those days if a man killed his rival in the heat of passion because the other man was trying to steal his wife, he had a fair chance of beating the rap. Raines' approach demonstrated a cold-blooded mindset that did not sit well with the authorities—the *Jackson Democrat* referred to the murder as a "*Cowardly Assassination*"—and this time there would be no out-of-court settlement.[20] Raines took to his heels with the law in hot pursuit and lived as an outlaw in the wilds of Nicholas County for the next two years. There were later claims that he had in fact been captured following the murder, but managed to escape.

And what of Louisa during this entire ordeal? Was she culpable in setting one man against the other? Death has a way of distilling men's characters into succinct epitaphs and for Andrew Raines this became "*wife beater.*" After the Pfost-Greene murders, the press took great pains to point out that "*like begats like*," recalling Andy's vicious temper and propensity for brutality, domestic and otherwise.[21] One can easily see how the older Morgan might have felt compelled to thwart such behavior, particularly if Louisa and her children were in obvious need of a champion, and how quickly Louisa, in turn, might have gravitated toward any kindness shown her. It is difficult to view John Morgan's mother as anything but victimized and with the death of her benefactor, Louisa and her children were once again left to survive on their own.

The deadly outcome of this tragic affair came as no surprise to anyone. U.S. Marshal Dan Cunningham wrote in his memoirs that sometime in 1877 Andrew Raines was tracked to a farm near Summersville and Jackson County officials sent a warrant for his arrest.[22] A local peace officer named Flem Rader discovered the fugitive sitting in an apple tree waiting for deer to approach a salt lick. When Rader ordered him to surrender, Andy raised his rifle. Rader fired first and Raines fell from the tree.

Meanwhile, Louisa gave birth to her fifth child, a daughter named Florence, who though she carried Morgan's name throughout her life, could not possibly have been his. Nor was she likely to have been Andy's.

It is unclear at what point the five children were divided up. Either after Andy's initial abandonment of his family or the murder of Clem Morgan, the paternal grandparents stepped in and took the older two, William and Melissa, leaving John and his two younger sisters with their mother. Then sometime after the 1880 census Abraham and Lucinda Raines picked up stakes and, like their parents before them, began moving the family westwards, ultimately settling in Wadena County, Minnesota.

By the time Andy was killed, Louisa was living in poverty and struggling to raise her remaining three children. She could not afford to let the grass grow under her feet in her newly attained legitimacy as a widow and as fate would have it, waiting in the wings was a well-established suitor who was more than twice her age and newly widowed himself.

On Nov 22, 1877, just a few months after Flem Rader shot her husband out of the apple tree and six months after the birth of Florence, Louisa married well-to-do farmer Joshua Parsons. Louisa and her children moved into his home on Grasslick, just 2 ½ miles from newly wedded Edward Greene and Chloe Koontz Pfost. Like Joshua Parsons, Edward Greene was also recently widowed and he also took a much younger wife, the widow of his friend Marion Pfost, and moved into her home.

At the time of his marriage to Louisa, Joshua and his three sons made up a bachelor's household. There were a great many emotional adjustments for this blended family to make and neither time nor tolerance was allotted for difficult transitions in those days. Louisa and her children had suffered untold trauma. Joshua had recently buried his third wife, along with his three youngest children following the outbreak of some terrible contagion. How welcome were the Raines children in this household? Who knows how well the son of a murderer fared at the hands of an elderly step-father who no doubt had little patience with youthful folly and exuberance. At least one family informant claimed that Parsons *"was mean to him."*[23]

Louisa lived only seven years following her second marriage, dying in 1884 at the age of 38, and leaving her three youngest children orphaned. John related to his erstwhile biographer, O. J. Morrison, that *"I was small when my mother left me,"* though because of birth date discrepancies, it is uncertain how old he actually was at the time. But notice that he says, *"when my mother **left** me,"* not when she *died,* but when she *left* him, since from his childhood perspective he had, in fact, been abandoned. It is not hard to imagine the traumatic impact a mother's death might have on a child followed by the harsh reality that neither the Raines nor the Rollins families, nor the Parsons, nor even the Morgans for that matter, would make room in their hearts or their homes for him. No one did for any length of time it seems, until Chloe and Edward Greene took him in when he was about 16 years old.

Morgan recalled that he was left to wander *"from place to place, staying from three to twelve months at a place, until about the year 1891."*[24] The fate of the orphaned John Morgan and his siblings wasn't all that unusual

for the times. Raising a large family in those days was often less a matter
of nurturing than of practicality and basic survival. Disease, injury,
and childbirth could render bevies of children fatherless or motherless
overnight, and if relatives were not on hand to take responsibility, someone
else in the community usually volunteered. This did not always mean they
were given much more than a roof over their head and enough food to eat.

Much has been made of John Morgan killing his *"foster family"* who
ostensibly took him in and treated him *"like as son,"*[25] but regardless of
his treatment, John Morgan was known to be a *"bound boy,"*[26] an orphan
placed with one family after another to work as a servant in return for
food, clothing, shelter, and a public education until he reached the age
of 21. Many such boys were exposed to maltreatment and long grueling
hours of manual labor, and they often became runaways, which may
explain John's unstable home life up until the time he was taken in by the
Greenes.

John Morgan, in a written confession included with a petition for
clemency sent by his attorney to Governor Atkinson, had this to say about
his own paternity:[27]

*I was born on the 7th of May, 1871, near what is now called Gay Post
Office in Jackson County, West Virginia…My mother married Andy Marion
Raines, and whether I am his son or a son of one Clem Morgan, I do not know.
I have always went by the name of Morgan.*

In fact at the time of the 1880 census, the three younger children
were still going by the surname Raines when they were living with Joshua
Parsons. Shortly afterwards, John and Florence started going by Morgan,
while Ida retained the Raines name. Though John Morgan may have
claimed he had no idea who his father was, the information he gave
Morrison during his interviews suggests that he believed himself to be
the son of Andy Raines.[28] This was also the common belief held within
John's community, because when people spoke of John Morgan after the
murders, they were quick to include *"alias Raines"* after his name or point
out that he was *"really a Raines."* Surely they would not have done so if
they harbored any doubts that he might have been the bastard son of
Clement Morgan. After the hanging, the editor of the *Jackson Herald* took
pains to clarify the matter:[29]

*Though bearing the name of Morgan, there can be no doubt that
the subject of today's execution was the son of Andy Marion Raines, who*

transmitted to his offspring his brutal instincts and propensities to take human life.

And the *Nicholas Chronicle* followed suit:[30]

Morgan, alias Raines, is the son of Andy Marion Raines, who came from Jackson to Nicholas Co many years ago and was killed while being arrested for murder.

Even the Raines' old neighbor, Henry Evans went on record regarding John's paternity:[31] *"I had no reason to believe at his birth that he was a Morgan, and since he has become a man his looks show him a Raines."*

John's first cousin Benjamin Raines whose information about John was passed down to his son, supplied another genetic marker when he remarked that John Morgan possessed what the family referred to as *"the Raines temper, a curse we all, even today, have to watch closely."*[32]

The following may be nothing more than a fabrication as John's reputation was partially demonized to make sense of his horrific actions, but if true, John's mother Louisa may have had the final word on the subject. Mrs. Francis Casto, one of the numerous Casto relations, recollected that Louisa frequently complained to her that, *"the hemp has grown to hang that boy."* To this prophetic comment, Mrs. Casto replied, *"Louisa, there is plenty of hickories, why don't you whip it out of him."* And then came Louisa's sorrowful rejoinder, *"Ah, what is bred in the bones cannot be beat out of the flesh."*[33]

But something more was at work in John Morgan's genetic legacy which may have contributed to his downfall—something that, no matter how hard he tried, he could not overcome. Although he did not live long enough for a definitive diagnosis, John Morgan without a doubt passed down the hereditary disease which his son Albert would later die from—Huntington's Disease—then known as *Huntington's chorea.* Today, HD remains a devastating diagnosis; its debilitating progression is incurable with no effective treatment.

Research indicates that in some families there is a preponderance of psychotic symptoms, some of which may signal the initial onset of the disease.[34] It has also been suggested that in these families, the HD gene may act to either unmask latent psychosis or predispose these individuals to develop such mental disorders.[35] Early onset can present with symptoms of cognitive decline, including disordered thought processes, speech, and behavior, sometimes leading to full-blown psychosis, and it always carries its own death sentence.

Morgan's son Albert died of Huntington's in the West Virginia State Hospital for the Insane in Spencer in 1942. William, John Morgan's older brother, died the year before in the Eastern State Hospital for the Insane in Pendleton, Oregon, though no cause of death is listed. There is no clear trail to indicate which of John's parents might have been the carrier.

End Notes

[1] Morrison, O. J., *The Slaughter of the Pfost-Greene Family of Jackson County, W.Va. A History of the Tragedy*, 1897.

[2] McWhorter, Lucullus, *The Border Settlers of Northwestern Virginia From 1768 to 1795: Embracing the Life of Jesse Hughes and Other Noted Scouts of the Great Woods of the Trans-Allegheny.* Hamilton, Ontario: Republican Publishing Co, 1915, p. 33-35.

[3] McWorter, p. 65.

[4] *Ibid.*

[5] Withers, Alexander Scott. *Chronicles of Border Warfare,* Cincinnati: Robert Clarke Co, 1895, online edition by Project Gutenberg, p. 137.

[6] Letter written to John Morgan's granddaughter, Phyllis Hall Thaxton, on 21 October, 1986 by a cousin, Pearl Kessinger of Murrayville, WV.

[7] Morrison.

[8] *Jackson Herald*, Ripley, WV, 17 December, 1897.

[9] Kessinger letter.

[10] *Jackson Herald.*

[11] *Ibid.*

[12] *Cincinnati Enquirer,* Cincinnati, OH, 04 November, 1897.

[13] *Jackson Herald.*

[14] *Ibid.*

[15] Kessinger letter.

[16] *Jackson Herald*

[17] Author's note: It is difficult to pinpoint Morgan's actual age. In both his interview with O. J. Morrison and his petition to the governor, John gives May 7, 1871 as his birth date which corresponds with Evan's report here. But in the same interview he told Morrison that he was 22 years old when he should have been 26. To muddy the water further, John listed his age as 23 on his marriage certificate that would have meant he was born in 1873. It was also generally held that he came to live with the Pfost-Greene family in 1891 at the age of 16, making his birth year 1875, the year of Clem Morgan's murder, which tallies with later reports that he was a babe in arms at the time.

[18] *Jackson Herald.*

[19] *Ibid.*

[20] *Jackson Democrat,* April 29, 1875 as referenced in the *Jackson Herald,* 10 December, 1997.

[21] *Jackson Herald.*

[22] Cunningham, Daniel W. *Memoirs of Daniel W. Cunningham: The Criminal History of Roane and Jackson Counties, West Virginia.* 1928. Located in the West Virginia Archives.

[23] Kessinger letter.

[24] Morrison.

[25] *Ibid.*

[26] Kessinger letter.

[27] *Jackson Herald.*

[28] Morrison.

[29] *Jackson Herald,* 17 December, 1897.

[30] *Nicholas Chronicle,* Summersville, WV, 19 November, 1987.

[31] *Jackson Herald,* 17 December, 1897

[32] Interview with Carlton Raines by Greg Matics, ***Ripley Star News*** 1993, undated

[33] *Jackson Herald,* 17 December, 1897.

[34] Tsuang, Debby, et. al. "Familial Aggregation of Psychotic Symptoms in Huntington's Disease," *American Journal of Psychiatry,* 157:12, December 2000.

[35] *Ibid.*

STRANGE SPELLS AND AN UNSETTLED MIND

More than a century after the crimes were committed there are still a surprising number of clues available to help attempt to explain why a likeable, *"good-natured,"* ordinary guy—a family man who was doing his best to make ends meet—suddenly transformed into a crazed ax-murderer.

John Morgan hadn't been himself lately. And that, his lawyer would argue, explained why Morgan grabbed a hatchet out of the kindling box and disrupted the breakfast preparations. John Morgan had, in fact, not been himself for some time, and in the weeks leading up to the murders people had taken notice. Chloe Greene and her daughters mentioned to their neighbor that John was *"acting queer."*₁ They admitted that they were beginning to feel increasingly uncomfortable around him. His wife Rebekah was nearly frantic with worry, so much so that she had been confiding in friends and neighbors, and asking them what she should do.

During the trial, Rebekah testified that her husband began having *"strange spells"* early in the spring of that year.₂ Later on, others noted that this onset appeared to coincide with a much-reported business transaction. John Morgan traded the old horse Chloe Greene had given him as wedding present for two younger ones and the difference in value left Morgan with a lien for $35. This was due in November around the time of the murders. These events may have been completely unrelated; then again, maybe not. For someone in Morgan's financial straits—a day laborer with a new baby and a wife to feed—taking on that kind of debt may have been one of the first indications of a significant lapse of judgment, and may have contributed to his later actions.

It seems unlikely that either Morgan, described as a young man with *"excellent sense"* and reputed to be *"conscientiously honest in the payment of his debts,"*₃ or the man he was trading with, would have entered into this agreement without both parties feeling confident in Morgan's ability to pay off the lien. But in the ensuing months it became evident that something had drastically changed. Sometime in the early spring John's thought processes began to unravel.

John hired out as a day laborer for several farmers, including the Pfost-Greene family, and Rebekah testified that John had been working

away from home on a regular basis ever since the previous March. He
left early in the morning to reach an outlying farm and was gone all day,
returning home in time for supper unless the lateness of the hour kept
him overnight. On those occasions, as was common at the time, he simply
bedded down in someone's barn or extra room.

Rebekah noted that in addition to his regular work hours, he
sometimes left home with the excuse that he was *"attending to business."*[4]
Yet he never said just what this business was. As Rebekah recalled, he
"seemed to want to be rambling all the time; his mind seemed to be unsettled."[5]

It may be no coincidence that John's problems became evident so
soon after the birth of baby Albert. Here was a man, orphaned at a young
age and set adrift, unwanted and unloved, who had at last found a sense
of permanence, love and nurturance in his marriage. And now his wife's
energies and affections were being absorbed by this helpless newborn. John
and *"Becca,"* as he called her, had been married just a little over a year and
she had every right to expect him to join in this parental doting. Instead,
John was inexplicably absent, both physically and emotionally, leaving
Rebekah to take care of the house, the chores, and their son all on her own.

While trying to explain to the jury how John's personality and
disposition changed so dramatically in the months leading up to the
murders, Rebekah referred to *"strange spells"* during which her husband
seemed to totally lose interest in everything at home, including herself and
their baby.[6] In the beginning these were only transient episodes, and after a
short time John would be his loving, charming self again. He would work
hard around the place and *"appear as lively and jovial as ever,"* then without
warning, *"his mind was away on something else,"* and he would grow distant,
uncommunicative, and disinterested.[7]

By summer she realized that the problems were getting worse, and she
sought help. Her friends were sympathetic, but could only agree that she
needed to *"get something done for him."*[8] Rebekah testified that she begged
John to seek medical attention on several occasions, but he always refused.

John refused because he knew that he could not tell anyone what was
bothering him. *"I could not get my mind to settle,"* he would lamely explain
when chores were left undone or incomplete, or he'd wandered off without
explanation.[9] How could he tell anyone that he had but one thought in
his head and it tortured him day and night? It had rooted deep and try as
he might, and it seems he did try, he could not dislodge it. John Morgan
was engaged in a life and death struggle against an insidious impulse over

which he was steadily losing control, and it would ultimately destroy two families and lead directly to his own death.

"About six months ago it come in my mind to destroy that family," he would later write in a letter to Governor Atkinson, *"and I could not keep from doing it…and yet I had nothing whatever against them."*[10]

I went different times to do it before I did it and nothing could ease my mind and when I would start there I would think and the spell would wear off…the idea of killing them would wear off and I would go back home, and still it would prey on my mind to kill them.

His description of this raging internal storm, and his desperate attempts to quell it, is compelling in its starkness.

I studied and it come in my mind not to kill them and I turned and went back home and I got in the house and set by the fire and the killing of these people so impressed my mind and I read a paper a part of the time and a Testament part of the time. I set there and nothing would relieve my mind and I got up and started again.

He was even able to identify the moment, at least from his troubled perspective, when his life began to spiral out of control. He had been visiting with his elderly next-door-neighbor, *"Granny Fisher,"* Chloe Greene's mother. The old lady made some off-hand remark about the baby being in short dresses, *"while its shoes were on,"*[11] a reference to the usual custom of keeping little boys as well as girls in dresses until a certain age, and in longer gowns until they were walking. Given their lean financial circumstances, Rebekah may well have kept Albert in whatever clothes she had available. Mrs. Fisher remarked that, *"to dress a baby that way she thought there was something lacking somewhere."* She may well have meant to criticize John's ability to provide adequately for his family or it may have been merely a thoughtless or teasing remark about parental judgment, but at any rate Morgan took it very personally.

…my wife asked me on one occasion why I was in such a deep study [but] *I made her no reply. I was ashamed of myself, but did not tell her what was the matter, and then this spell of killing this family would wear off I was just as I had always been, lively and treated my wife well.*[12]

Rebekah also related sleep disturbances—episodes of nocturnal wanderings in which her husband exhibited bizarre, even violent behaviors.

The most recent incident had taken place during the Casto family reunion. In addition to being related to the Castos on his mother's side, John's sister Florence was married to Enoch Casto. That September before the murders John and Rebekah spent the Saturday night before the reunion at the Casto home. At the trial both Rebekah and Enoch testified to the following incident.[13]

Rebekah and the baby were awakened during the night by John's fitful movements. Realizing that he was still asleep, Rebekah tried unsuccessfully to wake him. Alarmed, she called out to her in-laws for help. Enoch testified that his brother-in-law, *"lit out and run out doors and was gone, he hollered very viciously, and when I got out he was standing by the house some ten feet away."* [14] It was a chilly night and the family were all barefoot and in their night clothes.

"I followed right along and got hold of his left arm, then he turned and struck at me three licks, and then I went back to the house and dressed...then Mrs. Morgan and I both went after him; he was in the brush; he seemed to object to her taking hold of him."

They made several attempts to calm him, but John kept pushing them away and striking out. *"He screamed just wild and wicked; he hallooed several times, then he started and commenced singing or humming to himself low, then he next whistled."*

They tried shaking him and yelling to wake him up. Finally, he calmed a bit and Rebekah was able to lead him back to the house where the four of them congregated by the fire. They thought John was awake because he was talking to them, but soon realized that *"he* [was] *still wrong someway."* Rebekah kept at him until he finally *"came to,"* though he seemed disoriented and claimed to have no memory of the preceding events.

Episodes like these are most often caused by an arousal disorder which can trigger complex behaviors such as walking, dressing, eating, talking, or even driving a car without conscious awareness.[15] Some people experience sleepwalking off and on throughout their lives, but for others it is a sign of intense emotional pressure and conflict. Sleepwalking and fugue states can also be related to neurological conditions such as nocturnal frontal lobe epilepsy, or diseases of the central nervous system such as Huntington's or Parkinson's which cause deterioration in the movement centers of the brain that govern sleep paralysis.[16] It is not at all rare for sleepwalkers to enter a highly emotional state, which can lead to violent outbursts. Homicides have been committed during such episodes and in rare instances a diagnosis of sleepwalking has made a successful legal defense.[17]

After the murders, Rebekah stood by her husband, believing fervently that although he might have killed, he was not at heart a killer. She remained his most staunch supporter throughout the trial, doing her best to help John's attorney convince judge and jury of her husband's unstable mental state. After his execution, she continued her crusade for a more thorough investigation, reasoning that he was insane at the time of the killings and/or led astray by an accomplice who had yet to be apprehended and brought to justice.

Those closest to a mass murderer often notice the signs of psychological distress and mental aberration beforehand and try to find help or warn authorities. Next to the loss of life, one of the most grievous results of such crimes is the emotional burden carried by survivors. Left to retrace the outcome over and over again, they wonder if they could have done anything to prevent it.

Crimes committed in the heat of passion are at least recognizable in terms of cause and effect, but John's own confessions are evidence of pre-meditation, though possibly psychotic in nature. Robbery is at least a plausible motive, but as it turns out no money was found on John Morgan. He himself said, *"the idea never struck me to kill these people for money and I did not kill them for money."*[18]

In recent years a great deal of research has been conducted on rampage-style killings to help experts understand the driving forces behind these acts. Several common elements are applicable to the Grasslick murders. One in particular stands out: in most cases, family members and others close to the killer have commented on a sudden change in personality and behavior just before the incident.[19] Also notable is an over-reaction to feelings of humiliation, a sense of rejection, depression and despair, and the presence of psychoses manifested by command hallucinations and delusional thoughts.[20]

A history of family violence is often a deciding factor, and while much of this reflects learned behavior, it may be polygenetic. Childhood deprivation and abuse plays a critical role as well as the loss of parental affection and social support, and there are often reports of early instances of cruelty to animals and humans.[21]

For all intents and purposes, the widow Chloe Greene and her children—29-year-old Alice, 26-year-old Matilda, and 18-year-old

Jimmy—were Morgan's foster family, though it remains questionable just
how much of an emotional bond was ever forged. He was taken in as an
orphaned teen, fed, clothed, and in his own words, always treated *"kindly,"*
up until the day he moved out to set up house with Rebekah.[22] While the
motive for the killings may remain unclear, it is certain that he intended
to kill the entire family. He admitted this repeatedly, referring to them
as *"that family,"* and at one point discussed his initial plans to include
35-year-old Floyd Pfost, who had come home for a visit. [23]

Usually the goal of a family annihilator is either altruism, when a
deranged family member kills to *save* his or her family from a perceived
fate worse than death, or revenge, which may well have played a part
in the Pfost-Greene murders.[24] In nearly every instance there is some
type of catalyst in the killer's mind which irrevocably severs his sense of
relationship.[24] Whatever connection the killer may have felt has been
destroyed by the family's actions, which he perceives as causing his current
hardship, be it financial or a loss of self-esteem. Giving way to depression
and despair, the murderer blames his victims for all his difficulties, and
imagines that his life can only be set to rights through their destruction.
While it may be hard to imagine that an elderly family member's comment
about a baby's attire could have led to such catastrophic consequences, it is
just possible that in John Morgan collapsing mental state it registered as a
final straw.

End Notes

[1] *The Jackson Star News,* Ripley, WV, 27 February, 1991. (Interviews with Mary Chancey)

[2] Morrison, O. J., *The Slaughter of the Pfost-Greene Family of Jackson County, W.Va. A History of the Tragedy,* 1897.

[3] *Jackson Herald,* Ripley, WV, 17 December, 1897.

[4] Morrison.

[5] *Ibid.*

[6] *Ibid.*

[7] *Ibid.*

[8] *Ibid.*

[9] *Jackson Herald,* Ripley, WV, 17 December, 1897.

[10] *Ibid.*

[11] *Ibid.*

[12] *Ibid.*

[13] Morrison.

[14] *Ibid.*

[15] Yuhas, Daisy, "Sleep Violence: A Real Danger, Little Understood," *Scientific American,* 14 June, 2012. Retrieved from World Wide Web 02-13-2016

[16] *Ibid.*

[17] Lyon, Lindsay, "7 Criminal Cases That Invoked the 'Sleepwalking Defense'" *U.S. News and World Report,* 8 May, 2009. Retrieved from World Wide Web, 02-13-2016.

[18] *Jackson Herald.*

[19] Goodstein, Laurie and William Glaberson, "The Well-Marked Roads to Homicidal Rage," *The New York Times,* New York, NY, 10 April, 2000.

[20] *Ibid.*

[21] Muscari, Mary E. "How can I detect the warning signs of extreme violence in my patients?," *Medscape,* 03 September, 2009. Retrieved from World Wide Web 02-12-2016.

[22] Rueve, Marie E. & Randon S. Welton, "Violence and Mental Illness," *Psychiatry,* 5(5), May 2008, pp. 34-48. Online publication retrieved 02-12-2016.

[23] *Jackson Herald.*

[24] Kelley, Raina, "Why Ordinary People Murder Their Families," *Newsweek,* 18 February, 2009.

[25] *Ibid.*

EVENTS LEADING UP TO THE MURDERS

Morgan had the reputation of being *"honest"* and of *"good character,"* but some people, even those closest to him, had ceased to trust him in the weeks leading up to the murders. Rumor had it that John had recently taken one of his landlord's horses and made the rounds of outlying farms, trying to sell it for the sum of $25. He told people he was planning to purchase a tract of land.[1]

According to O. J. Morrison, another story made the rounds as well. Two weeks before the murders John Morgan rode over to visit a hired hand working for a local farmer named Samuel Simmons. Earlier in the year Simmons purchased a horse from Chloe Greene and still owed his final payment on the note. Allegedly Morgan wanted to know whether Simmons had paid up yet. The Pfost-Greene farm was known for its fine horseflesh and a few days before the murders another farmer, J. D. Skidmore, stopped by to look at one of Alice's animals and negotiate a deal. Alice wasn't home at the time, so he said he'd come back.

Morgan seems to have been remarkably aware of the Pfost-Greene business dealings. He reportedly rode over to see Skidmore, and after confirming that Skidmore wanted the horse, he asked if he would be paying cash. Skidmore told Morgan he would give Alice a check. At this point, Morgan clumsily over-played his hand, insisting that Alice would only accept cash.

Surely Skidmore wondered what Morgan was up to. True, the banks in Ripley had only been in business a few years. Banks were sometimes inconvenient to get to and many people still didn't understand or trust them. John's avowal that Alice wouldn't accept a check might not have seemed so outlandish were it not for these facts: the well-to-do Pfost-Greenes conducted multiple business dealings a year, no doubt made easier by the relatively new Bank of Ripley, and nearly everyone was aware that the new bank president was Alice's brother, Floyd Pfost.

If these allegations were all true, it would certainly seem that Morgan was trying to gauge how much cash the Pfost-Greene family might have on hand for reasons of his own. He was in such a bind that on October 27th, exactly one week before the murders, he forged a note from Chloe Greene to her son George, who owned the little store in nearby Fairplain, telling him to give John $5 and she would settle with him later.[2] George Pfost was no fool. He must have realized the handwriting was not his mother's. He also knew she kept more than $5 on her person. Nevertheless, George sent John home with groceries.

On October 29th, five days before the murders, 29-year-old Ed Southall was helping his older brother Charlie tend his acreage on the lower part of the farm belonging to Charlie's father-in-law, John Chancey. Ed, short for Edgar, was still a bachelor and known to carry a bit of ready cash. According to local gossip, Morgan showed up that Friday insisting that Ed go squirrel hunting with him.[3] But Southall had already promised to help his brother. Morgan left disappointed and young Southall lived to talk about what may have been a near brush with a fatal hunting accident.

The day after Ed Southall refused to go hunting with him, Morgan repeated the ruse with a slightly different twist. At one o'clock in the morning he awakened the Pfost-Greene household by calling for Jimmy to get dressed and come outside.[4] He explained that he had a couple of raccoons treed nearby and needed Jimmy's help to bring them down. Jimmy, along with Billy Chancey and the Southall brothers, was used to hunting with John Morgan—they'd grown up sharing escapades like this. Jimmy may have been somewhat irritated at being called out at such an ungodly hour, but it was, after all, the best time for coon hunting and he was still young enough to be game for a midnight hunt. On this night, however, something about John Morgan was decidedly off-putting and it worried Jimmy enough that he spoke of it afterwards.

Alice Pfost would later testify that Jimmy said that he and John had only gone as far as the stables, about 200 yards from the house, before John suddenly stopped and asked Jimmy if his mom had been paid yet for the colt she'd sold Simmons. Jimmy said she had not, but was expecting payment the next day.

Once again Morgan's half-baked plans were going awry. He walked on a few steps into the hay field, then stopped again. He said, "*We will go no further as it is too dark to see to shoot the raccoons.*"[5] Morgan kept up the pretense, calling out to a boy who was known to be staying with him at the time and then telling Jimmy, "*He will watch the raccoons till daylight.*" Then Morgan asked if he could bed down at the house for the rest of the night.

John later confessed that he had thought to kill Jimmy and the three women that night. So why didn't he? Was he relieved or angry that the money hadn't arrived? And since he asked to stay the night, did he consider killing the family with or without the extra funds on hand, only to change his mind as he lay there in the dark in Jimmy's room? Regardless, Morgan left the Pfost-Greene farm before breakfast the next morning without further mention of the treed raccoons.

Morgan was not sophisticated enough to create the signs of pathological subtlety and symptomatology imbedded in his confessions. The most heart wrenching of these became part of his attorney's last-ditch efforts to persuade Governor Atkinson to commute Morgan's sentence to life imprisonment or confinement in an asylum.

I went at times to destroy this family, and when I would get there the idea of killing them would wear off and I would go back home, and still it would prey on my mind to kill them and yet I had nothing whatever against them. I went there on Friday night before the killing to kill them. I went there late in the night; I left home in the night; When I got down between Pete Adams' and Mary Rollins' there I studied and it come in my mind not to kill them and I turned and went back home... I set there and nothing would relieve my mind and I got up and started again, and I went on down to Mrs. Greens' that time and I hollowed to Jimmie and he got up and opened the door and asked me what I wanted and I do not know just what I said to him, but I know he got his gun and we started and got up in the meadow and then we went back to the house. This thing of killing got off my mind and we went to bed...I got up the next morning and went home before breakfast and then the killing of the family kept baffling... [6]

Afterwards Jimmy told his mother and sisters about Morgan's odd behavior and they talked at length about what it could mean. Finally, as Alice reported at the trial, they concluded that John might be planning to rob them.[7] Chloe and her daughters shared these concerns with their neighbor John Chancey. Decades later Mary Chancey claimed that the girls had been afraid that John might harm them.[8] Mary was only nine years old at the time of the murders, but her father spoke of these events in later years and her memories for the most part tally with contemporary documentation. During an interview in 1990, Mary recalled that Alice and Matilda told her father about Morgan's *"funny actions"* and said they were afraid of him. *"He told them if John ever did get boisterous to just whistle for him and he would take care of it."* [9]

If anyone knew the violence men were capable of, that man was Civil War veteran John Chancey. When faced with what he believed to be women's fancies, he dismissed their intuition and offered well-intended reassurance. On the off chance they might have need of him, all they had to do was whistle. On the other hand, Chancey may have taken the women a bit more seriously than his daughter remembered. Local editor Henry Deem maintained that Chancey advised the women not to allow John to stay overnight again unless they first sent for him or some other neighbor.[10]

What was it like for this well-meaning man to come face-to-face with Alice Pfost a day or so later, bleeding profusely from her head wound and hysterical with fright? What was going through his mind when he reached his neighbors' property and found two women he would have protected with his own life wounded and breathing their last? What self-recrimination did he feel when he saw young Jimmy, just a few years younger than his own son Billy, lying there in the hog pen with his skull caved in?

For the rest of his life John Chancey must have wondered if he could have handled things differently. Someone had been whistling on the Pfost-Greene farm the morning of November 3rd, and Chancey hadn't heard him at all.

End Notes

[1] Morrison, O. J., *The Slaughter of the Pfost-Greene Family of Jackson County, W.Va. A History of the Tragedy*, 1897.

[2] *Ibid*

[3] *Ibid.*

[4] *Ibid.*

[5] *Ibid.*

[6] *Jackson Herald*, Ripley, WV, 17 November, 1897.

[7] Morrison.

[8] "Last Public Hanging," *Goldenseal Magazine*, Spring, 1990.

[9] *Ibid.*

[10] *Jackson Herald*, Ripley, WV, 18 December, 1897.

THE NIGHT BEFORE MURDER

In the confession that was sent to Governor Atkinson, Morgan gave a very disjointed timeline leading to the destruction of his foster family. The raccoon hunt episode occurred in the early hours of Sunday, October 31st. John did not linger the following morning, despite Chloe's expected payment that day, and though he claims to have set out again for the Pfost-Greene homestead that evening, he never arrived:

... I did not go all the way and went back. I do not now know how far I went. The first I recollect was there at the school house as I come back and, in fact, do not know that I went any further or not.[1]

On Monday, he spent half the day husking corn and then announced to Rebekah that he was going to take his horses to be shod. It was while he was attempting to shoe the horses at the home of George and Ida Lanham, his brother-in-law and sister, that the urge to kill returned in full force:[2]

... it seemed to me I was bound to go to Mrs. Greene's, but I went on to get the horses shod in their fore feet... I first went to my brother-in-law's... He is a blacksmith and he was hauling rock for his chimney, and said for me to shoe them myself. I turned two shoes for one of the horses' forefeet. Then this killing so impressed me that I could not take hold of the horses' feet. I then thought I would go right up to Mrs. Greens' to do the killing, but [it] wore off again...

Instead, he went to George Pfost's store and *"traded a little,"*[3] after which he went to his father-in-law's near Fairplain, where he intended to stay the night. He had supper with his in-laws, but was too restless to sit still and decided to head for home even though it was well past dark. Hiram and Nancy tried to persuade him to stay over, but he had to keep moving—*"nothing would do me but go"*—and he went home to his family.[4]

By this point in his narration, Morgan appears to have entered a manic stage of sleep deprivation. He has been wandering all hours, too restless to work or sleep, and is confusing his days and nights. He later commented on the dream-like quality of some of these episodes, including the murders themselves. The reader is left with a blurred impression of his comings and goings that wraps back and forth on itself like the winding stream of

Grasslick. The forged note he presented George Pfost was dated October 27th, and he'd gone home with five dollars' worth of groceries. Had he really gone back to trade on November 1st or had he confused the dates?

The next day was Tuesday November 2nd, the eve of the murders. Rebekah recalled that John got up as usual and spent the day husking corn before returning for supper. But he'd barely sat down before he abruptly left the table saying that he had to go over to Dug Shinn's *"on business."*[5] *"Dug"* was neighbor Rueben Perry Shinn, a deputy sheriff, and the brother of Sheriff James Owen Shinn. The two brothers farmed together near Fairplain.

John told Rebekah that he would be gone no more than three hours and promised to be home by 9 o'clock. Since it was already dark Rebekah asked him to take one of the horses, but John elected to walk and told her he planned to take the short cut over the hill. To do this, Morgan needed to walk in the direction of the Greene farm before bearing right to cut across the hill to Shinn Ridge—not that it really matters, because he never went there. John later claimed that he fully intended to visit Shinn when he first set out, but veered off track:[6]

Then I left home on Tuesday night but did not start to go to Mrs. Greene's. I started to go to Dug Shinn's and went out on the hill and it come over my mind out on the ridge that I should destroy this family. I then turned my course and went to Mrs. Green's and the killing again wore off my mind.

In 1993 there was a fascinating interview with one of John's cousins who told of a story handed down through the family. Carleton Raines, the youngest son of Morgan's first cousin Benjamin, told a reporter for the *Ripley Star News* that his father and an uncle, Ben Anderson, who worked for the Pfost-Greene family, were with Morgan on the eve of the murders. He contends that his father always believed that if he had only taken a different approach with John that night he might have prevented the tragedy.[7] The story, as related to Carleton Raines, was that Morgan insisted that Chloe Greene owed him money for work done over the summer—amounting to about $40—and the trio stopped off at the Pfost-Greene farm so he could ask for his payment. Chloe disagreed with John's assessment, but offered to settle the matter for $5 and some cast-off shoes and coveralls. Raines said that Morgan stood there with his head down in complete silence for several moments, then turned suddenly and walked away, leaving the other men to make their hasty goodbyes. When Raines caught up with his cousin, Morgan was allegedly in high temper, stomping and cursing.

The three were traveling the Grasslick road in the direction of Fairplain, which would have returned John home again within a few minutes. Raines claimed that Morgan and Ben Anderson lagged well behind him in deep conversation, which annoyed him since he was eager to be on his way to Ripley. Before long Morgan came to a complete halt, announcing that he was going back to stay the night with the Pfost-Greenes, "*as he often did, get his hair cut, and settle with Chloe for the $5 and clothes. He said he had no food in his house.*"[8] John started back the way they'd come, leaving Raines and Anderson to continue on.

Were Ben Raines and Ben Anderson really with Morgan that evening? There is no way to confirm this story after all these years. Neither Raines nor Anderson was called to the witness stand, and the only other people who would have known—Alice and John—never mentioned the incident.

But another mystery presents itself. Why did no one else mention this issue of payment that John believed was owed him? Alice all but denied that there was any type of confrontation when she said, "*he never spoke a cross word.*"[9] Still, the story handed down through the Raines family is that Morgan walked off as though insulted by Chloe's counter-offer. If this happened it should have been apparent to everyone that Morgan was very "*cross*" indeed. Not only did Alice fail to mention the visit earlier in the evening or the money John asked for, she said he stopped by to borrow a coat pattern. Yet the Raines revelation sounds genuine. John himself alluded to a discussion about money due him when he spoke at his sentencing, although he said nothing about Raines and Anderson being privy to it:[10]

> When I left there, there was five months and fifteen days' of my time that I never received a cent for but a pair of breeches and pair of boots for, and I went in, and was talking to them about it. I asked them if they did not really think that they ought to allow me something more than that for my work; that is all I said to them: they did not seem to like it very well, but everything went along all right.

While Ben Raines refers to payment owed from the immediate summer past, it would seem that Morgan was referring to the summer he first left the Pfost-Greene family—"*when I left there*"—which would have been before he married Rebekah. If so, he had either harbored a long festering resentment toward the family, or he was so desperate for funds that he began sifting through the past. He made one other startling claim during this same confession. While he never once mentioned his cousin Benjamin Raines, he laid blame for what happened the next morning squarely on Ben Anderson. And later still, on Alice.

For her part, Alice mentioned only his second visit, if indeed there was a preceding one, saying he showed up after dark. It was getting late by then and the family must have been less than happy to see him, particularly if he'd left in a temper only a short while before. It is reasonable to assume the family was on edge, but John *"talked as usual to all the household."*[11] Alice would later testify that, *"he never spoke a cross word to any of us, nor said a word when he was trying to kill us."*[12]

She testified that John came for a coat pattern to fit Opha Parsons, the seven-year-old son of a distant cousin, both of whom were visiting the Morgans at the time.[13] This is the same child Morgan pretended to call out to on the night of the raccoon hunt. No wonder Jimmy thought Morgan was behaving strangely. Did he really expect Jimmy to believe that he was ordering a seven-year-old child to spend the night alone in the woods while the two of them returned to a warm house? In any case, Chloe didn't own a pattern that size.

It was nearing bedtime and John had decisions to make. He tried to prolong the evening by asking Tillie to *"shingle"* his hair,[14] as she had so often done before, but Tillie was having none of it. She tried to put him off claiming it was too dark to see, but John was not dissuaded.[15] He used the haircut as an excuse to stay the night, asking if she would cut his hair the next morning, and in Alice's words, her sister *"reckoned so."*[16] While she may have preferred to refuse outright she could hardly do so without appearing overtly inhospitable which would have been unthinkable. John was no doubt used to cajoling Alice and Tillie to get his way during his years with them and he managed to do it again.

Morgan describes his last evening with the family: *"The family and me talked just as we always did, and Alice played the accordion."*[17] Somehow the addition of this one small detail—that Alice was a music lover and played the accordion—brings her to life far more than her own words about the ordeal she suffered.

There they sat—Morgan and his chosen victims, making small talk and listening to the music, watching the firelight reflect off the accordion as Alice's fingers danced along the keys. It was almost like old times. Almost.

No doubt the family was apprehensive, yet none of them took any action that might have altered the course of events. Did they even contemplate following John Chancey's instructions not to let Morgan stay the night without sending someone to fetch him? They went to bed that night suspecting they were harboring, at the very least, a man who might want to steal from them. Not more than 400 yards away John Chancey made his own way to bed, blissfully unaware of the horrors the morning would bring.

Did anyone at the Pfost-Greene farmhouse sleep that night or did they lie awake listening for any indication that Morgan was on the prowl? Had Chloe thought to move her money to a hiding place? Did the sisters chide one another for their fears and still shove a bureau against their bedroom doors? Or did they do what so many victims do—ignore the clamoring of internal alarms and dampen down their instincts for self-preservation?

End Notes

[1] *Jackson Herald,* Ripley, West Virginia, 17 December, 1897

[2] *Ibid.*

[3] *Ibid*

[4] *Ibid*

[5] Morrison, O. J., *The Slaughter of the Pfost-Greene Family of Jackson County, W.Va. A History of the Tragedy,* 1897.

[6] *Jackson Herald.*

[7] *Ripley Star News,* Interview with Carleton Raines by Greg Matics, 1993, undated.

[8] *Ibid.*

[9] Morrison.

[10] *Ibid.*

[11] *Ibid.*

[12] *Ibid.*

[13] Author's Note: According to trial transcripts, the child's name was *Ofa Parsons,*[10] but the transcriptionist made a natural spelling error in this case. Opha Litcher Parsons, not *Ofa,* was the seven-year-old son of a distant cousin of Morgan's, Anna Laura Rollins Parsons. We are told by Alice Pfost at the time of the trial that Mrs. Parsons was known to be living with the Morgan's. She may have done so, but no reason is given for this and it seems a bit odd since the Parsons had three other children younger than Opha at the time. Just how many people were in the Morgan household at the time? It was, after all, a very small house.

[14] Shingling refers to a type of man's haircut preferred in the late 1800s where the back was cut short and tapered down. This male hairstyle would later be appropriated

by the thoroughly modern flappers in the 1920s and transformed into the iconic *bob*.

[15] Audio Taped Interview with Mary Chancey by Betty Jean Fourney dated Jan 1986 when Mary was 97 years old.

[16] Morrison.

[17] *Jackson Herald,* 17 December, 1897.

MURDER MOST FOUL

The Pfost-Greene farmhouse was torn down many years ago, but Morrison describes it as *"a model old time country home."*[1] The photograph included in his murder pamphlet reveals a two-story structure with attic space and a multi-columned porch extending most of the length of the house. The house was a bit of a hodgepodge, with expansions and improvements made over the years as the family grew and prospered.

Generations of large families had lived in this house. The elderly Chloe slept in a downstairs bedroom at the back of the house. Alice and Matilda probably had bedrooms upstairs and Jimmy had a room which he may have shared with John Morgan in their earlier years.

It is amazing that the sole survivor Alice Pfost, who suffered an open head wound, could bear witness immediately following these events. It is not surprising that there are small inconsistencies in the accounts she gave on separate occasions and that her narrative does not always track.

Chloe and her daughters rose a little before 5 AM on the morning of

Photo taken of the Pfost-Greene farm shortly after the murders.

Wednesday, November 3rd.[2] The women lit oil lamps and lanterns since it was still dark out, washed their hands and faces, dressed for the day, folded away their night clothes and prepared to go about their chores. They then began lighting a fire in the sitting room and building up the fire in kitchen. Then they started breakfast preparations. John and Jimmy spent the night in the kitchen and Alice said that the young men did not rise until a little later.

In Morgan's version of these events, he and Jimmy got up sometime after four o'clock, and he sat chatting with the family—*"we were sitting around there talking some and after awhile they got up and lighted a fire and Jimmy and I started out to the stable."*[3] In his trial testimony, Morgan avoided any mention of the hog pen, but Alice stated that her brother went out to feed the hogs and John followed. And here too she made a point of saying that there was no hint of malice or warning in John's demeanor that morning. *"He…talked just as friendly and sensible as he ever was."*[4]

What happened next was surmised from the crime scene since no one witnessed the assault on Jimmy Greene. Mary Chancey recalled the theory that Morgan had hidden an old mattock in the corn crib to have a weapon close at hand,[5] and law enforcement testimony supported that conclusion. Whatever Jimmy might have thought John Morgan capable of, it is clear he never expected to be physically harmed. Jimmy turned his back on Morgan as he began to put corn out for the hogs. The attack came so suddenly that he had no opportunity to call out. He received three or four blows to the head with the mattock. Afterwards, his skull was crushed with a large rock. But why use two separate murder weapons? Did Jimmy surprise his attacker, who had already flung the mattock away, by surviving that first assault? Did Morgan enter a kind of berserk frenzy on discovering that Jimmy was still alive? Or is it possible there were two assailants using two different weapons?

Morgan gave several accounts of the murder of Jimmy Greene during his multiple confessions. He admitted to killing the boy, but in one confession said that he had only wielded the rock and that another man had struck the victim with the mattock.[6] On a separate occasion he repeated his claim that, *"I never struck but one lick and that was what I struck with the rock."*[7]

Jimmy's murder was very bloody, which presents another puzzle. Why was there no mention of blood on Morgan's clothing? Whether he used one or both weapons he should have been substantially blood splattered when he returned to the house, but no one seemed to notice. It may have been impossible to tell in the dim light of an oil lamp, but there was also no credible report of blood evidence on his person at the time of his capture.

Even Rebekah, in her testimony regarding John's arrival at their house later that morning, never mentioned anything amiss in this regard although he did arrive without his coat. Neither attorney seems to have addressed this issue at the trial. Two newspapers reported that his hands and clothing were covered in blood at the time of his capture, but since both these articles were inaccurate in practically every other detail, it is impossible to know if this was factual.[8,9] It is odd that no one—the neighbor who captured him, the sheriff, his deputy, the coroner, Alice, or Rebekah, all of whom described their close encounters with Morgan either before or immediately after his capture—noted this detail in their narratives.

While Jimmy was being murdered in the hog pen the women were going about their business indoors and still comparing notes about John Morgan and his odd behavior. Alice testified that Chloe admonished her daughters to *"treat John the best they could,"* for *"she did not believe he would hurt them,"*[10] but their anxiety only increased when Morgan came back to the house alone.

They asked where Jimmy was and Morgan replied that he had stayed out to check his traps. This might have been believable. After all, this was the best time for trapping since by fall the local game had reached their best weight and maturity. There was just one problem. The family knew that Jimmy had already checked his traps and brought them in the night before. His absence weighed heavily and a few moments later Chloe voiced her concern again, *"It is curious that Jimmy has not returned to the house."*[11]

John kept going in and out of the house—Alice said he did this a total of three times that morning—and whistled from the porch. When he came back in he told them he could hear Jimmy whistling down in the field. Alice said she went out on the porch to listen, but heard nothing. Their neighbor Mary Chancey would later recall this part of the story:[12]

> *Morgan walked out on the porch and whistled a little bit and looked up in the yard. He said, "Jimmy's coming. I hear him whistle." And they knew it wasn't Jimmy. It was Morgan whistling.*

The girls went back to the kitchen leaving Chloe and Morgan in the sitting room, but when Chloe left him to go back to her bedroom John joined Tillie and Alice in the kitchen, which Alice claimed was unusual for him.[13] She and her sister took the lantern and headed out into the dark to get buttermilk from the milk house. Since going for milk did not require both women, it seems obvious that they didn't want to be left alone with Morgan and wanted to discuss matters outside of his hearing. Alice said that as soon as they were out of earshot they once more remarked on Jimmy's absence.[14] Clearly, they feared that something had happened, but neither of them took this opportunity to look for their brother.

Back in the kitchen they continued their tasks. Alice began mixing the ingredients for biscuits. Morgan went back out on the porch a second time and seemed to be listening. This time he announced that he heard Jimmy coming toward the house. Then unexpectedly he said, *"I have slept in that room many a night."*[15] The women remained silent.

Morgan popped back out onto the porch and whistled a third time. What purpose did this serve? Did he really think he was fooling the two women with this pretense? Or was there something else afoot? This time when he came back in he washed his face and hands. Why, if he had blood on his hands, did he wait so long to wash up? Or had he cleaned up earlier in the watering trough?

Alice outlined what happened next.[15] She described John standing next to the wood box near the stove and she made a point of noting that they kept a hatchet there for kindling, though she denied ever seeing the weapon in John's hands. Tillie had taken over the biscuit preparation at the stove and was nearest to him. Alice was busy at the table and had her back turned. The moment had come.

As Tillie stepped away from the stove to pass between Morgan and Alice, Morgan made his move. Alice testified that her sister staggered back and cried out, *"Oh John don't kill me,"* and Alice turned in time to see Tillie grab for the edge of the table as she started to fall.[16] Alice began screaming and John struck her sister a second time. This time Tillie went down. Alice tried to run, but the table blocked her escape and John was on her in an instant, delivering a blow to her head that caused her to topple backwards onto the table. The attack on Alice gave the wounded Tillie the precious few seconds she needed to gather herself, and scrambling about on all fours she made for the porch. Once outside she started screaming for help. If only she had kept on going.

Tillie's screams drew Morgan's attention away from Alice and he started toward the back door. Alice believed that he meant to lock the door, either locking her in or her sister and any would-be rescuers out. With Morgan's attention divided between the two women, both were now managing to get clear of him. Alice slipped the confines of the kitchen by way of the pass-through closet near the stove. She ran through the sitting room and out onto the front porch, glancing back to see Morgan hard on her heels. He had just entered the sitting room when he suddenly changed course. Instead of following her out the front door, the logical action for a man whose victims seemed to be escaping, Alice said that he veered away and moved toward her mother's bedroom at the back of the house. Both girls were screaming by now and Chloe may have come out of her room to see what all the commotion was about.

Alice was bleeding copiously from her head wound and in her panic was not thinking clearly. There was a loaded gun in the corner of the sitting room.[17] It was within easy reach of the front door, but Alice ran past it on her way out.

Stunned and winded, she hid behind a pile of fence railings, expecting to see Morgan emerge from the house at any moment. Seeing that the coast remained clear she ran again, finding better cover in a corner of the hen house. A newspaper account of the trial included a piece of information that was not present in either Morrison's excerpts from the transcripts or in Alice's statement to the coroner. *The Wheeling Register* reported that Alice testified that from where she was hiding she could see the glow of lamp light from the windows. From the movement of the shadows she could follow Morgan's progress as he walked back toward her mother's bedroom. Interpreting Alice's remarks, the reporter wrote: *"Pretty soon Morgan came out, followed by old Mrs. Green who was trying to defend herself."*[18] Notice the syntax—Chloe *followed* Morgan out onto the porch—and the use of the word *defend* in this fashion would indicate that Chloe was defending not only herself, but her children and her home.

The article pointed out that Alice's testimony in court *"varies somewhat from her former statement,"*[19] referring to the deposition she made to the coroner immediately after the murders. In her earlier statement, Alice said that Morgan did not pursue her out of the house but turned immediately toward her mother's bedroom. Perhaps both scenarios occurred, but at different times. From the evidence recovered from the crime scene, a fierce battle was waged between the back room, the sitting room, and the front porch.

Chloe locked her bedroom door against her attacker at some point because he broke through with the hatchet, but Morgan was so disorganized that he may have disengaged to go after Alice and Matilda again. It is also clear that at some point this courageous old woman went after Morgan, backed by the efforts of her daughter Tillie who somehow managed to join forces with her mother.

Alice told the coroner that while she was hiding in the hen house she suddenly remembered Morgan's whistling charade and it dawned on her that he might have been signaling an accomplice.[20] As it turns out, Alice may have had good reason to believe that a second killer was lurking in the shadows of her yard that morning. Morgan would later assert that Alice knew full well there *was* an accomplice, but that was after he'd already sworn that he committed the crimes entirely on his own.[21]

End Notes

[1] Morrison, O. J., *The Slaughter of the Pfost-Greene Family of Jackson County, W.Va. A History of the Tragedy*, 1897.

[2] The time line for the murders, their descriptions and sequence are derived from the excerpts of trial transcripts and Alice's statement to the Coroner as found in Morrison, O. J., *The Slaughter of the Pfost-Greene Family of Jackson County, W.Va. A History of the Tragedy*, 1897, unless otherwise noted.

[3] Morrison.

[4] *The Jackson Herald*, Ripley, WV, 12 November, 1897.

[5] "Last Public Hanging", *Goldseal Magazine*, Spring, 1990.

[6] *The Morgantown Post*, Morgantown, WV, 17 December, 1897.

[7] *The Cincinnati Post*, Cincinnati, OH, 14 December, 1897.

[8] *The Morgantown Post*, Morgantown, WV, 4 November, 1897.

[9] *The Wheeling Register*, Wheeling, WV, 4 November, 1897.

[10] Morrison

[11] *Ibid.*

[11] *Ibid.*

[12] *Goldenseal Magazine*, Spring 1990.

[13] Morrison

[14] *Ibid*

[15] *Ibid*

[16] *Ibid*

[17] *Ibid*

[18] *Wheeling Register*, Wheeling, West Virginia, 6 November, 1897.

[19] *Ibid*

[20] Morrison

[21] *The Jackson Herald,* Ripley, WV, 17 December, 1897.

HELP COMES TOO LATE

Hiding at the hen house gave Alice time to gather herself. She knew she needed to get help. Her nearest neighbor, John Chancey, was only a few hundred yards away, but it might as well have been miles for the injured, traumatized Alice. Fortunately, the adrenaline coursing through her bloodstream helped numb the pain and fuel her muscles. A moment more to steel her nerve and she was up and running out in the open.

Alice fled through the corn fields, weaving drunkenly in her effort to stay upright and dodge the corn shocks. A gibbous moon shed light upon the scene, though mist hindered her visibility. Her breathing was ragged and she tripped over corn stubble and fell, rising again and again to lurch onward. Each time she looked back, expecting to see her pursuer. At last she reached the fence marking the edge of the Chancey property and began to climb, only to realize that she'd used the last of her strength. It was here that she heard Tillie screaming for her. *"Alice, do come back, and try to get the gun and help us."*[1]

Alice did not turn back. Within moments the sounds of screams reached her again—this time she was sure they were coming from both her mother and her sister. Later, as though she felt the need to justify her flight that morning, she explained, *"I knew where the gun was and that I could not reach her, and I did not go back."*[2] Morgan confirmed that the gun was kept in a corner of the parlor near the front door. He claimed he'd tried to get to it to defend himself when the women attacked *him.*[3]

Alice last saw her sister scrambling out the back door of the kitchen, yet somehow Tillie managed to get back inside the house, no doubt trying to reach Alice and her mother. She may not have made it past the sitting room where her body was found, but when Mary Chancey was interviewed in 1990, she claimed that Tillie joined her mother in the back bedroom and they locked themselves in.[4] Mary's version, which seems to have been substantiated at the time, could only have occurred if the younger sister was able to dodge Morgan and he had temporarily abandoned Chloe in the house to search for the two women outside. And why wouldn't he have done so? Why deal with a cornered half-blind old lady first, when two wounded but mobile young women are on the loose and possibly seeking help?

The theory that Tillie and Chloe were both locked in the back bedroom is a plausible one. It is certain that Chloe, either by herself or with her daughter, barred the bedroom door because Morgan took the hatchet to it, splintering it into pieces to get inside. It is hard to imagine that any mother, hearing the frantic screams of her daughters, would think only of saving herself and leave her children to the mercy of their attacker. If Tillie managed to reach her, however, and told her that Alice had escaped, the two of them might have locked the door against Morgan hoping to hold out until help arrived. But once Morgan broke through that door it seems impossible that Chloe could have fended him off and gotten out of her bedroom on her own. Surely Tillie must have been there as well, both women putting up the fight of their lives. Morgan would have concentrated first on one and then the other as he had done earlier in the kitchen, giving them just enough maneuverability to reach the front parlor. Here again, Tillie must have moved through the sitting room, by-passing the gun just as Alice did.

And what of the Wheeling reporter's commentary regarding the rest of Alice's testimony, that Morgan came outside *followed* by Mrs. Greene? Is this when Tillie joined her mother? And are we to believe that Alice turned and fled in the opposite direction when she saw her elderly mother up against Morgan on the front porch? Moments later as Alice reached the fence Tillie screamed for her to come back and help them. Why ask her sister to *come back* unless she saw her running away?

One thing is sure: Chloe died on the front porch still clutching the piece of her bedroom door she'd been using to defend herself. She may have followed Morgan out the first time, gone back inside with her daughter to reach the bedroom, and forged her way out a second time once he'd busted down the door. But it is also possible that Alice's view of her mother battling Morgan outside the front door occurred just minutes before her final collapse at the edge of the porch.

Regardless of the sequence there is no doubt that Chloe and Tillie were together in their final moments. John Morgan inadvertently tells us this in his sentencing speech, a curious and probably unconscious amalgamation of truth and fiction. He attempted to muster the ridiculous plea of self-defense, claiming the two women attacked *him* and that he had just been trying to protect himself and make his escape. Yet within the garbled fantasy he produced in court it is possible to discern several kernels of truth:[5]

The old lady come at me with a club and another girl with the gun and I says to them: "Do not hurt no one, and no one is going to hurt you;" the girl that got the gun, could not get it to work, so she just struck at me with it, and I throwed up my hand that way, to dodge the lick and kind of glanced it off, and I had the hatchet in my hand that fell over on her head as I knocked the lick off. Mrs. Greene was standing in the door with a club; that old lady—that mother that had protected me in many a thing—she struck at me with a club."

One of the more interesting aspects of Morgan's indignant description relates to the *"girl with the gun."* Somehow in all the chaos, and after she had shouted to Alice to come help them, Tillie Pfost managed to grab the weapon herself. Here was her one chance to save herself and her mother. She aimed at Morgan and pulled the trigger, only to have the gun either jam or misfire. She *"could not get it to work."* Morgan was telling the truth here. Tillie had already sustained two head wounds. Blood was streaming into her eyes. She was panicked and fumbling frantically. Any number of things could have gone wrong and so she ended up wielding the gun like a club. And Morgan struck back with the hatchet, blocking her blows, and knocking the gun away, and inflicting that last mortal blow across Tillie's forehead. The local editor described the wound *"as if made by the sinking therein of the poll of a hatchet"*—that is the blunted or rounded hammer butt of the tool rather than the blade itself.[6]

All the while Chloe had been hitting him with a piece of her bedroom door. Morgan was shocked by this, *"that old lady—that mother that had protected me in many a thing,"* he complained, *"come at me with a club."* Chloe was only five feet tall, but probably weighed as much or a little more than Morgan at around 150 pounds. His claim that Chloe used a club tallies with the reporter's notation about Alice's testimony as well as evidence found at the crime scene. And though Morgan adamantly denied ever hitting Chloe with the hatchet, she sustained multiple wounds during the course of the struggle. Bloody pieces of splintered wood from the bedroom door were found scattered throughout the house, which suggests that both women were using them as makeshift weapons. Chloe was found still holding a piece of the door with the bar latch.[7]

The memory of this final pitched battle lodged so vividly in the killer's brain that its reality fused with his fabricated version of events. Mother and daughter fought so valiantly for their lives that in Morgan's own words, *"it seemed like there was a crowd of people there fighting me."*[8]

It was no contest in the end. The two women, despite their courageous stand, were no match for the man with the ax. Tillie collapsed from that final blow and Morgan now gave his full attention to her mother. The mortally wounded Chloe staggered out onto the front porch and fell off the edge. She had been struck at least three times with the hatchet. It was finally over, although there was still the matter of Alice to attend to.

But miraculously Alice had escaped. She reached the safety of the Chancey farm and what follows are Mary Chancey's recollections of her arrival.[9]

Mary's brother Billy was going about his chores in the barn when he thought he heard someone cry out. He stepped outside to listen and spotted Alice trying to climb the fence that bordered their property. He ran to help and half-carried Alice across the stream and up to the house.

Alice was "*hysterical*"—which comes as no surprise—and at first the family couldn't make sense of what she was trying to tell them. John Chancey said, '*Alice, do quiet down and tell us what has happened. You know nobody's been killed*', to which Alice responded, "*Why John, looky here what he's done to me.*" Alice lifted her head and they saw that "*big clots of blood were rolling down from the top of her head.*" Chancey immediately started for the Pfost-Greene farm, but his wife stopped him, "*Goodness man, would you go up there when you don't know who is up there and what is going on?*"

John Chancey told Billy to collect Ed and Charlie Southall and waited impatiently for them to arrive. He had already cleared the stream by

The old Chancey homestead where Alice ran for help

the time he heard the younger men coming and he took off toward his neighbors at a dead run hollering, *"Come on, boys and come quick."*

There is a timing discrepancy between John Chancey's testimony and Alice's. Chancey states that he and *"the boys"* arrived on the Pfost-Greene property at around 5 AM.[10] Given that it took a few minutes to organize themselves afterwards, that would put Alice's arrival at around 4:45. Alice said that her family got up that morning only *"a little before five,"* but in Morgan's testimony, the day began closer to 4 AM and likely his memory is more accurate in this instance. There was a short span of time following Jimmy's murder in the hog pen, but once things started rolling again the rest of the carnage was over in minutes.

John Chancy had considerable experience with men trying to kill him and he took the lead: *"Boys, watch for the fire out of this Winchester and when you see it, fall to the ground."*[11] They ran on through the darkness, rifles at the ready. Their first indication of just how bad it was going to be confronted them when they stumbled over Chloe's body. John Chancey described the scene:[12]

"When I got there in front of the house Mrs. Chloe Greene was laying on her back with her head out off the porch and her feet up against the porch, struggling in her blood."

Chloe was moments away from death. The front door was partially ajar and Charlie Southall shoved his way inside, heedless of the danger. He said later that once they'd found Chloe he stopped being afraid.[13] He just wanted to even the score. They found no sign of Chloe's attacker, but by the firelight they made the next grisly discovery. Matilda Pfost lay in a pool of blood on the sitting room floor; she too was still breathing.

The men made quick work of searching the house and then brought out the feather ticking from Chloe's bed and laid it in front of the hearth.[14] They gently laid Tillie on the mattress and did their best to make her comfortable. John Chancey tried to get her to swallow a little whiskey, but though she opened her eyes and smiled in recognition, she could neither swallow nor speak.[15] One of the younger men went for help and soon other neighbors arrived on the scene. Billy rode to fetch the sheriff and the doctor, who lived near one another on up the creek.

It was too late to help Chloe, and they did not attempt to move her from where she had fallen. She died at sunrise and her body was still warm when Dr. John Bechtel arrived.[16] He found his former friend and patient

where she had fallen, her head and shoulders draped over the edge of
the porch. The 58-year-old country doctor, who also happened to be the
county medical examiner, had known this woman for nearly four decades.
He did his best to provide what comfort he could for Tillie, knowing that
she could not survive the day, and then as quickly as possible he went next
door to see to Alice. Afterwards he was left with the autopsies—measuring
entry wounds and gauging the depth of penetration—assisted by another
local physician, O. J. Casto.

When the men did not immediately find Jimmy Greene's body they
hoped that he had somehow survived, but at sunrise his bloody remains
were discovered in the hog pen. One glance told them that Jimmy was
beyond all human aid. There was nothing they could do but leave him for
the coroner.

> *James Green was lying dead near the hog pen, his head cut in several places
> and his brains scattered over the bloody ground. A bloody mattock lying near
> showed it had been used as the weapon of murder and a large rock had been
> hurled upon the defenseless head, mashing it, after deadly blows had been
> inflicted with the mattock.*[17]

By now Sheriff's Deputy Reuben Shinn was on the scene and a large
crowd was beginning to gather. Another neighbor, Andrew Anderson, was
on his way to Ripley with the news and Sheriff Owen Shinn, who had spent
the night in town, would be arriving later. Next door the Chancey farm
was also a hub of activity—Mary compared it to *"a beehive"*[18] —and it would
remain so throughout the day. Alice's remaining siblings would soon be in
attendance, along with various friends and neighbors, ministers, law officers,
and the neighborhood busy bodies intent on gathering all the news.

Word of the murders and Alice's accusations spread like wildfire,
rippling outwards from the tiny hamlets around Grasslick as one neighbor
hastened to inform the next in relay fashion. Meanwhile, sheriff's deputy
Reuben Shinn was left to organize an armed posse to hunt down John
Morgan.

End Notes

[1] Morrison, O. J., *The Slaughter of the Pfost-Greene Family of Jackson County, W.Va. A
History of the Tragedy*, 1897.

[2] *Ibid.*

[3] *Ibid.*

[4] *Goldenseal Magazine,* Spring 1990.

[5] Morrison, O. J., *The Slaughter of the Pfost-Greene Family of Jackson County, W.Va. A History of the Tragedy,* 1897.

[6] *The Jackson Herald,* Ripley, WV, 18 November, 1897.

[7] *The Jackson Herald,* Ripley, WV, 18 November, 1897.

[8] *The Jackson Herald,* Ripley, WV, 17 December, 1897.

[9] *Goldenseal Magazine,* Spring 1990.

[10] Morrison, O. J., *The Slaughter of the Pfost-Greene Family of Jackson County, W.Va. A History of the Tragedy,* 1897. [11] *Goldenseal Magazine,* Spring 1990.

[12] Morrison.

[13] *Goldenseal Magazine.*

[14] Audio Taped Interview with 97-year-old Mary Chancey conducted by Betty Jean Fourney, January 1986.

[15] *Goldenseal Magazine.*

[16] *The Jackson Herald,* Ripley, WV, 17 December, 1897.

[17] *Ibid.*

[18] *Goldenseal Magazine.*

HUE AND CRY

Morgan was outside searching for Alice when he heard Chancey shouting and the men coming through the field. He was out of time. Now he had to get away. If he had only caught Alice he might have been home free, but now the entire community would be after him.

Rebekah testified that her husband didn't arrive home until *"break of day"* around 7 AM.[1] If Morgan fled the scene at roughly 5 o'clock then he had nearly two hours to cover the mile and a half distance to his house. If he was moving fast he should have gotten there easily before 5:30, even if he was avoiding the road. What was he doing all that time? Did he hole up somewhere to compose himself? Was he washing the blood from his clothes? Was he hiding money? He denied stealing any and none was found at the time of his capture. Yet it appeared that money was missing from the household and pockets in the victims' clothing had been turned inside out. Morgan's coat was also missing and this led to initial speculation that he might have hidden both somewhere along his route. O. J. Morrison reported that:[2]

> *Mrs. Greene also had a pocket-book containing some gold pieces of rare date, which she always carried in her pocket; this was gone. It is the opinion of many that the coat that Morgan wore at the time he committed the crime, and which he concealed and refused to tell where, if it is ever found, this money and pocket-book will be found with it.*

Ultimately, this theory would be discounted.

Whatever the reason for the delay, Morgan's actions after the murders do not reflect the urgency of a man on the run. Rebekah's testimony describes what happened after his arrival.[3] She was tending to Albert and her morning chores when John walked in and wandered through the house, ignoring both her and the baby. Though she repeatedly tried to talk to him, he did not respond. O.J. Morrison relayed a very different story, presumably as told by Morgan during their interview.[4] While Rebekah described a subdued, dazed, and non-verbal spouse wandering aimlessly from room to room, Morrison portrays him as rushing in and excitedly shouting, *"All of them are killed down to Chloe's."* Rebekah is supposed to have asked, *"Law, who done it?"* To which Morgan cryptically replied, *"You will hear who.*" Though far more Shakespearean in tone, this conversation probably never happened. The Morrison interview took place more than a month after the murders, on the very eve of John's carefully planned escape. He was no longer the panicked fugitive suffering from the after-effects of his own violence. He was now famous, and had begun to consider how his actions were going to play out in print.

According to Rebekah, after several minutes of aimless pacing John took his gun down and walked out of the house. She grabbed Albert and ran after him, staying hard on his heels as he charged up the road toward Jim Fisher's house. When they got there, Rebekah ran to the door to ask Jim for help—to *"assist me to do something with him, because something was wrong"*—but Chloe's half-brother was away from the house that morning. Only his wife Nancy and Chloe's mother Susanna were at home.

John headed directly for a corn shock and began violently tearing it apart. Ripping off several ears of corn, he started toward the hog pen. Finally he responded to his wife's incessant imploring, telling her that Fisher had asked him to feed his hogs that morning and that's what he was aiming to do. Rebekah was not at all reassured, but since she'd left the house without extra wraps and Albert was chilled, she turned back to give the baby to Nancy Fisher. Nancy, who had taken rapid stock of these proceedings, urged Rebekah to get the gun away from her husband.

It must have taken a good deal of courage for Rebekah to move close to Morgan in his current state, but she did and asked him to please give her the gun. He refused and began feinting with it this way and that, forcing her to back away from him. Then, as she retreated, he threw the gun at her. She would later testify that she had no idea if he was actually trying to hurt her, but it should be noted that Rebekah's fortitude at this point may well have saved other lives. Thanks to her, Morgan was unarmed at the time of his capture. He took off again, cutting through Fisher's field until he reached the plank fence about forty steps away. He began dismantling it and made such strange noises as he did so that Rebekah was at a loss to describe them.

Horrified and unable to handle her husband alone, Rebekah reluctantly turned back. She watched him start off and then change directions several times before he finally made his way down over the hill. The next time she would see John he would be behind bars.

By this time, Andrew Anderson had reached Ripley with the terrible news. Sheriff Shinn was just calling the circuit court to order when he was interrupted. The presiding judge, Reese Blizzard, promptly suspended the proceedings and the mad scramble began. Knowing that his brother Reuben would be at the murder scene by now, the sheriff gathered his deputies—Henry Mahon, J. M. Weas, and George Nohe [5]—and set out for Grasslick. He stopped along the way to speak with Rebekah and learned that John had already been there and gone.

Prosecuting attorney James Seaman lined up his own entourage which included judicial representatives of varying degrees of importance, among them the assistant prosecutor, John Baker, and Marshall Archer, an ambitious young law clerk and former deputy sheriff who would later study for the bar. The coroner, David Brown, hastily began to assemble his jury of inquest, taking a few men with him and planning to add others at the scene. [6]

The procession from the Jackson County courthouse to the Pfost -Greene homestead was soon underway. Lawmen and officials, as well as hangers-on calling themselves assistants of every sort, made for whatever conveyances were at hand and joined the throng. Nearly two hours later the crime scene was overrun with several hundred people—Morrison claimed that *"fully six hundred"* had gathered by 10 o'clock.

The coroner's inquest convened on the spot, and after examining the bodies and the evidence, returned the verdict that both *"Mrs. Green and her son came to death at the hands of John F. Morgan."* [7] For the moment at least, Matilda Pfost was still among the living, as was her sister Alice.

By now all efforts to preserve the crime scene, if there ever were any, had been left by the wayside. Troops of onlookers tramped in and out of the house and the hog pen. It was chaos on a grand scale. Still, the coroner managed to secure the murder weapons—the hatchet and the mattock—as well as sections of the splintered bedroom door *"in whose hands Mrs. Green held the latch in her efforts to bar him out."* [8] There was no mention of the gun.

[Coroner] *Brown brought home the hatchet which is covered with blood, to which gray hairs of Mrs. Green adhere. The coroner also has parts of the door broken and split up by Morgan to get into the room to Mrs. Green. The parts of the door are also covered with blood.* [9]

Meanwhile, the fugitive had already been apprehended without any fanfare. Moments before Mr. Anderson galloped into Ripley, Reuben Shinn's father-in-law, George Shamblin, was riding through the pasture near his house about four miles from Morgan's home. Shamblin had been at the Pfost-Greene farm early on and had gone home to grab his horse and shotgun. He was on his way back to join an *ad hoc* posse when he spotted Morgan in his own backyard. The unarmed Morgan was *"compelled to surrender."*[10]

Two decades prior, Morgan's father, Andrew Raines, sat in an apple tree looking down at a constable who was pointing a gun at him and telling him to give himself up. Andy, never good with impulse control, raised his weapon and was shot dead on the spot. The apple may not have fallen far from the tree, but his unarmed son knew better than to argue with a loaded shotgun. He raised his hands in the air and shouted, *"Don't kill me, I'll give up."*[11] Backup arrived soon after and Morgan was shackled and strapped and on his way back to face the music.

The *Morgantown Post* offered this totally erroneous report of the capture the following day:[12]

> *About noon they found and captured Morgan in his hiding place in the woods. His clothes were covered with blood and upon his person was found the stolen $1,500.*

By now the full report had reached both the Morgan and Fisher households and emotional chaos reigned. Family members, friends, and neighbors gathered around both families, moving back and forth between the stricken Rebekah and her bewildered, frightened child, and Chloe Greene's distraught mother. The men had gone with Jim Fisher to the murder scene.

Jimmy and Chloe Greene had been gruesomely butchered and bludgeoned. Matilda Pfost lay dying from her wounds and Alice Pfost might succumb as well. Never in Rebekah's wildest dreams had she considered that her beloved husband could savagely murder anyone.

End Notes

[1] Morrison, O. J., *The Slaughter of the Pfost-Greene Family of Jackson County, W.Va. A History of the Tragedy,* 1897.

[2] *Ibid*

[3] *Ibid.*

[4] *Ibid.*

[5] *Ibid.*

[6] Author's note: The jury, according to Morrison, included Lycergus Mattox, a shop keeper from nearby Kenna and brother-in-law to O.J. Morrison; J. D. Skidmore, whose plan to buy Alice Pfost's horse was foiled; John Chancey; Chancey's brother-in-law and next-door neighbor, Henry Winter; the Sheriff's uncle, Solomon Harpold; 23-year old Daniel Crow from Ripley, one of Floyd Pfost's wife's relations; Adam Benson Parsons, one of Joshua Parson's sons who had been a step-brother to John Morgan; Adam Greenbury Parsons, a nephew of Joshua Parsons living in Fairplain; and local farmers George W. Rankin, John C. Hood, James W. Dorsey and Joseph McRay.

[7] Morrison.

[8] *The Jackson Herald*, Ripley, WV, 18 December, 1897.

[9] *The Morgantown Post*, Morgantown, WV, 4 November, 1897,

[10] Morrison.

[11] *Ibid.*

[12] *The Morgantown Post*, Morgantown, WV, 4 November, 1897.

LEGAL BEGINNINGS

While nearly every able-bodied man in the county was racing to join a posse, Coroner David A. Brown went to John Chancey's place to see if he could get any kind of statement out of Alice Pfost. Despite her injuries, he found her surprisingly coherent and able to describe the morning's events.

The only credible description of Alice's head wound comes from a Wheeling reporter who wrote that *"her skull is fractured and the physician's probe entered one-half inch,"*[1] which would have been a considerable injury, but not quite as serious as others claimed at the time. Nine-year-old Mary Chancey was suitably impressed by the amount of blood Alice was losing, but even small head wounds bleed copiously, and as badly traumatized and wounded as she was, she still managed to travel nearly a quarter of a mile for help. One thing is certain: she was not, as the *Morgantown Post* wanted its readers to believe, *"so horribly injured that her brains were oozing out of the terrible wound in her head and were scattered on her shoulders."* Still, she would wake up with a headache every morning for the rest of her life.[2]

Alice was already moving away from her attacker when he struck. The hairstyles of the time, which involved the coiling of waist-length hair into a bun or wrapping it around sausage shaped fillers called *rats* on the top or sides of the head, may have helped to divert or cushion the blow. There is no documented evidence of Alice having memory loss or confusion, and the description she gave the coroner the morning of the attack tracks fairly well, despite her initial bout of hysteria. She was also recovered sufficiently to appear in court two days later, giving virtually the same information. What follows is an excerpt from the affidavit taken by the coroner:[3]

I am Alice Pfost, the daughter of Mrs. Chloe Greene, who, as I am informed, lies a corpse at her residence. One John Morgan came to our house about 6 o'clock last evening. He came in and talked as usual. He had lived at our house for over five years. He claimed to mother that he came after a coat pattern for Ofa Parsons, who was living at his house. He talked on awhile and requested my sister Matilda to shingle his hair. My sister refused to cut his hair after night. He then wanted to know that if he stayed all night whether she would cut his hair the next morning. She told him she reckoned she could.

Alice went on to describe the events of the following morning, how Morgan followed Jimmy to the hog pen, but came back alone. Then she walked the coroner through the attacks, explaining that after his initial assault, Tillie made it out onto the back porch, while she ran though the sitting room and out the front of the house. She told Brown that she was afraid that Morgan had an ally because he had been signaling for someone with his whistling. And she admitted that her family had "*suspicioned Morgan before…,*" giving the details of the recent raccoon hunting stratagem. "*This was told me by my brother Jimmy, who they say now lies dead at the hog-pen.*" She concluded her narrative with her escape to the neighbors' home.

I left the house and came to Mr. John Chancey's. When I got to the bars I heard my sister scream for me to come back and get the gun. After I got further I heard my mother and sister both scream. I came right on to Mr. Chancey's.

In route to Grasslick Sheriff Shinn received the welcome news that George Shamblin had captured the killer and was bringing him to the murder scene in the bed of a farm wagon. Shinn deputized George's nephew, John Shamblin, and when George arrived with his prisoner in tow, the two men frog-marched Morgan down through the fields toward his old home. It all looked just as he had left it—the hay in stacks, the corn in shocks—except that now a great congregation of people surrounded the house and stood in the fields—hundreds of them. Old friends and neighbors were among them; some stood stiffly, silently, numbed with shock and grief; others moved toward him—agitated, aggressive, demanding blood.

Morrison describes what took place next. It was with some difficulty that Shinn and his men brought Morgan safely through the gauntlet and out into the garden. The lawmen would later recall how strangely their prisoner had acted from the moment of his arrest: "*He appeared crazy when arrested, and kept up his strange conduct after being taken in charge by the officers.*" Shinn agreed that Morgan was behaving oddly and would later share his observations in court: "*…his actions were very strange; he was making a noise, would spit at one, and different things like, and kind of grinning and hissing all the time; that lasted until we got him down to the fence near the garden…*"

It had been no easy task making their way through the milling throng and Shinn was increasingly anxious about crowd control. He had his men take Morgan down past the creek toward the barn, and did his best to calm the crowd. Shamblin sat with Morgan on a log out in the field and advised him to *"straighten up"* and stop acting crazy: *"...the people know you are sane; it would be better for you to straighten up and tell a straight story, if you know anything about this matter."*

Was Morgan feigning insanity so early in the game? Possibly. But his behavior also sounds remarkably like the sleepwalking episodes Rebekah later described, as well as his actions when Rebekah followed him to Jim Fisher's house. Could these have been stress-induced neurological responses? Vocalization and facial tics have been associated with early onset HD, including unintelligible speech, grunting, barking, and grimacing. Whatever the cause, Morgan eventually pulled himself together because some ten to fifteen minutes later John Shamblin informed the sheriff that Morgan was ready to talk. Hearing this, Shinn turned to Perry Greene, Jimmy Greene's much-older nephew, known to all as *"P.C.,"* and asked if he wanted to hear Morgan's statement.

By today's standards this gesture appears inappropriate and smacks of political grandstanding. A representative of the prominent Greene family is nearby, the prisoner has been captured within hours and brought to the scene of the crime, and now the sheriff is in position to offer up Morgan's confession. But most likely it was simply a sympathetic gesture from one friend and neighbor to another at a time of great loss. Shinn asked Morgan's permission to include Perry, and Morgan, who was also acquainted with Edward Greene's grandson, had no objection.

By now John Morgan was thoroughly spooked. The only thing separating him from the furious onlookers was an old rail fence and a handful of lawmen, and he was badly shaken from his walk down through the crowd. He told Shinn, *"I want the crowd kept away...I am ready to pay the debt, but I want to be protected."* And Shinn promised that he would do everything in his power to keep him safe. But to make it legal Shinn needed the coroner on hand to witness any confession, and David Brown was still at the Chancey farm interviewing Alice.

The role of the coroner was not a medical one in those days, but was instead a holdover from the English legal system when *"Crowners"* were assigned to investigate suspicious deaths on behalf of king and crown, and assess the estate of the deceased. The American practice of electing physicians to the office did not begin until the 20th century.

Morrison depicts David Brown as a highly-respected member of the

Jackson County bar whose life was an example of, *"…what an American boy of pluck can do, when he so wills."* Brown was only forty-three-years old and had held the coroner's office for the past few years while continuing his legal practice. He was an experienced prosecutor, and before coming to Jackson County had practiced in the town of Spencer in adjacent Roane County where he'd been involved in several high-profile murder cases related to the Bruen Land War. Brown had yet to realize the difficult role he would play as these events unfolded, or how they would impact his life. He would spend the rest of the fall and the Christmas holidays trying to save one man and bring another to justice. Sadly, he would not live to see another fall.

When Brown arrived back at the Pfost-Greene farm he found the prisoner shackled and guarded by John Shamblin. Upon learning that Morgan was planning to give a statement, his first thought was that the man had been intimidated into doing so, and so he warned Morgan not to agree to anything or make any kind of statement in his current circumstances. He explained the risks and consequences, and realizing that Morgan still seemed intent on talking, he pleaded with him to at least wait until he had a clearer head and was in the relatively safe confines of the jail.

Not at all sure the prisoner was fully cognizant of the legal ramifications, the ethical Brown wanted nothing to do with this chain of events, but he had little choice. When Morgan assured him that *"Yes,"* he understood what Brown was saying and that *"No,"* he'd not been threatened by anyone, Brown reluctantly agreed to witness Morgan's statement. Just as he feared, Morgan would later claim that he had no recollection of any of this.

Shamblin testified before the grand jury that when Brown finished explaining all the legalities, the prisoner stood up, looked the attorney in the eye, and said, *"Gentlemen, I am going to quit acting a fool, I want to make a true statement of this affair. I killed these people."* Shamblin took all the credit for Morgan's decision, believing that once he'd told Morgan that no one believed him to be insane, the prisoner realized the jig was up and decided to cooperate.

Morgan dictated the following:

"I, John Morgan, being duly sworn by D. A. Brown, Coroner of Jackson County, West Virginia, I am sworn at my own request and make this statement under oath free and voluntary, and I further say that the same is not extorted from me, nor made by me through any promise in the future. I killed Jimmy

Greene, Mrs. Greene and Matilda Pfost on the morning of Wednesday, the 3rd day of November, 1897. It was between 4 o'clock and daylight of said morning. I killed Matilda first, the old lady second and Jimmy at the hog-pen. I killed them in self-defense. I done the crime in defending myself.

Signed, J. F. Morgan

Obviously the prisoner was carefully coached though the first half of the statement so that it would be couched in the appropriate legal jargon, and it is not until the end that we hear the real voice of John Morgan: *"I done the crime in defending myself."* This was to be his opening gambit in the trial for his life. It was also just the first in a series of confusing and contradictory confessions.

What immediately catches the attention is the sequence he gives: *"I killed Matilda first, the old lady second and Jimmy at the hog-pen."* Is it possible that Jimmy was not dead when the women were killed? Did Morgan strike him with the mattock when he first followed Jimmy out to the hog pen, then later, while searching for Alice, discover that the young man was still alive and crush his skull with the rock? Or was someone else involved?

Within minutes of his statement Morgan was bundled off to the wagon and the sheriff pointed his little band of lawmen toward Ripley. Six weeks later the young murderer would be at the head of yet another cavalcade retracing a portion of this same route—this time to where the gallows waited just outside of town.

End Notes

[1] *Wheeling Register,* Wheeling, WV, 7 November, 1897.

[2] Audio Taped Interview with 97-year-old Mary Chancey conducted by Betty Jean Fourney (?) January 1986.

[3] *Jackson Herald,* Ripley, WV, 12 November, 1897. Copy courtesy of Mike McGrew.

[4] Morrison, O. J., *The Slaughter of the Pfost-Greene Family of Jackson County, W.Va. A History of the Tragedy*, 1897.

RIPLEY: A GATEWAY TOWN

The town of Ripley is near the center of Jackson County, just twelve miles west of the Ohio River and about midway along what used to be known as the Charleston-Parkersburg Turnpike. It is situated on a plateau surrounded by gently sloping terraces with the banks of Mill Creek to the south and Sycamore Creek to the north.

Tradition has it that it was named for a young circuit riding minister by the name of Harry Ripley who drowned on his way to his own wedding in the early part of the 19th century. The romance of the thing made such a deep impression on the citizens of the town then known as Jackson Courthouse, that the legacy of the seventh president was jettisoned in favor of an itinerant drowning victim.

The town may have taken its name from an unlucky minister, but it owed its existence to Jacob Starcher, who build the first gristmill on the banks of Mill Creek and donated the acreage for the county seat and courthouse square. The town's commercial district radiated out from there, its main streets named for the points on the compass, though in John Morgan's time South Street would be re-christened Lydia Street in fond remembrance of a certain lady *"much visited by the menfolk"*.[1]

Within two decades of its founding, Ripley's fledgling governmental body was faced with its first capital murder case. Both victim and murderer were outsiders, but the crime fell under Jackson County jurisdiction and its citizens did their duty. A ravine just outside of town where the gallows was built became known as Green's Hollow, named for Charles Green (no relation to the Pfost-Greene family) who murdered a fellow steamboat crew member.

At the time of the Civil War, Ripley was an isolated backwater with only 180 residents. When western Virginia broke away from the Confederacy the Union retained control of Jackson County, but there were Southern sympathizers in the town and skirmishes were commonplace, often between the Union infantry headquartered in nearby Ravenswood and a band of guerillas known as the Moccasin Rangers.

Farmers on both sides were routinely subject to depredation and retaliation; grain and livestock were stolen from Union families to provide food and transport for the opposition, and the Union Army burned the homesteads of suspected Confederate sympathizers.

Recovery during the post-war period was slow and each new election fueled ongoing feuds and re-opened old wounds. Those who had supported secession could no longer hold office or vote. Ordinary citizens pointed fingers at neighbors who were known or suspected to have been Southern sympathizers during the war, and accused old friends of past wrong doings.

Despite the years of discord, Ripley continued to prosper and grow. Major Charles Henry Progler, a first generation Swiss immigrant and builder by trade, was responsible for much of the town's architectural landscape over the next several decades. He also had a large woodworking factory in town which turned out furniture, buggies, spokes and wagons. As a young man he had witnessed the building of Charlie Green's scaffold and the early experience proved useful when the time came for him to build one for John Morgan.

A newspaper was needed to keep everyone abreast of all the new developments, and during the war years two ex-sheriffs, brothers John and William Greer, established the *Jackson Democrat*. Though the paper died out a little over a decade later, it was soon resurrected as the *Jackson Herald* by new owner and editor Henry Deem, a local teacher. It was considered one of the finest county newspapers in the state, described favorably in the trade as "*lively*" and "*readable.*"[2] The year before the Pfost-Greene tragedy, a second newspaper—the *Mountaineer*—also started circulation.

As the agricultural center of the area, Ripley was quickly becoming a gateway town. Steamboats plying the Ohio River made stops at Ripley Landing, located at the mouth of Mill Creek about thirteen miles away, and much of the area's livestock and goods were transported from there. In John Morgan's time it was also the site of the closest telegraph office and this long-distance commute was no small inconvenience to the swarm of reporters that would converge on the little town of Ripley, and contributed to their frequent erroneous reporting.

In the 1880s the railroads began to replace roads and rivers as the primary means of transportation. The Ripley and Mill Creek Valley Railway Line opened in 1888, establishing direct contact with the outside world and catapulting the little town into the Industrial Age. Next to the hanging of Charlie Green, the opening of the little railway was the biggest thing that had ever happened in Ripley, and everyone turned out to celebrate. The new depot was decked out in red, white, and blue bunting and the first train arrived festooned with flags and local VIPs. The gala was marked by the firing of cannons and rockets, and editor Henry Deem rhapsodized:[3]

The lady photographer setting up equipment in the foreground is Miss Susan King, who would later capture the images of John Morgan's execution. Photo courtesy of the Mike McGrew Collection.

The long-talked-about, much-desired, hard-worked-for, sometimes-almost-despaired-of, county-developing, wealth-creating, travel-accelerating Ripley & Mill Creek Valley railway now bears the engine and cars from the Ohio River road to Ripley.

Not everyone was enamored with the coming of the Iron Horse to Jackson County. Cinders from the locomotives started fires, the noise scared the horses, and everyone feared it would bring in more riffraff—*"more whiskey drinkers and people with low morals."*₄ Residents complained that they couldn't sleep because the firemen kept up a head of steam throughout the night.₅ As a compromise, the train was parked overnight a half mile down the track and peaceful slumber was restored.

Riding these rails was not for the faint of heart. The building of the railway into Ripley was no small feat, thanks to the rugged terrain, and while only a little over twelve miles in length, it incorporated thirteen trestles along with steep gradients and tight curves.₆ A special correspondent from the *New York Sun* made the train journey to Ripley to attend the hanging and included this description as part of his coverage:₇

This photo taken of the Ripley's muddy main street shows the Bank of Ripley with Pfost's drug store next door.

It is reached by a branch of the Ohio River Railroad known as the Mill Creek and Ripley branch, which railroad is referred to out there as resembling a plug of dog-leg tobacco, dog-leg being the crookedest kind of plug known. While the road is only thirteen miles long, it takes anywhere from an hour to three hours for the single passenger train to go the distance.

It was judged at the time as being *"in dangerous condition all along,"* and badly in need of repair.[8] In fact, a train wreck on the line occurred just before the large crowds started gathering for Morgan's hanging.

The Ripley and Millcreek Valley Railway served the little community for nearly seventy-five years, and although the line is no longer in existence, the station depot still stands on the western side of Mill Creek just beyond the bridge.

With the expansion of the railroad, West Virginia's timber business soared. A timber boom was built on Mill Creek to catch the logs coming downstream from the various clear cuts, and heavy rains during timber-cutting season were considered a godsend. Railroad ties and lumber were hauled to the train depot for loading, and during high yield seasons freight wagons might be backed up all the way through town and for a mile or

Starcher Brothers Mercantile. Photo courtesy of the Mike McGrew Collection

more along the Charleston Pike. Local businessmen made small fortunes. Much of Floyd Pfost's wealth was built on timber and he owned a lumbermill in town in addition to his other business interests.

The up and coming little town had just about everything it needed when it came time to host John Morgan's execution. It could boast several mercantile stores, including O.J. Morrison's, A.M. Carson's, the Ripley Merchandise Company, and Starcher Brothers, all of whom advertised heavily during the week of the hanging, *"On account of the Great Crowd and Jam Expected on the 16th"* (the day set for Morgan's execution), and seven hotels.₉

There were a couple of harness shops and blacksmiths, hardware stores and jewelers, confectioneries, a barber and a butcher, and at least one millinery shop and a shoe store. Five physicians practiced in town, along with eight attorneys. There were five churches and an opera house, but not a single drinking establishment due to Ripley's temperance leanings. Isaiah Vail, who owned the second woodworking shop, doubled as the town's undertaker.

At the time of John Morgan's trial about 500 individuals lived within the town limits, most on half acre lots that included a residence, barn, hen coop, pig pen and sometimes a garden. Streets were unpaved and in the dry season created a cloud of dust that blanketed everything and made breathing difficult. Rain made things even more challenging and mud was considered a major tribulation. For those living in Ripley, a hard rain meant crossing streets in ankle deep mud to reach the rough board walk on the other side, and loaded wagons might sink hub deep in places.

But there were worse aspects to living in town:[10]

"The town was infested with flies and rats. There were no screens on doors and windows so the flies could enter the homes at their pleasure... The horse and cow manure in every barn and scattered on the gardens made an ideal breeding place for millions of flies. Corn kept in cribs for feed for the livestock furnished food for countless rats. Anywhere in town, one could see rats scurrying from one building to another and dashing under the wooden sidewalks and across the dirt streets."

The last decade of the century was a watershed in the Nation's history, marking a shift to industrial development. Yet everything was not so thoroughly modern in Jackson County. In the fall of 1897 even the most progressive residents were caught straddling the new millennium with one foot still very firmly entrenched in traditions viewed as outdated, even *"barbaric"* by much of the nation.

And the proud citizens of Ripley were soon to be brought low by their portrayals in the northern press.

End Notes

[1] Crow, George Burton, *Ripley about 1900-1915, Jackson County History Vol 1972-1973.*

[2] Rowel's American Newspaper Directory, 1885.

[3] *The Jackson Herald,* Ripley, WV, 28 September, 1887.

[4] Moore, Dean W. *Washington's Woods: A History of Ravenswood and Jackson County, West Virginia*, McClain Printing Co, Parsons, WV 1971, p. 172.

[5] Crow.

[6] Dan Robie's *History of the B & O Line* at http://www.wvncrails.weebly.com.

[7] *New York Sun,* New York, NY, 19 December, 1897.

[8] *Jackson Herald,* Ripley, WV, 18 December, 1897.

[9] *Ibid.*

[10] Crow.

A MOB FORMS IN RIPLEY

Sheriff Owen Shinn was worried about taking his prisoner into town; word had reached him that a mob awaited him in Ripley and there was heated talk of lynching. Including his brothers Reuben and John, Shinn had five deputies, and he had just deputized John Shamblin and a few others to serve as guards. They discussed taking Morgan to the neighboring town of Spencer or even as far as Parkersburg. They also toyed with the idea of flagging down the train at a location several miles away so they could board Morgan without interference.[1] But jurisdiction had a very personal meaning for a man in his first term as sheriff, and eager to prove himself, Shinn decided he could handle things in town. This was his first mistake.

An excited throng was gathered around the courthouse and jail, and the *Clarksburg Telegram* reported that:[2]

As the officers were taking Morgan through the streets of Ripley to put him in jail, a mob wrought up to the highest pitch of excited indignation, formed in a few moments and closed in about the officers and their prisoner, with the avowed intention of taking possession of Morgan and stringing him up the nearest tree.

Shinn must have realized how badly he'd miscalculated as soon as he rode into town. "*The feeling of the people is indescribable, as the murdered victims were held in the highest esteem by all.*"[3] As John Morgan was pulled out of the wagon to be marched the final distance to the jail, Chloe's son George pushed forward and shouted, *"John, did you kill my mother?"* When Morgan nodded, George drew a gun from his pocket, but his brother Floyd grabbed his arm, saying, *"Now George, you be careful what you do. There's been too much of that done already."*[4]

By some accounts, the mob swelled to between four and five hundred individuals, many determined to take the law into their own hands. It was all Shinn and his men could do to keep pressing forward, trying to shield their prisoner, until they reached the comparative safety of the dilapidated jailhouse. They were too few to withstand any determined onslaught, however, and matters could have turned deadly at any moment.

The term *lynching* had been popularized by the press only recently. The

New York Sun, whose correspondent wrote so colorfully about Morgan, was the first newspaper to define the word and its origins.[5] One popular theory surmised that it evolved from the era of Charles Lynch, a Virginia planter and justice of the peace during the Revolutionary War, who was prone to inflicting various punishments on Tory lawbreakers.[6] The term referred to any form of vigilante justice—from tarring and feathering, to beating, burning, or hanging—when men in the street delivered retribution without benefit of judge and jury.

In 1903 the *Cleveland Gazette* reported that there had been 3,233 lynching incidents across the U.S., *"in one form or another,"* over the previous two decades.[7] The majority had racial overtones, but there were many examples of white-on-white violence, particularly of the so-called *"white-cap"* variety in which secret societies rode at night dispensing their own brand of law enforcement. Lynching was frequently sanctioned by society at large and by the press. The victim's race was quickly identified, his character swiftly judged, as illustrated by the inflammatory coverage and pejorative labels—*"fiend," "brute," "unspeakable wretch,"* and guilt was assumed with the word *alleged* nowhere to be found. The *Sun* editorialized that, *"sometimes the offence is so outrageous that the people rise up in their might and string the fiend up to the nearest tree."*[8] Some lawmakers even believed that while lynching might have its drawbacks, the advantages were greatly underestimated: *"…few innocent men are lynched and those that are so are not desirable members of society, and the custom is certainly a great deterrent of crime."*[9]

During the 1890s West Virginia witnessed at least one lynching per year along with numerous threats and aborted attempts.[10] Just a decade before, the *New York Times* published an account of the lynching of three young men, one of them only 16, conducted by a group of Klu Klux Klan nightriders from Jackson and Roane Counties.[11] There were most certainly men in the crowd that day in Ripley who knew how these affairs were conducted.

Not all newspaper editors were willing to accept lynching as the status quo. Reacting to yet another West Virginia lynching a few months after Morgan's execution, the *Wheeling Register* issued a scathing editorial under the headline, *"Giving the State a Bad Name": "If this sort of thing is to go on, West Virginia might as well abolish her criminal courts."*[12] As the new millennium approached, the state was just beginning to come to terms with what it meant to be civilized, as defined by the outside world, and many of its citizens were less than enthusiastic about what they might have to sacrifice to meet that standard.

The sheriff and his men had barricaded themselves in the jailhouse and it now appeared they were going to be overrun. Shinn's newly deputized lawmen must have been frantically wondering if their new sheriff expected them to open fire on their friends and relations to save an ax-murderer. Things might have turned ugly indeed had it not been for the courage and eloquence of one man.

There was a newly appointed circuit court judge in town that day. Judge Reese Blizzard had confidently convened his courtroom that morning only to have his proceedings preempted by the news from Grasslick. Just two weeks shy of his thirty-third birthday when he walked out of his courthouse to face down the mob, Judge Blizzard was as cool as his name and just as forceful.

He walked straight into the heart of the crowd without hesitating, raised his voice and began his appeal to their better judgment, imploring them *"to remember their duty as good citizens, to let the law take its own course."*[13] He reminded them that there would be no legal delays since the court was already in session and promised that *"swift justice"* would be meted out to the prisoner.[14] Blizzard was quite specific in his assurances, promising that he would summon a special grand jury, have Morgan indicted and tried immediately, and if found guilty, hanged within thirty days.[15] He would tolerate no delays in his courtroom, he assured the crowd, and in return all he asked was that they spare the life of John Morgan long enough for him to administer the law of the land.

Blizzard proved amazingly adept at crowd control. Impressed, the mob decided to adopt a wait-and-see attitude and slowly began to disperse. This wasn't Blizzard's first experience with a lynch mob. A decade earlier in Calhoun County, he had been appointed to defend a father-son duo by the name of Sickles who stood accused of murdering a well-respected young man in Blizzard's home town of Grantsville. The *New York Times* reported on a party of thirty men, disguised in bedsheets and blankets, who rode into town a few nights before the trial and stopped at Blizzard's front door. *"Great indignation was manifested at the outrage, and threats of lynching the Sickles were made, but excitement was allayed by promises of a speedy trial."*[16]

Blizzard ably defended the Sickles, though he made no attempt to dazzle the court with tricky legal maneuverings that might have delayed the outcome, and the expected guilty verdict satisfied the Grantsville nightriders.

A Lynching Averted in West Virginia by a
Judge's Promise of Speedy Justice

Headline from the *New York Times*, 06 November, 1897

There was a great to-do in the press about the Ripley mob incident and the trial that followed. Blizzard's stature took on heroic proportions almost overnight and inspired this effusive letter to the editor of the *Morgantown Post:*[17]

How overpoweringly grand and noble was the attitude of Judge Blizzard, who exercised the God-given power of oratory with such effect that the bloodthirsty crowd dispersed. All honor to this hero, who deserves to go down to remotest history side by side with Grant, Lincoln, and the nation's greatest men. These are the men we want in office, and in whose hands our rights and our liberty may be safely be trusted.

And indeed, it wouldn't be long before there was talk of Blizzard's candidacy in the next gubernatorial election. For the moment at least, the crisis was averted. The threat of vigilante justice would remain omnipresent throughout the coming weeks, however, as a constant reminder of the people's will.

End Notes

[1] *Parkersburg Sentinel*, Parkersburg, WV, 4 November, 1897.

[2] *Clarksburg Telegram*, 12 November, 1897.

[3] *Wheeling Register*, 5 November, 1897.

[4] This information comes from Mary Chancey's recollections recorded on two separate occasions, her interview with *Goldenseal Magazine* in 1990 and in an audio-taped interview with Betty Jean Fourney in 1986.

[5] Waldrep, Christopher. *The Many Faces of Judge Lynch: Extralegal Violence and Punishment in America*. Palgrave Macmillan. 2002, p. 22.

[6] *Ibid.*

[7] *The Cleveland Gazette*, Cleveland, OH, 16 May, 1903.

[8] *The New York Sun*, New York, NY, 30 July, 1894.

[9] Speech on "*Civil and Religious Liberty,*" given by the Hon Charles Joseph Bonaparte, as reported in *The New York Sun*, 19 January, 1898.

[10] Konhaus, Tim. "I Thought Things Would Be Different There": Lynching and the Black Community in Southern West Virginia, 1880-1933, *West Virginia History: A Journal of Regional Studies*, New Series, Volume 1, Number 2, (Fall 2007): 27.

[11] *New York Times*, New York, NY, 17 October, 1887.

[12] *The Wheeling Register*, Wheeling, WV, 2 April, 1898.

[13] *Morgantown Post,* Morgantown, WV, 4 November, 1897.

[14] *Ibid.*

[15] *Morgantown Post,* 6 November, 1897.

[16] *New York Times,* New York, NY, 18 June, 1886.

[17] *Morgantown Post,* Morgantown, WV, 9 December, 1897.

A BLIZZARD ON THE BENCH, CRIME REPORTERS, AND A MERCHANT PRINCE

The son of a Scots-Irish Methodist preacher, Republican Reese Blizzard was the youngest circuit court judge on record in West Virginia, having surprised everyone by winning the position in a primarily Democratic district. John Morgan entered Blizzard's courtroom in the second year of his term.

After presiding over the trial that resulted in West Virginia's last public hanging, Judge Blizzard went on to gain further recognition with his prosecution of Mary Harris Jones, the infamous *"Mother Jones,"* who was charged with breaking the injunction that banned striking miners from congregating. By the time Jones was tried in Parkersburg in 1902, Blizzard was well into his next role as U.S. District Attorney. Regarding this fearless Irish-American labor organizer, memorialized in the old folksong, *She'll Be Comin' 'Round the Mountain,* Blizzard was quoted as saying, *"She comes into a state where peace and prosperity reign. She crooks her finger and 20,000 men lay down their tools."* [1] He famously labeled her *"The most dangerous woman in America"* and she reveled in it. Later, when an attempt was made to rehabilitate her image by calling her a *"great humanitarian,"* Jones fired back, *"Get it straight. I'm no humanitarian. I'm a hell raiser."* [2]

Judge Reese Blizzard

Blizzard has been described as one of the earliest progressive Republicans in West Virginia. He strongly opposed strikes for instance, and yet he contended that companies were largely at fault for their refusal to improve working conditions. Many of his ideas were revolutionary, bordering on socialist, and his family ties are interesting. His brother Tim was a life-long coal miner and married to activist Sarah Rebecca Rogers, known fondly by the men of United Mine Workers District 17 as *"Mother Blizzard."* She tirelessly worked the coalfield strikes with Mother Jones, and later stood *"with a crowbar in her hand,"* alongside her son Bill when he led 10,000 armed coal miners in the Battle of Blair Mountain.[3] Bill Blizzard became an incendiary force in the union's early opposition to the coal operators, and in this instance even Mother Jones tried to hold him back.[4] How did Judge Blizzard feel, having sentenced men to hang for less, when his own nephew went on trial for treason?

From the beginning, Blizzard drew attention for the speed and efficiency with which he conducted business in his courtroom. Shortly after John Morgan's trial, he described his efforts to streamline court procedure:[5]

I look upon a court as a business established by the State for the welfare of the people. I conduct court as I would any other business entrusted to me... As a result we have cleaned up the dockets in about one fourth the time heretofore customary. I have 15 sessions of court a year in the district. These sessions used to run two or three weeks. Now they finish in three or four days.

Although he was noted for legal productivity and enabling the wheels of justice to turn like a well-oiled machine, he was equally devoted to ensuring that justice was preserved for the innocent. He had only two reversals in the state supreme court in his entire career—setting yet another state record.[6] He was also known for his love of harness racing and his horses were often in the winner's circle. In fact, it was gleefully bruited about at the time of Morgan's trial that the staid and sober Blizzard had recently adjourned court just so he could get to the fair in time to see his fillies run.[7]

The judge was not a man to be trifled with, and he was not always calm, cool and collected. A few years later he would create quite a stir when he forcibly evicted a former U.S. senator and longtime political adversary from his office in the U.S. courthouse. The man had the temerity to use Blizzard's telephone without first asking permission and the judge physically ousted him, *"giving him, it is claimed, several kicks as he went."*[8]

As news of the murders spread throughout the countryside it was feared the mob might regroup, and this time, if better organized, might prevail.[9] The authorities debated the feasibility of removing Morgan to nearby Ravenswood or Spencer, but by then it was considered too risky. Clusters of armed men milled about the courthouse, arguing loudly and claiming to guard the jail, which was described as a *"mere rattle-trap, and easy to escape from."*[10]

Journalists from as far away as New York City would arrive later. All of them provided blow-by-blow descriptions of the proceedings, complete with the hyperbole of the time and some amazing details, many of which were surprisingly accurate. The interest of the *New York Sun* was piqued early on, and its special correspondent came to town in time for the hanging. From the shadow of the gallows he wrote a long and wildly descriptive account of the *"shetting out of John Morgan"* that by turns both amused and appalled its readers. Well over a century later it has lost none of its power and appeal.

Some newspapers, like the *Pittsburgh Post Gazette,* focused most of their attention on the legal aspects, conducting in-depth interviews with Judge Blizzard and writing lengthy articles about his progressive ideas and crusade to modernize court proceedings to save taxpayer dollars. Others concentrated on keeping their readers on the edge of their seats with daily news of the *"West Virginia Desperado,"* along with interesting elements of local color.

As mentioned earlier, there was no telegraph in Ripley, the closest being located at the riverboat landing, and there were only a few telephones in the area. These were installed in the banks and larger businesses and connected on the Parkersburg to Charleston line. People depended on their hometown newspaper for the news.

1897, the year the Pfost-Greene murders were committed, has been called *"the year that defined American journalism."*[11] It was the year that New York City's news titans went head to head, battling for ascendancy in the headlines in such a dramatic fashion that the outcome determined the course of journalism well into the next century. Best-seller headlines were those with the greatest shock factor. To qualify as truly electrifying, the story needed to remind the reader of his or her own vulnerability. John Morgan's crimes met all the requirements. He was the boy next door, well thought of by those who knew him, and close to the family he murdered. He was a family man and to all appearances a loving husband and father, and if the rumors were true he'd once courted one of his intended victims. He used a hatchet, often referred to as an ax in those days, that messiest and most horrifying of Victorian murder weapons, and seemingly the weapon of choice. And his motive remained a mystery.

America at the turn of the century was a willing captive to a new spectator sport—sitting at the breakfast table and searching the daily headlines for news of the latest whodunit. While the upper crust may have frowned upon sensational novels and so-called *penny dreadfuls*, newspapers adopted the same successful formula. Every crime was transformed into a melodrama and the reading public of all classes hung on every word.

There was a customary format to crime reporting. First came the discovery of the bodies, including all the lurid details—some far too graphic for today's coverage. Then came the capture of the perpetrator, to be followed, or so it was hoped, by his or her full confession. And then the moment of truth: following a speedy trial, the verdict was rendered and the public was reassured that no matter how diabolical the deed, justice always triumphed. Threats of lynching were thrown in for good measure and in the way of all good morality plays, the curtain came down as punishment was meted out in the final act—the execution—the more appalling the better.

John Morgan was about to meet the press after a very full day. He'd narrowly avoided a lynching, and now he was being introduced to Henry W. Deem, editor and publisher of Ripley's *Jackson Herald*. Deem had been taking notes all day. True, it was only Wednesday; his paper didn't hit the streets until Friday and the big city dailies had the lead. But Deem held the hometown advantage, and the extra day gave him opportunity to ensure greater accuracy and detail.

When Morgan spoke with Deem that evening he continued to maintain his innocence regarding motive and intent, still claiming self-defense and *"telling a yarn not in the least plausible and apparently constructing it as he spoke."*[12]

Until almost the end, John Morgan seemed to be making it up as he went along. None of his confessions bore much relation to preceding ones, and each was more implausible than the last. As terrified as he must have been that first day of captivity, Morgan soon developed a taste for notoriety. In the days and weeks that followed he seemed to enjoy reading about himself and began to give more careful consideration to how his words might appear in print.

Another gentleman was also taking note of the day's happenings. Okey Johnson Morrison was in the crowd that day in Ripley, and though not a journalist, this young entrepreneur's business acumen is the only reason that anything resembling a historical record related to John Morgan exists. Morrison, who went by *"Oak"* or *"O. J.,"* was a 28-year-old shopkeeper from Kenna who had recently opened a second, larger establishment in Ripley. He had a reputation as an honest dealer of quality merchandise sold at bargain prices. His mentor, a local Irish peddler, had taught him to buy discounted goods in volume in big cities like Columbus, Cincinnati or Chicago, and then undersell his local competitors.[13] He once started a fashion trend when he returned to Ripley with several hundred derby hats, having procured the entire lot for just 65 cents. These sold at ten cents each and were worn by men and boys all over the county. Scrutiny of the photographs of the crowd around Morgan's gallows reveals a great number of derbies. Despite his humble business beginnings, O. J. Morrison would go on to earn the sobriquet *Merchant Prince of West Virginia* and before his death he would lay claim to a chain of fifteen discount department stores throughout the state.

Morrison has been described as possessing *"the mind to plan"* along with *"the ability to execute and the foresight to grasp opportunities conditions produce."*[14] When he was twelve he seized the opportunity presented by crowds at a 4th of July celebration to sell lemonade and some of his mother's pies. Barefoot, wearing overalls and with his hair slicked back, he tirelessly worked the crowd and by the end of the day he'd pocketed $21, a princely sum in those days.[16]

Okey Johnson "O.J." Morrison

O. J. Morrison attended the trial, obtained copies of the transcripts, and gathered photographs and drawings of all those involved. In return for John Morgan's story, he offered him $25 to be used for the support of his wife and child, as well as a new suit of clothes to wear to his hanging. In the short period between the commission of the crimes and Morgan's execution, Morrison produced a small souvenir booklet entitled, *The Slaughter of the Pfost-Greene Family of Jackson County, W.Va. A History of the Tragedy with a notice of the early settlers of Jackson County, A Sketch of the Family and John F. Morgan, and all connected. His Trial and sentence by the court: his confession: Escape from Jail and Recapture: His execution,* and as the title page proudly notes, it was indeed *Profusely Illustrated.*

On December 16, 1897, Morrison sold several thousand copies of his little murder pamphlet for 25 cents apiece. The atmosphere on that day might have easily resembled that earlier 4th of July celebration. Thousands picnicked on the hillsides, drinking moonshine and lemonade, and munching on hot roasted peanuts.

The festivities were interrupted just long enough for John Ferguson Morgan, looking rather dapper in his nice new suit and crush hat, to climb the scaffold, bow to the onlookers, and swing into eternity.

End Notes

[1] Fetherling, Dale, *Mother Jones: The Miners' Angel,* Southern Illinois Press, 1974, p. 85.

[2] Gorn, Elliot, *Mother Jones: The Most Dangerous Woman in America*, New York: Hill and Wang, 2001, p. 3.

[3] Reference to T. Paige Dalporto's lyrics for *"Ma Blizzard,"* as recorded by Mountain Whispers (2006) on *When Miner's March.*

[4] *The Charleston Gazette,* Charleston, WV. 26, May, 1922.

[5] *Indiana Gazette*, Indiana, PA 17 Nov pg 12.

[6] *The History of West Virginia, Old and New: Vol III,* 1923, Chicago: The American Historical Society, p. 4.

[7] *Morning Herald,* Lexington, KY 9 November, 1897.

[8] *Pittsburgh Daily Post,* Pittsburgh, PA, 17 June, 1903.

[9] *The Wheeling Register*, Wheeling, WV, 4 November, 1897.

[10] *The History of West Virginia, Old and New: Vol III,* 1923, Chicago: The American Historical Society, p. 4.

[11] Campbell, W. Joseph. *The Year That Defined American Journalism: 1897 and the Clash of Paradigms*. Routledge: 2006.

[12] *Jackson Herald,* Ripley, WV, 12 November, 1897.

[13] *Jackson Herald, "Morrison Edition,"* Ripley, WV, 11 January, 1950.

[14] Ruben, Mike. *"O.J.Morrison—a legend was launched,"* Jackson Star News, February, 1992.

THE DAY AFTER

The morning after the murders, Judge Blizzard convened the grand jury and called Sheriff Owen Shinn, Coroner David Brown, and Deputy John Shamblin to the stand. In short order three indictments were returned, each reading the same—that John Morgan "*…feloniously, willfully, maliciously, deliberately, and unlawfully did slay, kill and murder one* [the name of the victim], *against the peace and dignity of the State.*"[1] The State would try Morgan for only one of these—the murder of Chloe Greene. After all, one was all they needed to hang him.

An emotionally withdrawn Morgan was brought into the courtroom, described by Morrison as looking "*as cool as if nothing had ever happened in which he was concerned.*"[2] When asked if he had an attorney, Morgan surprised everyone by pointing to David Brown, who stood up and stoutly denied that this was the case. In the end, despite his efforts to avoid the matter, Brown was appointed to represent the prisoner.[3]

It must have been difficult for the attorney, a relative newcomer, to find himself in the unenviable position of defending the most notorious criminal the county had ever prosecuted. Judge Blizzard was not insensitive to his dilemma. The next day as he addressed the packed courtroom he explained that although David Brown had not chosen this role, he was duty-bound to give his best effort to this assignment, and under no circumstances was anyone to treat him with disrespect.[4]

Whatever the former prosecutor may have thought of this dubious honor, when Morgan was asked how he responded to the indictments, Brown stood ready with a plea of "*Not Guilty.*" He hurriedly conferred with his client and then demanded that John's wife Rebekah and his sister, Florence Casto, along with her husband Enoch, be summoned as witnesses. John's suggestion that the Castos might serve as witnesses suggests that he had some grasp of his only available escape route—a plea of insanity—since the Castos had witnessed some of his strange behaviors earlier that fall.

With John Morgan safely returned to his cell until the witnesses could be located, Judge Blizzard set about returning his courtroom to its normal state. There were cases besides capital murder on his docket, and in all the chaos, 70-year-old Ichabod Sayre, nicknamed "*Bird*" by his friends, had been nearly forgotten. He'd been sharing the jail with Morgan and had a ringside seat to all the activity, which, as far as Bird was concerned, had been the only bright spot in his otherwise dismal state of affairs. Now he stood before judge and jury and tried to explain why he'd shot his next-door-neighbor. Fortunately for both men, Bird's aim was off. Still, a jury of his peers found him guilty of unlawful shooting and Judge Blizzard sentenced him to a year in the Moundsville Penitentiary. At this, the old man broke down and cried.[5] For all he knew he might die there; at the very least he was going to miss the hanging. Happily, the septuagenarian did not die behind bars, and a year later returned home a more peaceable citizen.[6]

The combined courthouse and jail was a two-story building constructed in 1858 and it had recently been condemned due to its poor condition. Discussions for a new building were underway, but another twenty years would pass before these bore fruit.[7] The upper brick story housed the sheriff and the courtroom, while the ground floor contained both the cellblock and the jailer's residence.[8] The jail's massive tungsten steel doors are all that is left of the building now; they weigh 400 pounds apiece, stand approximately 10 feet tall and look to be indestructible. They could not, however, keep anyone in unless they were locked, a small matter that someone overlooked on the second night of December.

Morgan's trip upstairs to the courtroom that morning had involved further exposure to the angry crowd. Mentally unstable or not, the man was no fool. He understood that he was going to hang one way or the other unless he could get away. He asked for pencil and paper and sat down to write a letter to his sister Florence and her husband Enoch:[9]

"Well Enoch will you make up a squad of ten and come and take me out of here i herd mis mrs Wriley say that she will give up the Kees up come to night and bring a wrope and protend that you are going to hang me."

Morgan comes across as poorly educated, his communication rambling and disjointed. There is no hint of the craftiness he later demonstrated when he carefully planned and executed his jailbreak. This letter was immediately confiscated by Reuben Shinn, but Morrison preserved its contents, carefully including all of Morgan's spelling and grammatical errors.

There were a surprising number of people who remained quietly supportive of John Morgan, some of whom, it is assumed, later attempted to aid and abet his escape, or at least turned a blind eye while he did so.

Shinn and his deputies were well aware of this and remained vigilant, as did the "volunteer guards" from the would-be lynch mob.

That afternoon Ripley resembled a ghost town. Out on the Charleston Pike hundreds of people were making their solemn way by wagon, buggy or horseback, out to Grasslick to witness the burial of three of their friends and neighbors.

On a low, grassy hill overlooking what was once the old Pfost-Greene farm, stands a tall weathered obelisk inscribed with the names of the three victims, along with that of *"F. M. Pfost,"* and *"Serah."* On this memorial erected by her children, Chloe's name is spelled in the German manner— *Chloah*—and she carries the surname of her first husband, Francis Marion Pfost, the father of her surviving children, rather than that of Edward Greene. Both Marion and their 28-year-old daughter Serah preceded her in death and were buried in this small family cemetery. The Pfost-Greene cemetery remains well-tended.

In rural areas of central Appalachia old family cemeteries are often found near the homes of early patriarchs. Many of these lovely old family plots are over-grown and nearly inaccessible now, but the Pfost-Greene cemetery remains well-tended. It is a peaceful spot, filled with the sound of the wind and bird song.

In those days, funerals often took place the day after the demise, particularly in the summertime. In small communities like Grasslick funeral preparations were both a familial and communal responsibility, and embalming was rare. Neighbors arrived to bathe the bodies and assist with the laying out. Bodies were generally laid out on tables, though most families simply removed a door from its hinges, placed it on saw horses and set the coffin on top.

Undertaking in rural areas had not yet transformed itself into professional funeral directing and was still mostly a sideline business. Isaiah Vail had been part of the influx of new immigrants who moved into Ripley in the 1840s, and his mechanics and woodworking shop had been in business for decades. He also made caskets, which were displayed in a back room or on the second floor of the establishment which still bears his name. Isaiah was no longer living at the time of the Pfost-Greene murders, and so it fell to his son Joseph to supply the caskets.

Except for accidental or untimely deaths, the passing of a loved one was not necessarily a solemn occasion. On the first night or two after the death, friends and neighbors gathered in the family home to share memories, food, and drink and celebrate a life well-lived. Wakes might last well into the night, and then one or two individuals joined the family in holding a final candlelight vigil by the corpse throughout the lonely hours, praying for both the departing soul and the bereaved. The ritual of waking the dead was a very practical response to the long-standing dread that seized the Victorian psyche in the 19th century. Fear of premature burial was not just a hysteria born of over-active imaginations fed by Edgar Allan Poe's newly created horror genre and bloodcurdling newspaper accounts. It was not so much a matter of whether such unfortunate events really occurred, but how often.

Medical professionals favored a cautionary approach, urging the public to put off burial until the body showed signs of decomposition—in other words to watch and wait. Safety coffins were manufactured complete with breathing tubes, periscopes, telephones, and alarm bells, and the graveyard shift was created as watchers were hired to patrol the churchyards, alert for any signs of life. In the case of the Pfost-Greenes, however, there was never any doubt. The nature of the wounds and the amount of blood loss was unequivocal.

Entire rituals surrounded the funereal process in the late Victorian Age—from the clothing and jewelry that were de rigueur during the proscribed stages of mourning, to the memorabilia or so-called momento mori that were collected to be cherished long afterwards. Locks of hair were clipped to be woven into miniature mourning wreaths and mounted under glass, made into intricate jewelry or encased in lockets. Photographers were called upon to take portraits of the deceased posed with family members or carefully arranged amid beautiful floral displays. While today such traditions may be viewed as creepily grotesque, these were meant to provide comfort to the bereaved and were an integral part of the normal grieving process, even in rural Appalachia. In the case of the Pfost-Greene burials, however, there was neither the time nor the inclination for this kind of indulgence.

The wake was held the same evening as the murders even though the victims' blood still stained the porch and walkways, splattered the walls, and pooled on the floor.[10] Yet the remaining family members stoically persevered. Faith was all that was left them. Hymns were sung, scriptures read and prayers said, and individuals took turns witnessing—sharing favorite memories of the deceased and bearing testimony to their spiritual goodness. Outside, men huddled in groups, smoking, and discreetly drinking as talk turned to John Morgan and the price that must be paid for this outrage.

Just before sunrise men from Grasslick were up with shovels in hand. It was not terribly cold that morning. Still, the tramping of their feet left imprints on the lightly frosted earth and their breath sent gentle puffs of mist into the morning air. They stood for a moment on the hilltop watching the sunrise—the weather was clear—and then they began to dig, all of them keenly aware that this was no ordinary grave. This one had to be six-foot-deep as was traditional, but extra wide to accommodate three caskets lying side by side. The family would be laid to rest facing the rising sun in readiness for the rapture.

In preparation for the afternoon funeral, the bodies were carried out of the house feet first as was customary, and lined up along the porch in the same position. By three o'clock, the fields surrounding the old farmhouse were overflowing with people. The *Cincinnati Enquirer* claimed that several thousand attended the Pfost-Greene funeral.[11]

The family had been members of the Ephesus Baptist church and their pastor began the service by reading from the scriptures and intoning the promise of life everlasting. He also preached hell-fire and damnation to the biggest crowd he was ever likely to have at his disposal. Country funerals were lengthy affairs in those days—lasting several hours—and the attending crowds at the Pfost-Greene funeral remained standing in the cold until after sundown.

Mr. J. G. Childs of Portsmouth, Ohio received a letter from his mother who attended the funeral. A widow who had recently married a local miller, Elizabeth Chase and her husband Henry knew the Pfost-Greene family well, and were a part of the congregation that afternoon:[12]

It was the most awful sight I ever beheld. There were from three to five thousand people there. They had the three caskets in the yard by the porch so people could view their poor mutilated bodies. They were in very high standing in the community.

Following the service, the coffins were loaded onto wagons and the sad procession set off down the road. The family walked or rode in buggies immediately behind, and when they reached the path to the hill pallbearers stepped up to shoulder their burdens, while friends and neighbors followed behind carrying lanterns. At the graveside, the men used ropes to gently lower the bodies into the grave, one after another. The pastor offered a final benediction and the congregation took turns filling the grave by handful and shovel.

For now, it was finished. A mother and her children had been laid to rest—those last terrible moments of pain and horror were all behind them. Now it was for the living to find what comfort there was to be had in swift retribution.

End Notes

[1] Author's Note: Though the court transcripts no longer exist, the original indictments for the Pfost-Greene murders are housed in the West Virginia Archives.

[2] Morrison, O. J., *The Slaughter of the Pfost-Greene Family of Jackson County, W.Va. A History of the Tragedy*, 1897.

[3] *The Jackson Herald*, Ripley, WV, 18 December, 1897.

[4] Morrison.

[5] *The Nicholas Chronicle*, Summersville, WV, 10 November, 1897.

[6] *Mountaineer*, Ripley, WV, 10 January, 1913.

[7] *Cincinnati Enquirer*, Cincinnati, OH, 6 November 1897, Front page.

[8] House, John A., **Pioneers of Jackson County,** an unpublished collection of historical notes donated by his family to the Jackson County Library. Found on www.wvgenweb.org/jackson/jh_jackson.index.html

[9] Morrison, O. J., *The Slaughter of the Pfost-Greene Family of Jackson County, W.Va. A History of the Tragedy*, 1897.

[10] *Cincinnati Enquirer*, Cincinnati, OH, 16 December, 1897, frontpage.

[11] *Cincinnati Enquirer*, Cincinnati, OH, 6 November, 1897, frontpage.

[12] *Portsmouth Daily Times*, Portsmouth, OH, 13 November, 1897.

THE TRIAL BEGINS: FRIDAY, NOVEMBER 5, 1897

Crowds Thronged the Streets and Threatened to Make Good Any Error or Delay of the Law's Machinery

Headlines from the Wheeling Register, Wheeling, WV, 06 November, 1897.

Ripley was filled with strangers on the morning of the trial. The courtroom was packed to the rafters, leaving hundreds to congregate outside in the square. News spread that Alice Pfost, the fourth victim, was not dead or dying as reported. Instead, that morning she was going to appear in their midst like Lazarus rising from the tomb, the star witness for the prosecution.

As people jockeyed for position in the second-floor courtroom, Judge Blizzard cautioned the crowds to have a care. The building had been condemned and there were grave structural concerns with over-crowding.[1] The doorway and aisles were packed so tightly the sheriff and his deputies had to strong-arm their way through in single-file to move their prisoner into the courtroom. The *Cincinnati Enquirer* reported that a mob of at least thirty *"organized"* men from Grasslick had arrived in town around

The old Jackson County courthouse. Photo courtesy of the Mike McGrew collection.

midnight. Now they were overheard in the courtroom loudly announcing that, *"should the verdict be less than death...they would drag him out and hang him."* [2]

John Morgan must have known he didn't stand a chance. As he made his way from the jail to the courtroom the press of the hostile crowd made him nervous and agitated, but once inside he regained his stoic composure:

He did not appear in the least affected by the crowd of surly mountaineers that pressed him on every side. [3] Several reporters described Morgan as, *"indifferent, unconcerned, and careless."* [4]

The prisoner sat in the dock in a shiftless manner, a serious, vacant look on this thin, expressionless countenance. [5]

As soon as Morgan reached the bar, he scanned the courtroom and asked for Rebekah. After being assured that she was on her way, he took his seat next to Sheriff Shinn. Rebekah arrived about five minutes later, escorted by a deputy and looking *"haggard and wan,"* with nine-month-old Albert in her arms. [6]

The jury had been impaneled the day before and had remained sequestered at a nearby hotel. Though orders had been given that they were not to be exposed to any news of the murders, such a thing was impossible in a small town whose streets were filled with citizens loudly discussing events under hotel windows.

To start, a series of questions was asked, to which the jurors responded by nodding in unison. But when asked if anyone was related by blood or marriage to John Morgan, a slight hitch was encountered. A Casto was serving on the jury and the Castos were related to pretty near everyone, including John Morgan. J. B. Casto, being an upright and honest sort, spoke up: *"If he was born in our neighborhood, I might possibly be some relation to him but no blood relation."* [7] And when asked directly by Judge Blizzard whether he believed himself to be related, Casto responded as truthfully as he knew how: *"I would be about third cousin to his mother, if his mother was a Rollins."*

This peculiar understanding of one's pedigree—the implicit knowledge that to have been born into a certain community was to imply relationship to nearly everyone living there—was prevalent at the time, and to some degree remains so in the county today. Family lineage was one thing, but kinship had become a lateral heritage spreading out through entire communities and absorbing anyone with a particular surname. When

J. B. Casto replied, *"but no blood relation,"* he was referring to a possible relationship by way of marriage rather than direct blood ties. Marriage enlarged family ties; the brothers of one's wife were often referred to as *my brothers,* her cousins as *my cousins.* In that fashion, Rebekah Morgan's brother-in-law, Enoch Casto, was referenced as her *"brother."*

Blizzard took the issue of Casto's relationship very seriously and asked both attorneys to approach the bench for consultation. After some deliberation, the three of them reached the conclusion that Casto qualified as a relative. The judge asked the defendant if he had any objection to J. B. serving as a juror. Morgan did not, and the questioning continued. Were any of them related to Chloe Greene? Had any of them expressed an opinion or made up their minds about the prisoner's guilt or innocence? In response to this last question, the jurors to a man all lied and said, *"No, Sir."*

The court was now ready to hear the witnesses for the prosecution. Brown was prepared and his witnesses were at hand, but Prosecutor James Seaman's were not. Alice Pfost and Dr. John Bechtel had not arrived. When he learned that Dr. Bechtel was on his way into town with Miss Pfost, the judge ordered Sheriff Shinn to drive out to meet them, suggesting that the emotionally and physically fragile Alice be settled into a nearby house until it was time for her testimony.

During this interlude, a letter arrived for juror George Franklin, and he gave the Judge permission to read it.[8] Ax-murderers and their trials aside, Lydia Jane Franklin had a household to run. She needed flour and sugar, and various and sundry other items, and wanted her husband to please pick these up on his way home. Life went on.

Dr. Bechtel and Alice arrived in town shortly thereafter, but by this time the prosecutor was nowhere to be found. Court had been in session for a total of three hours and not a single testimony had been heard. Conditions in the crowded courtroom had become stifling, even with all the windows open. Judge Blizzard, loath to start the action so close to noon, reluctantly ordered a recess until 12:45. No one was permitted to move until the prisoner had been safely returned to his cell, and then, because of the dangerous condition of the building, the judge warned the audience to *"move out quietly lest a greater calamity befall the people of Jackson County."*[9] Nobody moved. No one wanted to risk losing their hard-won seats.

Judge Blizzard was not pleased. Little had been accomplished and the day was already half gone. This was not the way he was used to running his courtroom:[10]

My court starts like a mill. At 8 o'clock in the morning we begin business. If witnesses and jurors are not on hand, they get no pay. I call no one at the front door of the Court House. I hold no juries to wait for lawyers to get ready to try their cases. I run court from 8 to 12, and from 1 to 5:30 or 6. I draw the line on the attorneys, as well as on the others, and we do not consume time talking about nothing. I have noticed that the men in my district, who pay the costs of the courts, work long days and waste no time while they are at work. This being the case I see no reason why those who are employed by these men at carrying on the courts, should not earn the money in full days of honest attempts.

As part of his overall plan to streamline justice, Blizzard had enlisted the aid of an attractive young widow by the name of Anna McVay, the first female stenographer in West Virginia. Court reporters were rare before the 1920s and judges usually kept their own notes during the proceedings. Little is known about Mrs. McVay, sometimes spelled McVey. Anna later astonished the onlookers at Morgan's execution with her inclusion among the special dignitaries leading the procession to the scaffold. An even greater shock was in store when she climbed the scaffold and remained in full view throughout the proceedings, an unheard circumstance in those days,

The first female court stenographer in West Virginia, Mrs. Anna McVay

and one which made her the target of a good deal of criticism:[11] *"Her duties did not require her presence. She is the first woman in the state, if not in the United States, to appear on the scaffold at a hanging."*

But Anna's duties *did* require her to be on the scaffold. The progressive Judge Blizzard gave no consideration to her gender, only to her ability to do the job at hand. He and Sheriff Shinn requested her presence because Morgan had asked for ten minutes to speak to the crowd before the trap was sprung, and they wanted to ensure that every word he said was carefully written down.[12]

Not all members of the press were affronted by Anna's appearance on the scaffold. There were some, like the reporter for the *Cincinnati Post*, who were very taken with the pretty widow and found her devotion to her task quite admirable:[13]

Mrs. McVey, it is said, is the first woman stenographer who ever worked in the courts of West Virginia. She worked along as though reporting hangings was an ordinary affair, and bravely stood the ordeal. She seemed less concerned than many men who were present.

Whoever she was and whatever led her to resolutely enter a man's world, we have her to thank for the word-for-word transcription of the events in that courtroom. The excerpts included here are all taken from Morrison's *Slaughter of the Pfost-Greene Family*, as copies of the transcripts were provided to him just before his souvenir booklet went to press. Morrison may not have preserved everything in Anna's transcripts, but the material he used was carefully replicated and included the stenographer's obvious grammatical errors, misspellings, and colloquialisms, e.g. *"staid"* instead of stayed. The transcripts, even in Morrison's abbreviated format, provide an unusual window onto courtroom examination in the late 1800s. The originals have not survived.

End Notes

[1] *Cincinnati Enquirer,* Cincinnati, OH, 6 November, 1897, Front page.

[2] *Ibid.*

[3] *Pittsburgh Post-Gazette,* Pittsburgh, PA, 6 November, 1897, Front page.

[4] *Parkersburg Sentinel,* Parkersburg, WV, 6 November, 1897, Front page.

[5] *Ibid.*

[6] *Pittsburgh Daily Post.* Pittsburgh, PA, 6 November, 1897, Front page.

[7] Morrison, O. J., *The Slaughter of the Pfost-Greene Family of Jackson County, W.Va. A History of the Tragedy,* 1897.

[8] *Ibid.*

[9] *Cincinnati Enquirer.*

[10] *Indiana Gazette,* Indiana, PA, Nov 17, 1897. Interview with Judge Reese Blizzard.

[11] *The Evening Bulletin,* Maysville, KY, 20 December, 1897.

[12] *Cincinnati Enquirer,* 17 November, 1897.

[13] *Cincinnati Post,* Cincinnati, OH, 17 December, 1897.

THE BURDEN OF PROOF

Court reconvened at 1 o'clock and this time both counsels had their witnesses in hand. Alice Pfost was waiting in the wings nearby, resting from her long trip into town. Spectators hemmed in Judge Blizzard's desk and crowded around the jury, and despite repeated warnings men stood on tables and chairs in the back of the room.

Fifty-five-year-old James Seaman had been practicing law in Ripley for two decades. A staunch Republican, he'd been elected county prosecutor a decade before and had been re-elected the previous year. Despite walking with a limp due to a clubfoot, he cut an imposing figure, described by

Court room scene from the trial of John Ferguson Morgan. Blizzard presides from the elevated bench; Morgan sits to the left of the stove; Mrs. McVay is transcribing at the table. To her right is court clerk Marshal Archer, seated next to Prosecutor James Seaman.

one acquaintance as bearing a striking resemblance to Civil War General John McCausland and outlaw Frank James, both of whom sported the trademark handlebar mustache favored by Seaman.[1]

The State carried the burden of proof in the matter of John Morgan's guilt, and Seaman spent fifteen minutes of opening argument to that effect. There is no record that Morgan's attorney, David Brown, made any opening remarks, but this wasn't uncommon; defense attorneys often reserved their comments until the government rested its case.

Morrison included only those elements he thought would be of most interest to his audience. This makes it difficult to follow a particular line of questioning or the reasoning behind it, and the noticeable gaps in Morrison's selections seem maddeningly prejudicial at times.

Photograph of James A Seaman courtesy of the West Virginia Archives.

Brown was a highly respected, competent attorney doing his best to obtain a verdict of *"not guilty by reason of insanity,"* but it is hard to perceive his strategy using only Morrison's account. Witness testimony appears disjointed and ends suddenly without closure. A witness responds with information that would normally elicit further clarification, yet none seems forthcoming. To add to the confusion, Judge Blizzard took an unusually active part in the proceedings, hijacking first one attorney's role and then the other's, possibly in the hopes of moving things along.

Medical examiner John Bechtel was the first witness called by the prosecution. He began by explaining his long-standing connection with Chloe and her family. He described her as being over sixty years old, although he could not recall her exact age. She was only five-foot-tall and weighed between 150-160 pounds. She had been visually impaired, most likely from cataracts, and her physician believed she had been in danger of losing her sight altogether.

Bechtel attempted to demonstrate the exact nature of her wounds with the aid of a human skull. His written testimony is difficult for the modern reader to follow because of the antiquated medical terms and his use of the visual prop, but he confirmed that there were three wounds in all, at least two of them fatal.

The smallest wound was likely the result of the initial attack as Chloe faced her assailant. This was a cut to the temple just above her right eye, that was 1 ¼ inch deep. It was probably delivered in a short downward chopping motion since it was only about 1 ½ inches long and likely caused by the *heel*, that is the lower edge, of the hatchet. There was enough force behind the blow to create an indentation in the skull, but Bechtel believed Chloe might have survived this injury. This wound caused the *"discoloration or darkening of the face."*

The deadlier blows were likely delivered in quick succession once Chloe left her bedroom and got out onto the porch. The second wound was about two inches long and ran along the base of her skull. Chloe was turned away from her attacker, possibly trying to run, and he must have been standing slightly behind her and to the side, swinging his weapon in a horizontal fashion. Dr. Bechtel explained the consequences of this strike, which severed a major blood vessel:

> ...*inflicting that kind of a wound pressing in that way would necessarily affect one of the main circulations of the head, one of the main vessels carrying the blood; it is what is called the posterior of the longitudinal sinus; from that wound proceeded, in my estimation, the most of the blood the woman lost, which was quite a quantity; where she was lying, the grass and yard was covered and saturated; her feet were laying on the porch and her head laying out on the rocks;... that wound alone would have produced death in my estimation.*

The third and final wound, across the crown of the head, was four inches long, and Bechtel revealed that the probe he used to measure the depth of the wound dropped 2 ½ inches into the brain along the entire length of the fissure. This blow divided the cerebrum, which, Dr. Bechtel explained, likely *"affected the sensory and motor nerves to the extent of producing immediate paralysis."* The length of this final cut and its uniform depth suggests that it was caused by the full contact of the blade as the blow was being dealt over-handed. Chloe toppled backwards off the edge of the porch and then bled out.

Once he'd seen enough to determine the cause of death, Bechtel discontinued his examination:

*…we thought it unnecessary to make any further disfigurement of the
subject, so that they might be presentable to their friends—for in order to
make a thorough investigation, it is a great disfigurement of the countenance.
You see this puncture of the skull; there was evidently a corner of some sharp
instrument which went right down here; the bone, was separated undoubtedly
there; from this wound here I believe exuded as much as two ounces of brains; I
removed two ounces of brains that had exuded and lay on the floor, and the rest
of the brains that lay on the floor, I put back in and sewed it up.*

Dr. O. J. Casto, a licensed allopath, took the stand only long
enough to corroborate his colleague's testimony. Neither the jury nor
the courtroom audience needed to fully comprehend all the medical
terminology to be shocked and sickened by the graphic description of
Chloe Greene's final moments. Brown needed to move past it as quickly as
possible and declined to cross-examine either physician.

Next on the witness stand was Chloe's neighbor, John Chancey. He
described Alice's arrival at his home at five o'clock on the morning of the
murders and explained how he had then hastened to the farm where he
found Chloe lying on her back with her head off the porch. He identified
the hatchet as the one he'd found in the garden behind the house and
noted that it was still smeared with blood and gray hair. He also identified
the mattock he'd discovered laying up against the corner of the fence
palings near the house.

The *Jackson Herald* reported that Chancey further testified that he
found evidence of tracks following in Alice's footprints nearly halfway to
his house. This is a chilling indication of just how close Alice may have
come to perishing with her family, in which case John Morgan might have
gotten away with murder.

John Shamblin had been deputized to guard Morgan in the field
behind the Pfost-Greene property. His testimony is enlightening, even
though it was ultimately stricken from the record with regard to the jurors'
consideration. Shamblin told the jury that although he'd known Morgan
for years, the prisoner *"pretended"* not to recognize him that morning.
When Seaman began to ask him about Morgan's confession, David Brown
objected.

Before such a confession could be introduced, Brown declared, it had
to be shown that it was freely given without coercion or reward. Seaman
then asked Shamblin a series of questions about his interaction with the
prisoner, including whether he'd pressured Morgan or offered him any

inducements to confess. The deputy's testimony was interrupted by both
the counsel for defense and Judge Blizzard each time he postulated that
Morgan had been shamming in some fashion. But after each interruption
Shamblin returned to the same theme. Finally, he said:

> *I said to him—Mr. Morgan, if I were you, I would straighten up and
> not act this way; that the people know you are sane; it would be better for you
> to straighten up and tell a straight story, if you know anything about these
> matters.*

At this point, Morgan's attorney asked that Shamblin's entire testimony
be *"stricken out,"* and surprisingly, Judge Blizzard agreed, ruling that *"unless
something had intervened"* the evidence was *"improper."* But something, or
in this case someone, *had* intervened.

David Brown, in his role as coroner, had arrived just in time for
Morgan's confession and had been forced to witness it against his better
judgement. Now Brown desperately sought to prevent it from being read
into the record. He was in a dilemma regarding Seaman's questioning of
the deputy. Shamblin was adding support to Brown's own contention that
Morgan had been out of his mind, even though the man's personal opinion
that it was all an act made for a certain risk. But the first order of business
was to block the introduction of the confession and failing that, Brown
needed to make a case for its having been made under duress.

Blizzard knew from the beginning, of course, which way the wind was
going to blow. He dismissed Shamblin from the stand and replaced him
with the defense counsel. Brown had to have known that he was going to
be forced to testify against his own client, but he did not do so willingly.
By now, the prosecutor had the original signed confession in his hand
and asked, *"Mr. Brown, is that your signature?"* Well of course it was. Still,
Brown did his best to explain his grave misgivings about whether Morgan
had even understood what he was doing. He addressed the judge:

> *Your Honor, my objection to this affidavit is that the prisoner was in the
> custody of two officers, and I don't think, under the law, that this affidavit
> ought to be allowed to go to the jury, unless it is shown it is by his own free will
> and a voluntary statement without any promise of protection. I don't think it is
> a proper document to go to the jury.*

Blizzard again took over the proceedings, put Shamblin back on the
stand, and began his own line of questioning. He asked Shamblin to

repeat everything he had overheard that morning between Coroner Brown and the defendant. Shamblin repeated all the warnings Brown had given Morgan, along with the fact that Morgan had said that he understood the consequences of proceeding with his statement. He firmly denied that either he or Sheriff Shinn had tried to influence or threaten the prisoner in any way.

Then Blizzard turned his attention to the matter of Morgan's apparent state of mind and his bizarre behavior at the time of his capture. Shamblin described Morgan as *"acting crazy"*—tearing at his clothes, raving incoherently, and pretending not to know him. He repeated how he'd told Morgan to quit shamming because everyone knew he was sane. The judge then asked:

Q: Was this conversation you had with the prisoner, had in relation to the matter regarding his insanity or regarding his confession that he was going to give? You say you told him it would be better for him to straighten up. Did that apply so some question of his insanity, or did it apply to the facts he was going to state?

A: I told him it would be better for him not to go on that way, that it was the opinion of everybody that he was just putting it on.

Q: Was that in regard to straightening up or the confession that he was going to make?

A: That was in regard to straightening up, the confession came afterward.

The judge continued his attempts to clarify, *Does the Court understand from you that you told him it would be better for him to straighten up and not feign insanity?*

A: I told him I thought it would be better to straighten up and tell all he knew about the matter.

Blizzard wasn't getting anywhere with Shamblin. After several minutes of going around in circles, Blizzard finally told the jurors that all testimony regarding conversations between John Morgan and John Shamblin as recalled by the deputy were to be disregarded. Only Morgan's statement— that is the confession itself—as given to Mr. Brown was to be admissible.

Brown objected to all of it. The only path available to him was a plea of insanity. With the judge's ruling, Shamblin's testimony regarding John's bizarre actions prior to the confession was now blocked from cross-examination. And regardless of Blizzard's admonishment to the jury to disregard the deputy's conversation with Morgan, the damage had been done. In the jurors' minds, any odd actions on the murderer's part were all play-acting. And the confession was still going to be allowed.

Brown's secretary, Mr. B. L. Rudman, was called to testify as to the circumstances under which Morgan's confession was made. Rudman confirmed the coroner's warnings to the defendant, and when the prosecutor asked him to read the confession aloud, Brown shouted, *"I object!"* He was overruled. Finally, everyone got to hear what all the fuss was about:

> *...I killed Jimmie Greene, Mrs. Green and Matilda Pfost, on the morning of Wednesday, the 3rd day of November, 1897...I killed Matilda first, the old lady second and Jimmie at the hog-pen...*

Now the cat was among the pigeons. For the first time since testimony began, David Brown stood to cross-examine. He had been forced to testify against his own client and now his own secretary was being used to magnify his actions and turn them against him. His cross-examination of Rudman, however, was nothing short of bizarre. Brown was obviously grasping at straws here—hoping that Rudman might be able to present him with some misstep in his own actions as coroner, some flaw in his language or explanation that Morgan might have misunderstood, but the loyal Rudman gave him no opening. His boss had, to the best of his ability, covered all the legal bases at the crime scene that morning and had overlooked nothing.

The prosecutor, knowing that Brown's only recourse was the insanity defense, intended to use Sheriff Shinn to prove that Morgan had been canny enough to pull the insanity card early on, only to discard it as soon as he'd gotten a good look at the hostile crowd at the murder scene. James Seaman led Shinn through his description of Morgan's behavior when he and his deputy walked him down to the house:

> *...his actions were very strange; he was making a noise, hissing, tearing his clothes; occasionally he would hallo; he would spit at one, and different things like, and kind of grinning and hissing all the time; that lasted until we got him down to the fence near the garden, and the crowd gathered around us so extensively...*

Then he recalled the difficulties he had managing the mob and Morgan's appeal for protection. "[H]*e did not want to die like a dog,*"

Shinn testified. Morgan told him, "*I am ready to pay the debt, but I want to be protected.*" And Shinn had promised, "*… that I would protect him as best I could there, as far as I could, that is all the inducement, if that is an inducement, that I offered him.*"

Then Seaman hammered home the point that neither lawman had anything to do with John Morgan's decision to confess his crimes:

Q: When Mr. Shamblen said that Morgan wanted to make a statement, he did not say what he intended to state, did he?

A: No.

And just like that Morgan's "*confession*" morphed into a "*statement,*" a word less likely to entangle. Judge Blizzard informed the jury that the defendant's "*statement*" to Coroner Brown was evidence, however John Shamblin's testimony regarding his having instructed Morgan to "*straighten up and tell all he knew about the matter*" was still off limits. It all seemed a bit like slamming the barn door not just once, but a second time for good measure, once the horse was out.

By now the attention of the courtroom audience, not to mention the jury's, was on the wane with all this legal wrangling. Add the physical discomfort of too many bodies packed tightly into that small space— one account claims that between 1000 and 1200 people were crammed into the little courtroom$_2$— and folks could be forgiven for allowing their thoughts to wander and dozing off from time to time. The only sensible threads they had to hold on to were Dr. Bechtel's horrific, albeit clinical, cataloging of Chloe's injuries, and the recitation of John Morgan's confession. Mr. Seaman waved the bloody hatchet and mattock in front of his audience to regain their focus, and then entered the weapons into evidence. The transcript also mentions, "*and other missiles.*" And then Miss Alice Pfost entered the courtroom.

You could have heard a pin drop. Veiled and swathed in deepest black, Alice stepped through the door, and supported by her sister-in-law Flora Pfost, made her way slowly to the front of the courtroom and sat down. The effect of her dramatic entrance was lost on no one. "*[A]nd when her veil was carefully thrown back, her pale, sad face was a mute appeal to the jury.*"$_3$ This was the moment they'd been waiting for—Alice Pfost was about to bear witness against John Morgan.

Imagine this beautiful young woman, suffering from head trauma, post-traumatic stress, and bereavement of an inconceivable nature, walking into a suffocating courtroom, and facing the man who had murdered her family and tried to murder her—a man, if accounts are to be believed, she may have loved. Later, Sheriff Shinn pointedly told a journalist that throughout her entire testimony, *"the girl could not look at the man who had so terribly wounded her."*[4]

Asked when she had last seen the defendant, Alice was quick off the mark: *"Wednesday morning, of course!"* Her voice was weak and whispery and she spoke in a halting fashion as she led the jury through the horrors of that morning:

On Wednesday morning, we got up a little before 5 o'clock; my brother and John Morgan got up a while after we all got up, and he followed my poor little brother out to the hog-pen to feed the hogs and murdered him, I know he did, for he never came back, and John Morgan came back, went in, and talked to mother and us awhile, and when my sister and me went to get breakfast he followed us out into the kitchen and stood around out there, and as my sister was making bread for breakfast he struck her, and as I looked around, he tried to murder me, and he run after my sister and struck her again, and I had strength enough to get up and run to Mr. Chancey's for help.

Alice said that she never once saw the hatchet in John Morgan's hands, and when she first saw Tillie fall in the kitchen, she assumed he'd struck her with his fist. Even when he turned his assault on her, Alice said she never saw the weapon. Nor did she see him strike her mother, although she had seen him turn back toward her mother's bedroom after following her out of the kitchen.

The reporter for the *Wheeling Register* was present in the courtroom that afternoon and he recorded several details from Alice's testimony that were not included elsewhere. He reported that Alice had one last glimpse of her mother before she ran for help:[5]

She could see by the lamp light from where she was hiding in the chicken coop, that Morgan was going in her mother's room, and pretty soon Morgan came out on the porch followed by old Mrs. Greene, who was trying to defend herself and where she was afterwards found struggling in a pool of blood by John Chancey.

The questioning continued:

Q: After you left the house and before you reached Mr. Chancey's did you hear your mother's voice in any outcry?

A: Yes, sir, I heard them both screaming, my sister called for me, and says: "Alice do come back, and try to get the gun and help us." I knew where the gun was and that I could not reach her, and I did not go back.

Alice repeated her earlier assertions that there had been no trouble between the family and John Morgan beforehand, although, she admitted, they had grown suspicious because of his comments and actions. She repeated Morgan's excuses for dropping in and spending the night— borrowing a coat pattern and getting his hair cut. "[H]*e talked on friendly and finally went to sleep in the same room with my brother.*"

Throughout Alice's remarkable testimony, her answers were clear and forthright, and as physically weak as she was, they denote a certain amount of inner strength and confidence, even a hint of defiance, as when she answered the prosecutor's question regarding when she last saw Morgan: "*Wednesday morning, of course.*" Righteous anger was evident as well when she says that "*he followed my poor little brother out to the hog-pen…and murdered him, I know he did, for he never came back.*" And the emotional disconnect was thoroughly clear. Throughout her testimony, she referred to her attacker only as *Morgan* or *John Morgan,* but never once as *John.*

The prosecutor also questioned Alice as to whether she had seen anyone else at the house that morning, or had any reason to believe someone else might have been there, to which she replied that she had not. Here again, the perceptive Wheeling correspondent pointed out the interesting variance between Alice's initial statement to the coroner and her court testimony. Alice did not repeat in court that John Morgan had been out on the back porch whistling, nor did she mention her fears about an accomplice. The prosecutor wanted to demonstrate that, other than the family, there was no one at the house that morning except John Morgan— that he was the only one who could have committed the crimes and had done so alone.

On the other hand, Alice had already told David Brown that when she was hiding from Morgan she realized that there could very well be two people stalking her in the dark. "*I was afraid that someone else might come, for the reason that Morgan went out on the porch before that and whistled.*" But Brown chose not to cross-exam Alice and so this discrepancy was never questioned.

At some point in the prosecutor's enquiries that afternoon, the motive of robbery must have been addressed. Both the *Cincinnati Enquirer* and the *Clarksburg Telegram* took note of the fact that there was no direct evidence to indicate Morgan had stolen anything, although Alice testified that Morgan expressed interest in whether Chloe had received the money for the colt she sold.

Alice was the last witness called by the prosecution and she had coherently and succinctly damned John Morgan. Everyone was noticeably affected by her harrowing tale and no one was in doubt as to the outcome. Though the process had seemed to drag on interminably, it had actually taken only a little over an hour for the State to present its entire case.

End Notes

[1] Donnelly, Shirley. "Tales of the Old Stomping Ground: Part II," *Beckley Post-Herald,* Beckley, WV, 8 November, 1961.

[2] *Cincinnati Enquirer,* Cincinnati, OH, 6 November, 1897.

[3] *Pittsburgh Post-Gazette,* Pittsburgh, PA, 12 November 1897.

[4] *Wheeling Register*, Wheeling, WV, 6 November, 1897.

[5] *Ibid.*

THE INSANITY DEFENSE

John Morgan's life dangled by a slender thread that could easily turn into a rope. His attorney had a chance to avoid the death penalty if he could convince the jury that his client had been mentally incompetent when he committed the crimes. Brown's strategy relied upon two witnesses, both of whom gave evidence as to Morgan's deteriorating mental condition over the past year.

Unfortunately, the jury was already biased against this tactic. Prior testimony by the law officers inferred that John had feigned insanity at the time of his capture. There had also been a good deal of negative publicity over the past several years regarding the so-called *"insanity dodge,"* some of which had originated in that very courtroom.

At the turn of the century there was no organized catalog of mental diagnoses, and no two medical experts could agree as to what constituted insanity. In fact, the introduction of the insanity defense had turned into an embarrassment for both legal and medical professionals. Too often shrewd lawyers abused it to help guilty criminals avoid well-merited punishment, and physicians were being paid top dollar to act as partisans in these strategies. Newspaper editorials like this one from New Orleans' *Times-Picayune* were scathing:[1]

> *The plea of insanity as a defense for men on trial for serious crimes is coming to be one of the most dangerous obstructions in the way of justice... Every great soldier, writer, artist, musician, inventor, is a maniac. Edison is one of the maddest of them all... every criminal is insane...the more atrocious the deed, the more marked is the insanity...But if the insanity "dodge" is to run "wide open"...then the courts will become mere playhouses in which is enacted the roaring farce after the bloody tragedy.*

For several decades, the American legal system had been applying Britain's *M'Naughton Rule* as a standard test for criminal liability: Was the defendant aware of what he was doing, did he understand the consequences, and did he know right from wrong at the time he committed the act?[2] The test required the testimony of alienists, experts in forensic medicine, who were most usually medical governors of asylums for the insane.

Testimony of this nature oftentimes did more harm than good. When President Garfield was shot by Charles Giteau the previous decade, a team of twenty alienists were equally divided about his culpability.[3] And in the end, he'd still been hanged, although most attorneys agreed that if the victim been anyone other than the president, Giteau would have been judged "irresponsibly insane" and committed.[4] Brown believed that the *"Irresistible Impulse Test"* applied to his client, but how was he to convince a jury of that? David Brown had less than a day to prepare for Morgan's trial, and he had no access to experts on such short notice.

Brown did what he could with the limited time and resources at his disposal. He approached two local physicians in town, Dennis Casto and L. F. Campbell, neither of whom had any training or background in mental illness, and asked them to evaluate his client. Campbell, the older and more experienced of the two, visited with Morgan on the second night of his captivity and again on the morning of the trial. He informed Brown that Morgan was not insane, but rather was a case of *"extreme depravity."*[5] Dr. Casto concurred.

Having observed Morgan closely just after the murders, and after talking with Rebekah, Brown was convinced that something was wrong with the man. He was hoping that Rebekah would prove persuasive when it came to swaying the jury.

Rebekah Morgan made for a very sympathetic figure in the courtroom, sitting near her husband and holding little Albert on her lap. Only about ten percent of the assembly that day were women, but nearly everyone had compassion for this distraught wife and mother who might be left to raise a young child on her own:[6]

Her appearance was inexplicably sad. She did not weep but her face, drawn and haggard showed how much she has suffered. She…told in a most straightforward way without concealment, a number of instances of when her husband had been apparently out of his right mind.

Compared to the surprisingly collected Alice, Rebekah's mental state can easily be construed from her testimony. Initially even the simplest questions confused and distressed her. When asked to state where she lived, she responded, *"That is no fair question. I am so tore up I don't know where I live. I lived on Grass Lick."* Rebekah was not being disingenuous. She didn't expect to stay at their current home, but wasn't sure when or where she would be forced to move. And when asked how long she and John had been married, she answered, *"Two years the 27th of last February,"* when based on their marriage certificate their second anniversary would have been the *next* February. Poor Rebekah would be a widow by then.

In response to Brown's questioning, Rebekah informed the court that John had been absent from home the evening before the murders, and went on to give a coherent description of John's return to the house the morning after. She stumbled now and again with Brown's questions—"*I can't really say I'm so mixed up*"—but he carefully walked her through the rest of her testimony as she explained about her husband's strange behaviors, the odd noises he sometimes made, and the frightening sleepwalking episodes.

He has changed a great deal within the last six months...I noticed something wrong with him this spring, late in the spring...I had mentioned it at different times to some of my neighbors...they told me they thought there must be something wrong, and that I ought to have something done for him. I tried to get him to see a physician, but he would not do so. I have persuaded him at different times to have something done.

Finally, in response to Brown's question about John's activities on the night before the murders, she replied:

He told me that he was going over to Doug Shinn's on business; he told me he would be back by 9 o'clock; he said he would not be gone over three hours, or about 9 o'clock.

During James Seaman's cross-examination, Rebekah was asked about John's business with the sheriff's brother, Reuben ("*Dug*") Shinn: "*By the way of refreshing your recollection, did he say anything about going to borrow some money of Shinn?*"

This was an interesting question, suggesting that the prosecutor was privy to information about why Morgan might have originally headed toward Shinn Ridge that night. Henry Deem later reported in the *Jackson Herald* that after the sheriff and his brother questioned Morgan, they concluded that he might have been planning to rob *them*—but for some unknown reason ended up at the Pfost-Greene farm instead. This scenario, however, seems unlikely.

Rebekah claimed she didn't know why he might have been going to Shinn's. In fact she obviously had little or no knowledge of the reasons behind any of his goings and comings.

Brown next called Morgan's brother-in-law, Enoch Casto, and the jury listened as John's sleep walking incident at Bear Fork was rehashed along with other out-of-the-ordinary behaviors.

With the conclusion of Enoch's testimony, at about 3:30, David Brown rested his case and the prosecutor began his closing arguments. Seaman's speech was considered quite *"splendid,"* *"strong and convincing,"* and lasted about fifteen minutes.[7] Brown then spoke eloquently for the next half hour. Morrison did not include excerpts from either speech in his murder pamphlet.

This was Brown's last opportunity to convince the jury of his client's disordered mental state, and though some called his defense *"rather weak"* and said that it *"fell short,"*[8] there were those who found his arguments to be *"strong"* ones. One reporter said that Brown presented such a *"touching picture,"* that many of the jurors were in tears throughout.[9] By the time the State finished the summation—*"in a neat little sixteen minute speech"*—the time was exactly 4:23, according to the obsessive O. J. Morrison who watched the clock throughout the proceedings. The trial lasted only three hours and twenty-three minutes.

The time had come. Judge Blizzard charged the jury with deciding whether murder had been premeditated in the first degree, or committed without malice of forethought in the second degree. In the case of first-degree murder, he informed them, they could specify a sentence of life imprisonment if they so desired. If they offered no such recommendation, the penalty would be death.[10] At 4:27 the jury left to begin their deliberations.

Nearly everyone in the courtroom had been there since eight o'clock that morning, yet no one considered leaving at this stage. They sat quietly, conversing in subdued tones, and waited. John Morgan waited with them. A sea of faces either glared at him or studied him quizzically, but they had long ceased to register. Even the presence of his wife and child had not engaged his attention. *"He maintained a remarkable stoical demeanor"* throughout.[11]

At 5:28, the door opened and the jury walked back in. Brown knew this couldn't be good. He had hoped they would spend more time in debate. As the clerk was handed the small slip of paper from the foreman a hush fell over the assembly. Then slowly and carefully, he began to read: *"We the jury, find the prisoner guilty of murder in the first degree."* No recommendation for life imprisonment was given.

The stillness lasted only a second more and then came a storm of applause. Hats were thrown into the air and cheers rang out. Blizzard gave the crowd a moment or two of celebration and then pounded his gavel. It took several minutes to restore order, and throughout it all John Morgan sat as still as a stone.

To a man, the jury had voted for murder in the first degree, but when it came down to the actual punishment, one of them balked at the wording "*with no recommendation,*" which automatically defaulted to death by hanging. That man was A. D. Arnold, and he had stood firm, at least in the beginning, arguing in favor of life imprisonment.[12] Brown's arguments moved him, he said, and though he believed that Morgan was guilty of the crimes, he did not believe that he deserved to hang. Within the hour, however, he had succumbed to pressure from his peers and reluctantly gave in.

The judge capped the day with a short speech. He wanted to thank the citizens of Jackson County, he said, for their forbearance in a case that had aroused so much strong emotion. He thought they had behaved admirably, and so he warmly congratulated them before concluding:[13]

While we have laws and officers of disposition to see them rapidly and fully enforced, it is a matter of much gratification to see the people willing to let the law take its course in a case of this kind. We have published a record for ourselves in the rapid execution of the law, and while this Court is on the bench, I declare that it shall never be accused of negligence or dalliance in the matter before it.

The condemned man was led cautiously from the courtroom and returned to jail, and court was adjourned until the following morning. As newspaper editor Jim Comstock famously riposted decades later, "*The only way Morgan's lawyer could have kept him from hanging was to shoot him.*"[14]

End Notes

[1] *The Times-Picayune,* New Orleans, LA, 21 June, 1896.

[2] Crotty, Homer D. *History of Insanity as a Defence to Crime in English Criminal Law,* 12 Cal. L. Rev. 105 (1924).

[3] Available at: http://scholarship.law.berkeley.edu/californialawreview/vol12/iss2/3

[3] Noll, Richard. *American Madness,* Harvard, 2011. p. 153

[4] "The Defense of Insanity in Criminal Cases and Medical Expert Testimony", *The American Lawyer,* Vol 15, Number 7, July 1907, p. 310.

[5] Morrison, O. J., *The Slaughter of the Pfost-Greene Family of Jackson County, W.Va. A History of the Tragedy,* 1897.

[6] *Parkersburg Sentinel,* Parkersburg, WV, 6 November, 1897.

[7] *Wheeling Register,* Wheeling, WV, 7 November, 1897.

[8] *Wheeling Daily Intelligencer,* Wheeling, WV, 6 November, 1897.

[9] *Parkersburg Sentinel.*

[10] *Wheeling Register.*

[11] *The Iola Register,* Iola, Kansas, 8 November, 1897. Front page.

[12] *The Jackson Herald.*

[13] *Parkersburg Sentinel.*

[14] *West Virginia Hillbilly,* 18, August, 1979.

I AM NOT THE MAN

It was Saturday, November 6th, just three days after the murders. All the major newspapers in the state as well as several out-of-state papers went front page with lengthy accounts of John Morgan's trial. Most praised both judge and jury and remarked on the swiftness with which judgment had been passed. The verdict had been read just sixty hours after Alice Pfost first raised the alarm. More than one paper announced that the guilty verdict, as terrible as it was, had spared John Morgan's life for at least a few more weeks:[1]

Had any other than a verdict of death been returned it is not probable that the prisoner would have lived through the night, as the mob was ready to take him at little notice.

Long before the courthouse opened the next morning an immense crowd had gathered to hear the judge pass sentence, and when the doors opened just before 8 o'clock, *"a surging mass of humanity"* streamed up the steps and into the courtroom.[2]

More reporters had arrived overnight. In addition to the local editors, two Wheeling papers were represented, along with the *Morgantown Post,* the *Parkersburg Sentinel,* and the *Clarksburg Telegram.* The *Cincinnati Enquirer* provided on-the-scene coverage along with two Pittsburgh dailies. Several national newspapers, like New York City's *Sun* and the *Times,* provided coverage from a distance.

With great difficulty Owen Shinn and his deputies managed to get Morgan through to the front of the courtroom. By now the prisoner had begun to lose some of his composure. The judge started the proceedings by asking him if he had anything to say, to which Morgan replied, *"Why, I have lots I would like to have stated."*[3] This was Morgan's opportunity to impress his audience, and he certainly did so. His version of events was so totally disorganized, so obviously fabricated, and so hopelessly convoluted that no one took him seriously, and the man who had heretofore been known as *"scrupulously honest,"* began building his reputation as *"such a liar."*

"I am not the man that did the crime," he began.[4]
I know this about it that death will be my portion, I suppose, but I hain't

the man that done the murder; just give me a little time, and I will tell you all about it. Some of the people tells me I signed a paper; I might have done it… don't dispute that, but if I did, I have no recollection of it.

Well, this wasn't unexpected. But now, for the first time, Morgan claimed that someone else was involved:

Where is that man Floyd Pfost at—you know when he was at home on a visit, very likely some of you know when he and his wife were out there on a visit, there was a man living there on their place got into a little dispute about the crop; he thought that he did not get such ground as he ought to have; he had taken a lease; he did not get to sow wheat on the corn ground as he wanted to; he said he did not expect it to do another man any good, if he could not get it to use. He come to me four times to get me to help destroy this family; I told him I would not do it; I would just as soon think of destroying my mother if she were living, and my own sisters as to molest that family of people; I told him that I would not do it; he come to me the evening that Mr. Pfost made his return back to Ripley, and he says, "now is the chance to make the drive," and he says, "now is the time to do the work;" I says, "I am not going to do any such thing;" nor I did not; and he says, we can work on them so nice, they have got a gun down there; we can get them out by saying we can go shoot squirrels; get Floyd and Jim out," and I told him "I would not hurt that old lady to the very last, and I did not."

Morgan finally identified the other man as Ben Anderson and said this wasn't the only time Anderson approached him about the matter:

"…he come to me once after. He wanted to know of me, if I would not go with him and help do the work, and I held out and told him that I would not, and I did not. I say it was an evident fact that I was there that night, but I did not kill no one."

This time around, Morgan adamantly denied hurting anyone but Alice, and this, he claimed, was an accident:

What I done, gentlemen, I am not ashamed of. What I done, I done to get out, and I did not hurt no one, the only one that was hurt the worst by me, was the one that is living to-day; the one they called Alice. She was the only one I hurt, and I did not do that intentionally, and did not do it with any intent whatever of destroying or killing the family. What I did, I did to get out of the way; we had all been in a friendly good humor, and had treated each other right. I had staid there with them some five years, five months and fifteen days, and many a thing was done for me in the way of life's comfort and many's the thing I have done for them… When I left there, there was five months and fifteen days' of my time that I never received a cent for but a pair of breeches and pair of boots for, and I went in, and was talking to them about it. I asked them if they did not really think that they ought to allow me something more than that for my work; that is all I said to them: they did not seem to like it very well, but everything went along all right.

Even these careful calculations are indicative of his obsessive thinking. John Morgan had carefully kept track of his time at the Pfost-Greene farm and what he felt was owed him in return for his labor. As far as he was concerned he had not been sufficiently compensated. But surely, he was not so naïve as to expect anyone in the courtroom to believe what he said next.

I seen the girls had peculiar actions. I did not know what to think of it; one of them started into the house and she threw the hatchet at me as I went through into the house and it struck some place about the door facing. I went into the room there; was standing by the door; the door was right over this way and the gun set in the corner this way, that I aimed to get into. I got into the room and could not get out.

The old lady come at me with a club and another girl with the gun and I says to them: "Do not hurt no one, and no one is going to hurt you;" the girl that got the gun, could not get it to work, so she just struck at me with it, and I throwed up my hand that way, to doge the lick and kind of glanced it off, and I had the hatchet in my hand that fell over on her head as I knocked the lick off. Mrs. Greene was standing in the door with a club; that old lady—that mother that had protected me in many a thing—she struck at me with a club. I did not hit that poor old woman with a purpose of destroying her, but just hit enough merely to get out of the way. I don't know which one it was that struck at me with the gun, I just aimed to make my escape and get out of the way.

He rambled on in this fashion and then described the attack on Chloe Greene. Though he ultimately admitted his involvement in the deaths of Matilda and Jimmy just before he was hanged, he continued to deny that he had anything to do with Chloe's death. This he consistently blamed on Ben Anderson.

As I went out of there, here is this man that I was telling you about coming, the man that I know, I seen this man strike this poor old woman, as he struck her again, I could see she was staggering. There was a big light in the house; I could see this man very plainly; he stood with his axe raised and I seen him hit this poor old woman, knock her down, and hit her after she was down.

Aside from the obvious fact that Morgan was lying about his own culpability, this is a fascinating statement, an unrehearsed tangle of truth and patent falsehood that is nearly impossible to decipher. He maintained, *"I am not the man that did the crime,"* and accused fellow farm-worker Ben Anderson. At the same time, he claimed that he fought back in self-defense because the women attacked *him*. One of the more interesting aspects of Morgan's statement centers on, *"The old lady come at me with a club and another girl with the gun,"* a statement that may have been legitimate. His memory of the women's courageous last stand appeared to have vividly lodged itself in his mind. And he seemed to reflect true surprise and indignation when he recalled that, *"that mother that had protected me in many a thing,"* struck out at him.

But he shied away from calling his victims by name. Not once did he use Matilda's name, for instance, referring to her instead as *"the other girl"* or *"the girl that got the gun."* And there was his oblique reference to *"the one they called Alice"*—the woman he had thought to marry. Is it possible that Morgan always viewed this family with the objectivity of a sociopath, or did he inadvertently provide clues as to his mental state and the need to create emotional distance from his victims?

Ben Anderson was indeed living with his wife and children on or near the Pfost-Greene property at the time of the murders. He may even have quarreled with Floyd Pfost and Chloe over a misunderstanding about his lease of their acreage. Then we have Morgan's assertion that it was Ben Anderson's idea to lure Floyd Pfost and Jimmy Greene into ambush by inviting them to go squirrel hunting. It may have been too soon for the entire story to have been pieced together regarding John Morgan's actions in the days leading up to the murders, but if Ed Southall was in the courtroom that morning the implications of John's similar invitation to him must have been unnervingly clear.

Allegations of an accomplice did not surface during the trial itself, and it is only after the fact that there is any mention of this possibility. Reporters found the idea newsworthy, and it wasn't long before Sheriff Owen Shinn began his own investigations. There was more to come about Ben Anderson, as well as darker, more startling revelations, but on this day the courtroom audience was only interested in one man, and that was John

Morgan. He had been found guilty and the time had come to hear what Judge Blizzard had to say about the matter.

Reese Blizzard regarded John Morgan's entire speech as a pack of lies and he spoke from the heart when he addressed the young murderer who stood in front of him:₅

There is nothing that lasts, nothing that is enduring and permanent except truth, there is nothing that will live after you, or live after all of us, except the truth; it is impossible for a falsehood to live long. And the Court desires to impress upon you the necessity of telling only the truth in view of certain and almost immediate death, and your welfare hereafter. It would be as much as you can do to atone for the wrong which the Court is satisfied you have committed. You may give an entire statement of the facts, but nothing which you can say will extenuate your guilt or release you from the sentence that is to be passed upon you.

Between you and your God, however, there is a statement you can make, the truth, the whole truth, and nothing but the truth...and now it becomes, under the law, the duty of this Court to pass the sentence of death upon you. The Court approaches this task as reverentially to God, in a different spirit from which you passed the sentence of death upon those helpless victims for whose murder you are now convicted. The Court approaches it with all pity, with all possible mercy.

He acknowledged the difficult role allotted to Morgan's attorney, David Brown, and let it be known that he expected the public to treat the lawyer with utmost courtesy:

It is right under law for all persons to have a full, fair and impartial trial, assisted by counsel. It was, indeed, a courageous act on the part of counsel.

And finally, he offered praise for Rebekah Morgan, as *"one more monument to the character of noble womanhood,"* revealing the depth of his own sincere admiration for female resiliency and devotion:

...it only renews in the bosom of this Court the feeling that if the mother of our Savior had not been a woman, his blood, perhaps, would not have been sufficient to extenuate the sins of the world.

Finally came the words everyone was waiting for:

"It is the sentence of this Court that you shall be confined in the county jail of this county until the 16ᵗʰ day of the coming December, 1897,... and on that

date that you be taken from the county jail of this county by the Sheriff of this county, and hanged by the neck until you are dead, dead, dead: and may God have mercy upon your soul."

This time there were no shouts of jubilation, no public demonstrations. A heavy silence lay over the assembly. Rebekah Morgan was standing in the rear of the courtroom with tears streaming down her face. She moaned aloud and, clasping baby Albert to her breast, she fainted, dropping slowly to the floor.[6]

Morgan barely looked at Rebekah as he was being led back to the jail. Several ladies gathered round as Dr. Bechtel tended to her, and only when she had been safely carried out of the courtroom did the crowd begin to disperse. Reporters raced for the train station and the telegraph office at Ripley Landing.[7]

Several newspapers erroneously proclaimed December 17th, rather than the 16th, as the date scheduled for Morgan's execution. Custom dictated Friday as *hangman's day*, and the 17th was indeed a Friday. But the progressive young judge had chosen a Thursday instead.[8]

Reese Blizzard was the man of the hour, and several publications, like the *New York Times,* made much of the fact that he had just set a record for the speediest exhibition of due process in the history of the state.[9] Many touted his approach as the perfect panacea for lynching, one Pennsylvania reporter claiming, "*...the lynching problem has at last been solved. A quick witted young West Virginia judge has arisen to confound the lawless...*"[10]

And Pittsburgh's *Daily Post* was lavish in its praise of the "*Blizzard on the Bench:*"[11]

SWIFT RETRIBUTION: A Blizzard on the bench—Judge Blizzard, by the way—has shown how lynch law may be avoided and the law of the land allowed to take its course.

The judge had endeared himself to the people of Jackson County through sheer force of will and expediency. He had energetically fulfilled his promises, though technically Morgan's date with the hangman was scheduled beyond the thirty days he originally pledged, and as he passed through the crowd surrounding the courthouse that Saturday there were many who hailed him as "*our next Governor.*"[12] Not all the reviews were so positive, however:[13]

The man who commits murder in these days generally survived his victims *long enough to put the county to anywhere between $25,000 and $50,000 expense in the way of trials, expert testimony and high-priced officials. Occasionally we find a case in which the machinery of justice is so slow in operating that we are reminded of the famous trial of Warren Hastings, whose trial was begun in one generation and whose acquittal came in the next. But there are exceptions when the other extreme is reached. One of these occurred recently in Jackson County, West Virginia.*

No one was blind to the fact that John Morgan would have probably been lynched by the Ripley mob on the day of his arrest had Blizzard not intervened, and the newspapers never hesitated to remind people of this.

MORGAN CONDEMNED TO HANG

Fleet Justice Overtakes the Brutal Jackson Murderer—- Quickest Trial in Criminal Annals— Crowds Thronged the Streets and Threatened to Make Good Any Error or delay of the Law's Machinery.

Excerpt from the Wheeling Register, Wheeling, WV, 07 November, 1897

One emblazoned headline was far more blatant. It read:[14] *"THE MOB BULLDOZES THE JUDICIARY."*

And as the long week of horror and dismay drew to its close the people of Jackson County would find a reason to give thanks. The long drought that had begun back in August was nearly over. The rains began the following day and the creeks started to rise.

End Notes

[1] *Wheeling Daily Intelligencer,* Wheeling, WV, 6 November, 1897.

[2] *Wheeling Register,* Wheeling, WV, 7 November, 1897.

[3] Noll, Richard. *American Madness,* Harvard, 2011. p. 153.

[4] "The Defense of Insanity in Criminal Cases and Medical Expert Testimony", *The American Lawyer,* Vol 15, Number 7, July 1907, p. 310.

[5] Morrison, O. J., *The Slaughter of the Pfost-Greene Family of Jackson County, W.Va. A History of the Tragedy,* 1897.

[6] *Ibid.*

[7] *Ibid.*

[8] *Morgantown Post,* Morgantown, WV, 6 November, 1897.

[9] *Cincinnati Enquirer,* Cincinnati, OH, 6 November, 1897.

[10] Weekly Register, Point Pleasant, OH, 17 November, 1897.

[11] *New York Times,* New York, NY, 7 November, 1897.

[12] *Indiana Gazette,* Indiana, PA, 17 November , 1897.

[13] *Pittsburgh Daily Post,* 07 November, 1897

[14] *Adams County Free Press,* Corning, Iowa, 9 December, 1897.

THE PETITION

The following week citizens of Jackson County got back to their usual routines—buying and selling cattle, hogs and sheep, and milling grain, timber, and rumor. They read with disappointment that Judge Blizzard had no plans to become a gubernatorial candidate. *"The thought of being a candidate,"* wrote the judge to the editor of a local paper, *"has not occupied a moment of my time. I have too much business demanding my attention to chase rainbows that are three years off."*₁ John Morgan's execution was now only a month away and the judge expected nothing to interfere with the law running its course.₂

And that was precisely what the law was doing. On November 14ᵗʰ, a Sabbath, Attorney David Brown sat down with his client to map out their next strategy. He hadn't wanted to defend Morgan, but he was honor-bound to do everything he could to prevent the death penalty. He wasn't ready to let go of the insanity plea and there was still the question of Ben Anderson's involvement. How could that be resolved if the star witness was dead? David Brown had one last card and he played it on November 18ᵗʰ, less than a month before the execution date. He traveled to the state capitol in Charleston to meet with Governor George Atkinson, taking with him John Morgan's carefully crafted petition for clemency and yet another confession.

The petition began in the usual way by pointing out a few minor flaws in the court proceedings. For example, the time of Morgan's execution, *"between the hours of 10 o'clock in the forenoon and 2 o'clock in the afternoon,"* had been announced after Morgan had been returned to his cell, rather than in his presence as required by law.₃ The real focus, however, was upon the *"great haste"* with which the petitioner had been forced to go to trial in response to threats of mob violence and Blizzard's promise of *"speedy justice:"*₄

[The] *petitioner says that the Court refused to give him longer time to make defense… and that this petitioner was rushed and hastened into trial, and by reason of this extreme and unusual haste in the trial…great injustice resulted and was done to this petitioner.*

Brown argued that the state constitution, which *"guarantees to every citizen a reasonable time to prepare for his defense"* had been ill served, and a very different verdict might have been returned if Morgan had been treated fairly. The judiciary had indeed been bulldozed by the mob, [5] and because of this the petitioner asked to have his sentence commuted to life confinement in the state penitentiary.

Morgan's accompanying confession was extraordinary. It portrayed a confused and frightened young man, struggling with the truth and trying to understand how his life had spiraled out of control. Although his thoughts were still disordered, he attempted to present a reasonable timeline and coherent description of events: [6]

> *The idea of killing this family first began to work on me about 6 months before I did the killing. It seemed to me that I had to kill them and then it would wear off and I would come to myself and I would say to myself I would not kill them for the world, and I want to say now that I never had any spite or hatred toward either of them. They always treated me kindly.*

He described in detail how over the summer the compulsions to destroy the Pfost-Greene family came upon him in waves, causing him to feel restless, ill at ease, and unable to focus, and then receded leaving him confused and dazed. Back and forth his words tracked across the pages as he did his best to explain how the pendulum of his reasoning swung first one way and then the other. And then came the fateful day when it fully overcame him: [7]

> *When we all got up the next morning, this thing of killing then flew over my mind and it appeared to me they were fighting and I did the crime, but I do not recollect much about it. Me and Jimmie went to the hog pen and I suppose I killed him there, but to tell the truth, I do not know just how I done it, and further I do not know where I got the mattock nor where I left it, but I suppose from what they said, I used the mattock on Jimmie and what I done when I went back to the house I do not remember, but I suppose I killed Mrs. Green and Matilda Pfost, but it seemed like there was a crowd of people there fighting me, and I supposed I used the hatchet in killing them, but where I got it I do not now remember and what I did with it I do not know. What Alice said I suppose was the truth and I cannot say when I left there nor where I went, but it seems to me that I was back at the place that day, but it is only a dream to me.*

At this juncture he veered off subject to focus on Granny Fisher's comments about the baby's short dresses and shoes. Had John Morgan

Governor George Wesley Atkinson

been a sophisticated schemer and manipulator he could hardly have written a more compelling example of a mind in the throes of disorganized and delusional thinking, or a more classic portrayal of the *"irresistible impulse."* There is no governor on this type of mental aberration, no sense of morality strong enough to override it once the course is set.

While there was a certain level of honesty in Morgan's confession, he still stopped short of taking full responsibility for his actions. For instance, he glossed over the act of murder itself when he said, *"I suppose I killed..."* His inability to recall these events in any detail and his subsequent declaration that he had no memory of his capture and confession sounds like patent falsehood or shifty legal maneuvering. Yet he may have been telling the truth in these instances as well. Due to various causes, amnesia can occur after the commission of a violent crime.[8]

In today's world John Morgan would have been subjected to brain scans and frontal temporal lobe imaging to rule out the possibility of degenerative brain disorders, or lesions. He would have undergone a battery of psychological testing and be interviewed by a host of psychiatrists. But in Morgan's day, not even the alienists who later evaluated him assigned any significance to his disjointed ramblings.

Oh, that I could of kept this thing of killing this family off! This impression removed from my mind, but it still clung to me. Oh, that my God might have stricken me down before I did this horrible deed! This family was friends of mine, and why should such an impression steal over me and take complete control of me for no purpose but to cause the destruction of my own life and the death of Mrs. Green, Jimmie Green and Matilda Pfost? Why was it not otherwise provided or ordained? Why should such a wicked design seize the mind and prey upon it until the same was carried into execution? Was it ordained or was I seized and controlled by the Devil? Whatever may have been the cause of this crime is unforeseen and unknown to me.[9]

This time he made no mention of Ben Anderson.

Brown thought he had a decent shot at commutation. Governor George Atkinson was known to be a sympathetic man who never shied

away from speaking his mind or taking an unpopular stance if he believed
it was the right thing to do. [10] Despite his Republican roots, Atkinson was
a moderate progressive and a crusader for workplace reform, civil rights,
and greater equality in immigration laws. He was also the first Republican
to have been elected to the office in 26 years.

Only recently the governor had commuted the death sentence for
Seymour Gray, a black man convicted of murder the year before, to life
imprisonment, based on his belief that Gray *"had not exhibited malice
toward his victim."* [11]

Atkinson had already generated a remarkable amount of unfavorable
news coverage in his short tenure as governor, and by fall of 1897 his
outrageous remarks and attendant scandals had drawn political fire and
ridicule across the nation and as far away as Europe. He had recently
pardoned Scott Kimes of Parkersburg for shooting his brother-in-law after
finding him in bed with his wife, and declared that his only regret was that
Kimes hadn't succeeded in killing the man, that he *"should have practiced
with a revolver or double-barreled shotgun...."* [12]

The *New York Tribune* expressed horror and contempt for Atkinson's
"wholesale invitation to murder", and labeled him *"a leader of barbarians".* [13]
Brown may have hoped the governor would welcome the opportunity
to demonstrate that he was the enlightened leader of a civilized state by
commuting Blizzard's death penalty to life commitment in an asylum. But
there was another, more personal matter which made the governor hesitate
to pardon anyone else at the moment or cross swords with a popular young
judge.

Earlier in June Atkinson had married the beautiful, rich widow of
Judge Gideon Draper Camden, a well-known socialite who rose from
obscurity to wealth and status by marrying well and often. Myra Atkinson's
first husband died, amazingly enough, when he confused whiskey with lye
one dark night, [15] and while still in her twenties, she married the 75-year-
old millionaire judge.

The press made much of her previous marriages, particularly the fact
that Camden had given her $100,000 for marrying him and promised her
his entire estate. [16] Naturally his heirs viewed their father's nuptials with
considerable ill grace and grabbed the first opportunity for revenge. The
following appeared in the New York Times one month before the Pfost-
Greene murders: [17] *"The trial of the wife of Gove. Atkinson of West Virginia
began here yesterday... The charge is forging the name of her late husband...."*

Facing possible imprisonment if convicted of forging Camden's will and several receipts, Myra responded that, *"if she should be convicted and sentenced her husband would pardon her".*[18] After that the governor was a marked man. The *Cincinnati Enquirer* conducted a state by state survey to gather the reactions of other governors, and the ongoing debate further embarrassed West Virginians.

> *The question of Governor Atkinson's duty if his wife should be found guilty of forgery and sentenced to the penitentiary…has become the fad for discussion among country literary societies, and every country paper coming to hand these days contains editorials on the subject.*[19]

It is no wonder Atkinson was now a trifle skittish where pardons and commutations were concerned. Myra's trial ended in a hung jury just days before the Pfost-Greene murders and the case promised to drag on in the headlines. West Virginia's governor was being depicted as both barbarian and buffoon. And the judge in charge of Mrs. Myra Davis Camden Atkinson's various hearings and trials? None other than Reese Blizzard.

The governor may have been reluctant to plunge into yet another media maelstrom by commuting the death sentence for the so-called *"Triple Murderer of Jackson County,"* yet when Atkinson read Brown's petition he was indeed concerned. He didn't want it said that he had sent an insane man to the gallows and so he arranged for a couple of experts to give him a definitive answer.

He first contacted Dr. Thomas Camden, who for eight years had been the superintendent of the West Virginia Hospital for the Insane, formerly Trans-Allegheny, in Weston, and asked him to go to Ripley to assess Morgan's mental state. Coincidently, Thomas Camden was Myra Atkinson's step-nephew, presumably one that did not stand to inherit. The governor also invited Dr. Lewis Van Gilder Guthrie, current superintendent of the Insane Asylum in Spencer, to examine the prisoner.

The older of the duo, Dr. Camden, had been overseeing treatment at Trans-Allegheny for twenty-five years. Originally a light and airy building with beautiful, spacious rooms and well-manicured grounds, the Weston hospital had been founded on the theories of *"moral treatment"* advocated by influential Quaker, Dr. Thomas Kirkbride, who believed that comfortable conditions, cheerful lighting, and a nurturing, humane environment increased the odds of returning a patient to functional living.[20] Unfortunately, by the time of John Morgan's assessment, this concept had fallen by the wayside and Trans-Allegheny was simply warehousing the chronically and, all too frequently, criminally insane.

By 1890, Weston's State Hospital for the Insane was so full that a second state hospital was built in Spencer, with the uninspired name of the Second State Hospital for the Insane. Its first superintendent, Dr. Lewis Guthrie, was broadly respected with regards to his approach in diagnosing and treating mental illness, and in later years he became well known for his treatises on innovative clinical care.

Governor Atkinson chose well. In their day, these men were among the most experienced and well-trained alienists in the field. The two gentlemen paid a visit to John Morgan on November 23rd, purportedly without explaining who they were or what their purpose was, although undoubtedly Morgan knew what they were up to. Afterwards, Dr. Camden allegedly told someone, probably at the jail, that Morgan claimed to know nothing of any murder committed by him or anyone else, and before long it was rumored that the two physicians were convinced that Morgan suffered from mental illness and were going to report this to the Governor.[21] Fears of the lynch mob resurfaced and once again contingency plans were formulated to move the prisoner out of Ripley.

The prosecutor, James Seaman, had his own concerns about Brown's petition and decided not to wait on the outcome of the medical evaluations. He sought out the same local physicians, Campbell and Casto, who evaluated Morgan at the time of the trial. After obtaining notarized statements from each of them, to the effect that John Morgan was sane and *"a case of mental depravity,"* he too rode into Charleston to meet with the governor.[22]

Seaman's visit proved unnecessary. The reports of the experts matched those of the local physicians. Dr. Camden and Dr. Guthrie were confident that John Morgan was indeed mentally disturbed in addition to suffering from moral depravity, but they also believed him to be fully culpable.[23] There was nothing to justify a pardon or commutation of his sentence.

The governor announced his intention to support the death penalty and the wheels of justice continued to turn along their inexorable course.

End Notes

[1] *Clarksburg Telegram,* Clarksburg, WV, 18 November, 1897.

[2] *Ibid.*

[3] *The Jackson Herald,* Ripley, WV, 17 December, 1897.

[4] *Ibid.*

[5] Author's Note: The term bull doze came into use in American slang after the Civil War when it was first introduced by the press in reference to intimidation tactics used by bullies, often in the South, to keep newly-freed African Americans from exercising their rights. Originally it referred to the use of a bull-whip to coerce an animal or slave into submission and the "dose" was the amount of punishment inflicted. Eventually the term bulldozer meant anyone who used scare tactics to threaten someone else and often was used in reference to vigilante mobs.

[6] *Jackson Herald.*

[7] *Ibid.*

[8] Bourget, Dominique & Laurie Whitehurst, "Amnesia and Crime," *Journal of the American Academy of Psychiatry and the Law Online*, December 2007, 35 (4) 469-480. (Retrieved from the WWW 02-01-2017)

[9] *Jackson Herald.*

[10] *Men of West Virginia, Vol I,* Biographical Publishing Company, Chicago Ill, 1903, p. 315.

[11] *Marietta Times Leader*, Marietta, OH, 30 January, 1896.

[12] *New York Daily Tribune*, New York, NY, 13 August, 1897.

[13] *Ibid.*

[14] *Hutchinson News*, Hutchinson, Kansas, 4 December, 1897.

[15] *Milwaukee Journal*, Milwaukee, WI, 11 October, 1897.

[16] *Ibid.*

[17] *New York Times*, New York, NY, 11 November, 1904.

[18] *New York Times*, New York, NY, 4 October, 1897

[19] *Cincinnati Enquirer*, Cincinnati, OH, 11 October, 1897.

[20] Kirkbride, Thomas S., *On the Construction, Organization and General Arrangements of Hospitals for the Insane,* Philadelphia: J.B. Lippincott, 1880; reprint, New York: Arno Press, 1973, p. 37-40.

[21] *Wheeling Register,* Wheeling, WV, 27 November, 1897.

[22] Morrison, O. J., *The Slaughter of the Pfost-Greene Family of Jackson County, W.Va. A History of the Tragedy*, 1897.

[23] *Wheeling Register,* Wheeling, WV, 28 November, 1897.

THE FAREWELL CONFESSION: DECEMBER 2, 1897

Although the jail here is a mere rattle-trap, and easy to escape from, there is little danger of Morgan attempting to take advantage of its weakness. Precautions against such an event, however, will be taken, volunteer guards patrolling the locality day and night until the morning of the execution, not to prevent mob violence, which is a thing of the past, but to see that the prisoner does not get away.

Front page excerpt from Pittsburgh Daily Post, Pittsburgh, PA, 07 November, 1897.

Whether truth or the fiction that passes into folklore, much has been made of accounts that John Morgan swore from the first he would not hang. Owen Shinn grew tired of being questioned by reporters on this matter and countered all challenges with assertions that Morgan would indeed be hanged on the 16th of December and everyone was invited to come see it happen.

Ripley's jail was on the ground floor at the rear of the county courthouse. It was in very poor condition, though this had little bearing on the events that followed. Thanks to an observant Parkersburg reporter with time on his hands and a column to fill there is a detailed description of its layout.[1]

A corridor, approximately five feet wide and fifty feet long, extended from the front entryway down through the center of the building, dividing the ground floor into two separate apartments. From the standpoint of the outside entry with its heavy tungsten steel doors, the prison area took up the entire left side. The apartment on the right side of the hallway served as the living quarters for the jailer, 47-year-old Benjamin Franklin Riley, his wife Jenny, and their four children. Frank Riley was experienced, and was respected throughout the county.[2] His wife Jenny also worked at the jail, providing meals and cleaning with the help of her older daughters. These were strange accommodations for a family and they came with some inherent dangers.

Entrance into the prison area could only be gained from the hallway through a heavy iron-barred door that was to be locked at all times. Inside the prison area there was a large free-standing iron cell divided into two smaller *"cages,"* each measuring roughly six feet by three feet and standing seven feet tall. The enclosed cells were extremely small and prisoners were sometimes allowed supervised exercise in the larger cellblock.

Despite his cramped accommodations and the death sentence hanging over his head, Morgan was beginning to enjoy himself after a fashion. He was experiencing rare, undivided attention, first from the newspaper reporters, and now from O. J. Morrison, who was telling him he was going to put his story in a book that thousands would read.

On the 2nd of December, John Morgan began dictating his *"true"* and *"final"* confession to O. J. Morrison who was going to pay him $25. In addition to the promised cash, Morrison had brought Morgan a brand-new suit to wear on the gallows, a pair of shiny new shoes, and a crush hat. The merchant also promised to give a percentage of the proceeds of the book sales to Rebekah and Albert.

Morrison's idea for capitalizing on Morgan's story was by no means a new one. The American public has always loved true crime and these types of printed souvenirs, generally referred to as *murder pamphlets,* followed a long-standing tradition that began six centuries before in England with the cheap, one-sided broadsheets sold to crowds at an execution.

By the 19th century, murder pamphlets had evolved into small paperback booklets—true crime's answer to British *penny dreadfuls* and American *dime novels*, providing cheap pulp escapism. The booklets usually had lengthy descriptions of the crimes, the more titillating the better (though as these things go, O. J. Morrison's publication pales in comparison), trial transcripts and confessions, and sometimes, depending on the date they were printed, reports of the actual execution. Their covers were usually illustrated with portraits of the victim, or the criminal, usually holding his weapon.

They averaged twenty-five pages in length, although the more horrific the crime, the longer the booklet. *The Fall River Tragedy,* for example, published in 1892, offered a 312-page account of Lizzie Borden and the murders of her parents. *The Holmes-Pitezel Case: The History of the Greatest Crime of the Century and the Search for the Missing Pitezel Children,* written in 1896 by the Philadelphia detective who doggedly tracked America's first serial killer, H. H. Holmes, ran upwards of 500 pages.

Oftentimes the criminal penned his own pamphlet. Of note is the 1868 publication of *The Life and Crimes of Joseph Eisele, alias John Schafer, The Parkersburg Murderer, Written by Himself.* Schafer, a respected German merchant living in Parkersburg, West Virginia, killed two individuals with a hatchet, and was caught attempting to murder a third. He included a full confession in his autobiography, complete with the fact that he immigrated to America to avoid arrest for his first hatchet murder in Germany. His purpose for publication was to provide a small sum of money for his wife and young child. As to his motive for the killings, Schafer wrote, *"I always committed those crimes under the pecuniary necessity, when pressed for my debt."* 3

The preface, written tongue-in-cheek by Eisele's publisher, with very few changes might easily have applied to John Morgan: 4

"We believe it is customary to preface popular sketches of great criminals with a bit of romance, in the shape of a family drama, a story of disappointed affection, or other fatal incident supposed to have exerted a predestinating influence upon the hero's life. We regret not being able to follow that time honored usage on this occasion. The gloomy subject now before us is not the result of a sudden freak of fate, not the growth of a day, but the logical effect of a chain of causes founded in nature, opportunity and education... The object of these pages is merely to depict the man as we know him by his deeds good and bad, and to unite in a brief, plain, but faithful record, the leading facts of the criminal's 'dark and terrible' career among us which, at the hand of human justice will terminate upon the scaffold..."

Murder pamphlets were for the most part out of vogue by the 20th century. Nonetheless in 1931 the defense attorney for Harry F. Powers, West Virginia's infamous, *"Bluebeard of Quiet Dell,"* requested a change of venue, arguing that the circulation of a murder pamphlet entitled *The Love Secrets of Bluebeard,* along with articles in detective magazines and a murder ballad called *The Crime of Quiet Dell,* had inflamed the minds of the Clarksburg populace to such an extent that his client could not get a fair trial. 5

These were biased accounts and often the author had his own personal agenda. Morrison quickly picked through pages of trial transcription, choosing only what he considered the most interesting aspects and closed with a final sentence or two stating that the murderer of the Pfost-Greene family was executed on December 16th. This last bit was written on faith some days before the hanging since Morrison was on his way to Cincinnati to have his manuscript printed in time to be sold at the big event. He'd had less than a month to complete it and very nearly lost his opportunity altogether when Morgan escaped on the very evening of their final interview. Several thousand were sold as souvenirs and they represent the most complete contemporary record of the affair in existence. John Morgan later complained that O. J. Morrison had gotten it all wrong.[6]

Henry Deem, editor of the *Jackson Herald,* later reported on Morrison's experience during the last interview.[7] Apparently, Morrison was left alone with Morgan to conduct their conversation in private. Morgan had been allowed out of the cage for the occasion and the two men sat by the pot-bellied stove. Morrison complained to Deem that the prisoner's conversational style was extremely confusing and hard to follow. Frustrated, Morrison challenged Morgan's version of events, *"You know that wasn't why you killed those people."* Morgan sprang to his feet, exclaiming, *"Well, g__ d___, that's the way it's going to go anyway, and if you don't like it—,"* and made as if to grab the heavy iron poker near the stove.

The guards returned soon after and the badly shaken Morrison abruptly exited the jail. He'd had quite enough. As he left, he told the guards that if he ever had another occasion to speak to their prisoner he wanted backup.

Morgan gave what were meant to be his final words of farewell during this interview:[8]

I had a good wife; she was always good and kind to me; she had talked to me time and time again about my soul's salvation. If I had only listened to her I might not have been in such a condition to-day: this is an awful trying thing, knowing that I will have to die and leave my darling wife and child. I hope that God will reward her for the kindness she has shown me through this trouble.

I ask God to forgive me for the way I have done. I ask in the name of God, for the people never to throw this awful crime up to my lovely child or dear wife. My desire is to go from this world to a better one. This is for a warning to all who reads it. May God forbid that no one ever harbors an evil thought of this kind in their hearts. I am thankful to the ministers who have called on me since my confinement, and praying with me and instructing in the way of a better life. I thank the jailer and family for the kindness they have shown me since I have been here.

I am also thankful to my guards for the way they have treated me. I am thankful to the sheriff of Jackson County, the way he has treated me up to the present time. This brings this all to a close, and I bid you all farewell, and pray to God that he may take care of my dear wife and child.

John F. Morgan

John Morgan was putting on quite an act. This was to be his final
scene and it was important to get it just right. If Morrison had thought
about it, he might have realized that Morgan at times appeared to be in
remarkably good humor for a man facing the gallows. At other moments,
when he was making his farewell remarks for instance, he donned a more
sober and repentant attitude as befitted the occasion.

The guards had been watching Morgan closely ever since Brown
delivered the bad news about his clemency petition and they noticed their
prisoner had begun acting rather suspiciously. What was all this business
about bloodhounds, they wondered.₉ He wanted to know everything. How
fast could they run? Could they track a man in the rain? It was all rather
peculiar. Still they chalked it up to nervous chatter in response to his fear
of hanging. It was hard to take the young man too seriously. He cracked
jokes and made them laugh; they had to keep reminding themselves that
this was the same murderous *"arch fiend"* who had brutally murdered two
helpless women and a boy.

That evening after Morrison left the jail there were two guards on duty.
Fillmore Riley, known to all as *"Fil,"* and erroneously labelled *"Phil"* or
sometimes *"Phillip"* in the papers, was the jailer's first cousin. The second
guard, Charlie Jewell, was just getting back on his feet after a rough patch.
He and his first wife had lost an infant daughter the year before, followed
by his wife's demise from consumption shortly after. He was newly married
to his widowed sister-in-law and trying to merge the two families.

Fil and Charlie worked in so-called *death watch* shifts—three hours
on and three hours off—and Sheriff Shinn had given them specific
instructions to check on their prisoner every two hours to make sure he
was alive and well.₁₀ Suicide attempts were common among prisoners
facing execution and Morgan's guards had been warned repeatedly. Because
it was difficult to be with a condemned man day in and day out, the jailer,
Frank Riley, had started spending time with the men for added support.
All three were together in the large cell room on this particular evening.

In his farewell speech, Morgan made a point of thanking Frank
Riley and the guards for their kindness. In truth, it seems these men
were amazingly lenient with a prisoner convicted of such awful crimes.
Regardless, Morgan had only a few weeks left on earth and there was
mercy in these men. It became their habit to allow him out of his cell in
the late afternoon so he could stretch his legs, warm himself by the stove,
engage in a little conversation, and watch them play checkers.

From where they sat at the stove the men had a clear view through the locked and barred door separating them from the hallway. They could see anyone requesting admission and at the same time keep a close eye on their charge. No one was allowed in to see the prisoner unaccompanied by the jailer or without a guard present. At least those were the regulations laid out by the sheriff. But if Henry Deem's report about Morrison's interview earlier in the day was accurate, the rules weren't always followed.

Afterwards Frank Riley related the story of Morgan's escape in great detail to the *Parkersburg Sentinel* reporter.[11] That evening from five o'clock until shortly after eleven, Riley was keeping the men company. Morgan sat with them while they played game after game of checkers. He feigned an inconceivable lack of familiarity with the game, asked all kinds of questions about their contest, and told them how exciting it was. But after a few hours he began to flag and announced he was ready to turn in. He wasn't feeling so well, he told them, and he hadn't been sleeping. He was hoping to fall asleep early and didn't want to be awakened for supper. The men were sympathetic. As Morgan walked back to his cage he told them to be sure to let him know how their contest turned out.

Phil, Charlie and I were standing with our backs to the cage when he went in. We heard him moving about for a few minutes and then all was quiet. When I looked next (at) his bed a few moments later I thought he was in bed with a paper over his face as he had been in the habit lately of sleeping to keep the light out from shining in his eyes.

Instead, Morgan accomplished a masterful subterfuge. He deliberately left his old shoes sitting beside the stove and walked in his stocking feet back to the darkened area of the cellblock where his cage stood.[12] Once inside he quickly changed into Morrison's new suit and arranged his old clothes and blankets to look like a body at rest. Then he laid a copy of the *Cincinnati Times Star* over his pillow.[13] This had been his habit the past few weeks, lying on his cot day or night with a newspaper over his face, claiming the light hurt his eyes. Satisfied that all his props were in place and the men's attention was still on their game, Morgan picked up his new shoes and tip-toed out of his cage again, slipping around to the back and quietly climbing on top. Here he stretched out in the dark and waited. All this he managed within a few feet of his guards.

After dark, an oil lantern kept near the stove provided the only light for the room and the men carried it with them if they were inspecting the cages and their occupants. Otherwise, it was quite dark inside. It was a rainy, overcast night and the windows at the end of the cell area offered no light.

Time dragged interminably, but eventually the men put up their checkerboard and Frank Riley stepped over to lock Morgan's cage, calling out to Morgan as he did so to ask how he was doing. He heard a muffled *"very well."* Frank Riley was hard of hearing and so later when his son Jimmy came in, the jailer asked him to listen for the sound of Morgan's breathing and was reassured when the boy said he heard him. Frank continued to stand watch while Fil and Charlie bunked in the nearby cell. At 11 o'clock he woke his cousin and the two sat by the stove exchanging pleasantries and were joined by Jenny Riley. From time to time, one of them walked around the cages listening for Morgan's breath.

Sometime afterwards Fil Riley was on his own. Frank and Jenny had left him and Charlie was still asleep. He decided he needed coffee and some dinner and so he crossed the hall to the Riley's kitchen. First though, he checked to make sure Morgan's cell door was still securely locked. Then he walked out the door of the cellblock without locking it behind him.

Fil Riley's failure to lock the cell room door was a critical error in judgment and one that Morgan obviously counted on, though the only reason for him to have done so was if he'd observed it happening before. On the other hand, he might have had a backup plan. That iron poker was nearby and if the door had been locked, all he had to do was flatten himself against the wall and wait for Fil's return.

The moment Morgan had been waiting for had finally arrived. Silently he shimmied down off his cage, mindful of the other guard asleep in the second one, slipped on his new shoes, and then walked across the room and through the unlocked cell door into the hallway. There he light-footed it down the corridor and quick as a flash he was out the front doors of the jail. The doors were massive and impossible to open and close silently. Fil Riley heard them clang shut, but although it was going on midnight he did not go to investigate. Later he said he thought a member of the Riley family had been going or coming. Who else could it have been?

One Indiana journal offered its own priceless version of how Morgan fooled his minders:[12]

Morgan sold his confession for $25, and with this he bought a new suit. This served as a disguise to some extent.

He had a good head start and would be well on his way before his guards even realized he was gone. Within minutes of his escape it turned midnight. A new day would soon be dawning—the 3rd of December—the one-month anniversary of the murder of the Pfost-Greene family.

End Notes

[1] *Parkersburg Sentinel*, Parkersburg, WV, 4 December, 1897 *Ibid.*

[2] *The History of West Virginia, Old and New*, Vol II, Chicago, IL: The American Historical Society, Inc., 1923, pg. 628.

[3] Eisele, Joseph, *The Life and Crimes of Joseph Eisele, alias John Schafer, The Parkersburg Murderer, Written by Himself.* Inland River Books, 1868.

[4] *Ibid.*

[5] *Utica Daily Press*, Uttica, New York, 17, November, 1931.

[6] *Cincinnati Post*, Cincinnati, OH, 17 December, 1897.

[7] *The Jackson Herald*, Ripley, WV, 18 December, 1897.

[8] Morrison, O. J., *The Slaughter of the Pfost-Greene Family of Jackson County, W.Va. A History of the Tragedy*, 1897.

[9] *Parkersburg Sunday News*, Parkersburg, WV, 12 December, 1897. [2] *Utica Daily Press*, Uttica,

[10] *Parkersburg Sentinel.* [11] *Ibid.* [12] *Somerset Herald*, Somerset, PA, 8 December, 1897.

[13] *Jackson Herald*, Ripley, WV. 18 December, 1897.

[14] *Osgood Journal*, Osgood, Indiana, 9 December, 1897.

MANHUNT

Initial reports claimed Morgan was tracked to his home on Grasslick, where "*he procured a shot-gun, which he loaded heavily, and left in the direction of the mountains.*"[1] None of this was accurate. He was unarmed at the time of his capture. He did not go to Grasslick, at least not at first, nor to the mountains which might have saved him. Instead, he made a beeline for Rebekah and Albert who were staying with her parents. As soon as he was out of the jail he slipped into his new shoes, tied a bandana around his head to ward off the cold and damp, and jogged for about two and a half miles down the Charleston Pike until he came to a farm belonging to Asbury Casto. Here he stole a horse, threw a blanket over its back to protect his new suit trousers, and using only a halter, rode hard toward Fairplain, some six miles further south. Leaving the Pike, he rode along Poverty Ridge and arrived at Hiram Hall's farm shortly after one o'clock in the morning.[2]

At this point his brilliant escape plan lost all momentum. Instead of obtaining provisions and a fresh mount and getting underway, Morgan spent the better part of the night with his family, and it was well after five in the morning before he started out again. He later insisted he had no intention of remaining gone—he only wanted to see "*Becca*" and his son. "*He said he couldn't have lived had he escaped except apart from his wife and child and preferred to die.*"[3]

Given everything that followed, perhaps this was true. Having achieved his driving objective, he seemed to lose interest in actual escape. No doubt Hiram and Rebekah, knowing the sheriff might be at their door at any moment, urged Morgan to be on his way. And he did leave eventually, with a change of clothes and a satchel to carry them in, along with another coat, hat and vest, a little tobacco, and a bottle of liniment.[4,5] He probably could have obtained a weapon from his father-in-law if he'd wanted one badly enough, but he did not. Later it was assumed Morgan never intended to resist arrest if cornered.[6]

After leaving the Halls, Morgan returned to the Charleston Pike. When he reached George Shamblin's farm he turned the horse loose and crossed the fields on foot, cutting through the woods to climb the ridge above Grasslick. He was now headed southeast toward Bear Fork and his sister Florence's home about nine miles away. To get there he was forced to backtrack along the same route he'd taken the morning of the murders. Surely, if he had hidden money before his arrest, he would have taken time to retrieve it.

Just before dawn on December 3rd, one month to the day and almost the hour when the horrible sequence was set in motion, John Morgan stood looking down on the Pfost-Greene farm. Later he told a reporter he stopped by the farmhouse just long enough to dig into the winter storage pit and fill his valise with apples, and then he moved on.[7]

But that wasn't quite true. There may have been more to that visit than Morgan ever admitted. He remained at the Pfost-Greene farm much longer than the time required to grab some fruit. There was someone living in the house after all, someone John Morgan expected to see out feeding the livestock and milking the cows—someone he may have wanted to talk to. And that someone was Ben Anderson.

While John Morgan had been enjoying his family reunion, all hell was breaking loose in Ripley. When alarms were shouted around 3:15 in the morning, people woke up thinking the town was on fire, a common enough occurrence, but the fear and excitement was no less intense as word of Morgan's escape began to spread.[8]

Not long after Morgan slipped out the front door of the jail, Fil Riley returned from his dinner and took stock. His prisoner was still asleep; Morgan's hat, coat and shoes were lying where he'd left them beside the old wood stove. The sound of the rain against the windows seemed almost peaceful and it felt good to be indoors on such a night. All was well. And so, Riley kicked back until 3 o'clock in the morning when Charlie Jewell relieved him. Charlie was immediately suspicious. Morgan hadn't moved an inch in all those hours and Charlie couldn't hear him breathing. At first he thought the prisoner had somehow managed to kill himself. He grabbed the poker to move the newspaper off the pillow and was dumbfounded.

Imagine the consternation when the discovery was made—all the cursing, the blaming, the utter frustration, and dread. Charlie ran up the street to the Maguire House where the sheriff's brother Reuben was staying—the two men had been taking turns in town until the hanging. Reuben sent Charlie on to Fairplain to inform Owen, while he stayed behind to raise the alarm. It was a wet, miserable ride and Charlie had plenty of time to imagine the sheriff's reaction to the news. How could Fil have been so careless?

Along the way he discovered Asbury Casto's horse running loose in a schoolyard and this ultimately misled the lawmen, who surmised that Morgan was headed southeast toward Kentuck, out beyond Kenna. The Lanhams, Morgan's sister Ida and her husband George lived out there.

Charlie Jewell reached the Shinn residence near daybreak. Trusting his brother to organize the men in Ripley, Sheriff Shinn and Jewell roused the Grasslick neighborhood and sent men off in search parties. Then the two of them headed to Hiram Hall's farm.

Shinn got no help from Rebekah or the rest of the Halls. It seemed obvious Morgan had been there, but Rebekah refused to say if or when he had arrived or how long ago he had left. *"Don't ask me Sheriff. I don't want to tell you a lie and I don't want to talk."* [9]

Shinn made several false assumptions and they cost him and his posse several wretched, unnecessary hours in the saddle. He was certain that Morgan, like his father before him, was headed for the mountains. If John had done so he might have eluded his pursuers entirely. Because despite his head start of several hours, he was not all that far away. Unfortunately, Shinn abandoned his initial search area and rode back to Ripley where his brother was busy overseeing the manhunt. By now everyone believed Morgan had a head start of nine to ten hours. [10]

Word that the convicted ax-murderer was loose in Jackson County ignited the populace, yet it was no easy feat to find enough men to go after him. As the *Wheeling Register* explained, *"Although Morgan is of small stature it is plainly visible that there are very few people here who do not fear him."* [11] Old friends, neighbors and acquaintances knew John to be a savvy hunter and woodsman, and when finally cornered they believed he'd have nothing to lose. It was one thing for the younger men, some of whom relished the opportunity to pit themselves against a dangerous felon, to join an exciting manhunt. It was quite another for family men concerned about the safety of their women and children at home.

And then there were those who did not want to see him captured. Morgan had a good many relatives and friends in the area, and some, though horrified by his crimes, hoped he might yet escape the hangman's noose. Still, by the time Owen Shinn and his brothers left town they had managed to deputize nearly 250 more men, aided by unsubstantiated rumors of a $500 reward. [12] The men were under strict orders to take John Morgan alive, although if found many doubted he would live to see the gallows.

Shinn rode with his brothers, Reuben and John, the two guards who were eager to salvage their reputations, and John Shamblin. Deputy Shamblin, a former constable, was highly regarded by the locals as "*the nerviest man in the county,*" and they had great faith in his ability to find Morgan.[13]

It wasn't long after the escape that the news hit the wires, and reporters once again converged on the scene. Much was made of the way Morgan outsmarted his captors and he was described as "*shrewd*" and "*very smooth.*" "*Morgan's escape is one of the slickest in criminal history,*" read the *Clarksburg Telegram.* A front-page headline on the *Los Angeles Herald* read, "*Played a Sharp Trick,*" and the *Salt Lake Herald* headlined with "*Fooled His Jailers.*" The law did not fare well since the escape was "*easily accomplished.*" Owen Shinn was surely apoplectic by now. He and his men were being severely criticized for their negligence, "*after their many boasts of his security and the wide advertisement of the plans for his execution.*"[14]

Officials were sent to Huntington to cover the freight trains coming in from both the Ohio and Chesapeake & Ohio lines. They also brought bloodhounds in from Huntington, but because of the incessant rain the animals proved useless right from the start.[15] Posses were seen coming and going from Ripley throughout the day and most of the night, but there was little to report beyond the fact that Morgan had stolen a horse and ridden south.

As the hours stretched on the rumor mill cranked up. Morgan captured! Shots fired! Men killed! *The Denver Post* ran with news of a fabricated bloody shootout in which the sheriff, despite being so badly wounded, "*he will lose his left arm,*" still managed to put a bullet through Morgan's heart.

Some West Virginia reporters claimed these rumors had been started as "*jokes*"—hoaxes deliberately planted for the sensation-seeking out-of-state newshounds who published them as fact,[16] but it was no laughing matter for the local citizenry who were living in constant fear. John Chancey's daughter, Mary, had her own recollection of those terrible few days. "*After Morgan's escape,*" she recalled:[17]

"*...the community was tore up and scared a-plenty. A bunch of us would stay at each other's home at night for I don't know how long. This is how we did it for weeks before we got our nerves settled down.*"

Mary gave the impression Morgan was at large for several weeks, and no doubt that was the way it seemed to a nine-year-old. It was the stuff of nightmares for a child. Overnight, her friend John had been transformed into the bogeyman, and she and her family were greatly traumatized by the ordeal.

Morgan reached Florence and Enoch Casto's home on Bear Fork a few hours after leaving Rebekah. Afraid of being seen, he remained hidden in the woods near the road and waited for the sun to go down. He watched as the sheriff and his men met up with another posse led by Wilson Slaughter, the Casto's neighbor, and listened intently as Shinn issued instructions.[18] All this waiting around meant several more hours of cold, wet exposure. What was so important about seeing his sister that Morgan risked losing another full day of travel? Here was yet another instance of inaction that made no sense. It seems that Morgan simply didn't know what to do next.

His sudden appearance amid his Casto kin created quite an uproar. John asked for some supper and warmed himself by the fire, and it was later said he debated whether to give himself up.[19] After eating a hearty meal and drying his clothes he must have felt a little more optimistic about things because he soon headed out again. After all the time and trouble to get there he stayed barely an hour. Perhaps he wasn't welcomed or maybe he was behaving badly. Morrison related that just before leaving he asked for a book of matches, then told his sister and the man he called *"brother"* that if they told anyone he'd been there he would come back and kill them both. Just to make sure they got the message, he threatened to haunt them if he was captured and killed.[20,21]

This tale may have been manufactured by the couple to explain why they aided and abetted a murderer. If John *did* threaten his sister, Florence either didn't take him seriously or decided the best defense was a good offense, because the first thing she did was head for the neighbors. Unlike Rebekah, who kept her silence, John's sister told everyone, and the first person she came across was Festus Slaughter.

Brothers Festus and Wilson Slaughter were distant cousins of John Morgan and up until now they'd held him in some regard. Wilson's posse was already combing Bear Fork for any sign of the murderer. Once Festus informed him that John was in the vicinity, a determined Wilson Slaughter lost no time picking up the trail and, along with some Casto relations, was soon in pursuit.

By now it was obvious Morgan was heading straight for the Pocatalico

River, and the men on horseback were rapidly closing the distance. As he crossed the ridgeline Morgan looked down and saw his pursuers riding directly below him.[22]

End Notes

[1] *Wheeling Register,* Wheeling, WV, 5 December, 1897.

[2] *Cincinnati Enquirer,* Cincinnati, OH, 7 December, 1897.

[3] *The Jackson Herald,* Ripley, WV, 18 December, 1897.

[4] *Wheeling Register,* 5 December, 1897.

[5] *The Jackson Herald.*

[6] *Parkersburg Sentinel,* Parkersburg, WV, 6 December, 1897.

[7] *Cincinnati Enquirer.*

[8] *Parkersburg Sunday News,* Parkersburg, WV, 12 December, 1897.

[9] *Wheeling Register,* 06 December, 1897.

[10] *Parkersburg Sentinel.*

[11] *Wheeling Register,* Wheeling, WV, 4 December, 1897.

[12] *Ibid.*

[13] *Pittsburgh Daily Post,* Pittsburgh, PA, 05 December, 1897.

[14] *Wheeling Register.*

[15] *Ibid.*

[16] *Parkersburg Sentinel.*

[17] "Last Public Hanging," *Goldenseal Magazine,* Spring 1990.

[18] *Parkersburg Sentinel.*

[19] *Jackson Herald,* Ripley, WV, 18 December, 1897.

[20] Morrison, O. J., *The Slaughter of the Pfost-Greene Family of Jackson County, W.Va. A History of the Tragedy,* 1897.

[21] *Parkersburg Sentinel.*

[22] *Jackson Herald.*

LOST

When John Morgan left Florence and Enoch that night he faced a miserable five-mile hike along the Pocatalico and into Roane County. All his planning had gone into that one bold stroke back at the jail and he'd given little thought to what came next. Instead of fleeing the area, he had spent his first hours of freedom visiting family. Now he was just hours away from capture. He had gone without sleep for more than forty-eight hours and he was cold, wet, and frightened. What may have once been familiar countryside was now transformed into an alien landscape by winter darkness, freezing rain and perhaps his own inner demons.

Realizing he needed to put some miles between himself and Slaughter's posse, Morgan stole the first horse he came across and rode blindly through the night. Mile after mile he rode, believing that he was widening the gap between himself and his pursuers. Sometime during that headlong flight he lost all sense of direction, and as the night wore on he became increasingly disoriented. By the time there was light enough to see, his predicament was clear. He had ridden hard for several hours only to find himself within a hundred yards of where he had stolen the horse.[1] After his re-capture Morgan admitted to a reporter that he was *"greatly discouraged"* by this development, and so he built a fire in the woods and sat down *"to ponder the situation."*[2]

John Morgan was not the only man who was wet, cold and *"greatly discouraged."* While Morgan was pondering his disheartening circumstances, Owen Shinn and his men were riding back to Ripley empty-handed. They had spent the previous day searching the area around Hiram Hall's farm on Poverty Ridge, the Casto's on Bear Fork, and the Lanham's farm around Kentuck, and ended up staying the night with George and Ida.[3] The sheriff was hard-pressed to reassure his frightened constituents. He learned that bets were being taken on Morgan's ability to elude his pursuers and the odds were not in the law's favor. He swore he would run the man to ground, but hedged a bit, just in case:[4]

The sheriff believes that Morgan will be soon captured. A human wall, he believes, surrounds the fugitive and if he escapes through it, it will be by his splendid knowledge of the country and under cover of darkness.

Eager to shore up faith in his promises, Shinn ordered that construction on the scaffold be continued. Nothing, especially the prisoner's temporary *at large* status, was going to delay John Morgan's date with the devil, now less than two weeks away.

Crowds of anxious people stopped by the factory to measure Major Progler's progress on the scaffold.[5] After he was back in jail, Morgan allegedly told Shinn he had been disappointed to find the gallows site empty when he rode by on the night of his escape. He said he'd planned to leave a dummy hanging from the braces.[6]

At least the newspaper correspondents were enjoying themselves. Like alchemists, the sensationalists among them had stirred the rumor pots for the past twenty-four hours, transforming an absence of information into titillating headlines with the help of local mischief-makers. They reported on gun battles and Morgan's death in a hail of bullets, as well as information like this:[7]

Sheriff Shinn and posse, who spent the night in a fruitless search for John Morgan, the triple murderer, returned to Ripley early this morning. The County Court met shortly after the sheriff's return and raised the reward for Morgan's capture from $500 to $1,000.

There was no reward. There had been some discussion about one early on, but the county court had been unable to convene to approve it.[8] The papers choose to overlook this minor detail and by the time retractions could be printed the damage was done. Blissfully unaware of the truth, hundreds of armed men combed the hollows and hillsides, thoughts of all that reward money a constant balm for their developing chilblains and saddle sores.

Meanwhile, totally dispirited and suffering from exposure, Morgan rested by his campfire, tended his own blisters—Morrison's new shoes had been a very bad idea and the liniment wasn't helping much—and considered his options. He'd about given up any real hope of escaping, but aside from sitting around waiting for a posse to arrive, possibly with bloodhounds, he had no choice but to keep moving. He turned the second horse loose and started walking toward the little village of Walton, about ten miles away. But it wasn't long before his sore feet got the better of him.[9]

He was barely six miles from Florence's house where he'd been the previous evening when he decided to stop at a farm belonging to Armisted Harper.[10] He introduced himself by the name of Hickman and asked if he could come in to get warm and have a bite to eat. Once he was off his feet again and his belly was full, his spirits lifted and he began to regale the Harper family with stories of the dangerous ax-murderer on the loose, telling them all about the clever outlaw and his brilliant escape tactics.[11]

The Harper children listened wide-eyed as the stranger said that even now John Morgan was running for his life somewhere along the Great Kanawha River in the direction of Huntington with a furious posse and baying bloodhounds in hot pursuit. Harper later claimed he had no idea the man who sat with him and his family by the fireside was the fearsome John Morgan.[12] Morgan also happened to be related, a cousin on his Gandee grandmother's side, though neither seemed aware of the fact at the time.

Once he finished his meal and his yarn-spinning, exhaustion set in again and the foot-sore Morgan offered his host a dollar to take him on into Walton by horseback. Isabel Harper wasn't happy. This man Hickman came out of nowhere, frightening her and her children with his stories of an escaped slaughterer of innocents, and now her husband was riding off and leaving them all alone.

Of all the aliases Morgan could have chosen, why Hickman? The answer can be found in accounts of a protracted gun battle occurring on November 7, the Sunday morning after John Morgan was sentenced to hang. Hard on the heels of the bloody Jackson County murders, the last stand of the locally famous Milton Hickman and his band of outlaws against U.S. marshals made front page news across the country. Morgan had been avidly reading the papers and he knew all about Milton Hickman.

That Sunday morning Hickman and his men were seated, along with his sweetheart, among the congregation of a Methodist Episcopal church in the midst of the small mountain settlement of Muddlety, WV. [13] The minister had just started the doxology when a U.S. marshal stepped into the doorway and demanded Hickman give himself up. What came next was a veritable bloodbath. Hickman's gang grabbed their rifles and opened fire and several Methodists joined the affray either out of sympathy for the outlaws or sheer outrage at having their sermon disrupted.

The ensuing battle raged for nearly two hours during which both Hickman and the marshal were killed, along with several members of the congregation including a mother and child. [14] Pulpit and altar were totally destroyed, windows were shattered, and pews, walls and ceilings were riddled with bullet holes. If the accounts are to be believed, upwards of two hundred bullet holes were tallied in the walls alone. Its bloody reality aside, this final blaze of glory was just the kind of outlaw romance that appealed to the young felon who fancied himself a desperado. Following Hickman's demise John Ferguson Morgan was now the most wanted man in West Virginia, and there was still more to come in his own personal outlaw saga.

SLAIN AT THE ALTAR

Hickman, after having raided the mountain towns so often that all the natives were in abject terror of him, met a little brown-faced daughter of the mountains, with whom he fell in love. Through her influence he was induced to attend the little log meeting house and listen to the exhortations of the circuit evangelist.

He was kneeling at the altar—the altar at which he was soon to be married—and professing religion when Marshal Rader's posse surrounded the place and made an attack. Hickman, kneeling at the altar, leaped to his feet.

"Trust in the Lord," he cried, "but keep your grip on your Winchesters!"

From the Wilkes-Barre Record, Wilkes-Barre, PA, 10 November, 1897.

End Notes

[1] *Jackson Herald,* Ripley, WV, 18 December, 1897.

[2] *Cincinnati Enquirer,* Cincinnati, OH, 7 December, 1897.

[3] *Jackson Herald.*

[4] *Wheeling Register,* Wheeling, WV, 5 December, 1897.

[5] *Ibid.*

[6] *Ibid.*

[7] *Norfolk Virginian,* 05 December, 1897.

[8] *Parkersburg Sentinel,* Parkersburg, WV, 4 December, 1897.

[9] *Ibid.*

[10] *Jackson Herald,* Ripley, WV, 18 December, 1897.

[11] Morrison, O. J., *The Slaughter of the Pfost-Greene Family of Jackson County, W.Va. A History of the Tragedy,* 1897.

[12] *Parkersburg Sentinel.*
[13] *Wheeling Register*, Wheeling, WV, 10 November, 1897.
[14] *New York Times,* New York, NY, 10 November, 1897.

THE ROAD TO WALTON

Harper and Morgan began their seven-mile journey to Walton around sunset. It had continued to rain all day, and what began as an uncomfortable ride was about to get even more so. Soon after they started out they were joined by a circuit-riding minister by the name of William Ballard Parsons. Circuit riders moved from one small outlying congregation to another, preaching the gospel and marrying, baptizing, and burying. Unfortunately John Morgan was well-acquainted with this one. Parsons and his wife, the local midwife, had a farm not far from John and Rebekah, and Morgan's step-father, Joshua Parsons, had been the man's uncle. Additionally, "Bal" Parsons had prayed mightily for John's salvation a few years back during a lengthy revival service. John had *"professed conversion,"* though Parsons had harbored reservations even then.[1] The two men recognized each other on sight, but neither chose to acknowledge the fact.[2]

It is unknown whether Morgan had his own mount or was riding double behind Harper, in which case he could hardly have made a run for it, even if he'd wanted to. Parsons had no way of knowing whether John Morgan was armed like everyone said he was, and no doubt wanted to avoid a dangerous confrontation. In any case, this curious trio simply carried on through the rain and growing darkness with Armisted Harper apparently none the wiser. As they rode, Parsons began to plan. He knew a large reward was being offered for Morgan's capture and now, praise the Lord, the money was practically falling in his lap.

Just as they reached the outskirts of Walton, two more riders were spotted coming their way. As John peered at them cautiously from under the brim of his rain-soaked hat his heart must have turned over. He had once called these men friends![3] Was everyone he knew on that god-forsaken Walton road that night?

Billy Chancey, the young man who rescued Alice Pfost as she escaped her family's murderer, was as cautious as the preacher. He too chose not to confront a man he believed to be armed and dangerous. Neither did Chloe Greene's half-brother, John Morgan's next-door neighbor Jim Fisher.[4] Editor Henry Deem reported that the two men *"spoke to him in passing,"* but O. J. Morrison claimed that neither man had heard of Morgan's escape and failed to recognize him in the dark, which seems highly unlikely.

This was a time when chance meetings were an opportunity for sharing the latest gossip from distant neighborhoods and these men were coming from the direction of Walton where an active manhunt was underway. What really occurred between this odd little band of travelers and the two newcomers? After a word or two of greeting, Jim Fisher and Billy Chancey rode on by. Word would soon get out that they had encountered the fugitive.[5]

When asked by the Sheriff why they hadn't captured him, they replied that they didn't have any business fooling with John Morgan.

Wilson Slaughter had been on Morgan's heels since he'd left the Castos the night before. He'd found where the killer had stolen a horse, and though puzzled at first by his erratic changes in direction, it didn't take him long to realize Morgan had been riding in circles all night. His hopes of running him to ground began to soar when he discovered the remains of the campfire and realized his quarry was on foot again. When Slaughter and his men reached Armisted Harper's farm they learned from Isabel that Morgan had eaten supper with them and then gone on to Walton with her husband. If she had been concerned before, the truth about her dinner guest must have terrified her.

Slaughter was determined to press on in hopes of overtaking the riders, but the men with him were exhausted, as well as wet, cold, and hungry. They were farmers and family men, and now that they were about to corner the killer they may have been in favor of waiting for the sheriff. Resolute and riding hard, Slaughter quickly out-distanced the rest of them, but he was still about an hour behind Morgan and his companions when they reached Walton.[6]

Shinn and his posse were a couple of hours behind Wilson Slaughter. Shortly before noon that day the sheriff and his brothers had returned to their homes to obtain fresh mounts and dry clothes, and having received word that Morgan was headed toward Walton they were quickly back on the trail. It must have been galling for Shinn to learn how close he'd been to John Morgan on Bear Fork, but these back-country roads were a veritable maze and Morgan had been on foot at the time, cutting cross-country through brush and heavy timber. A father-son duo now rode with the Shinns.[7] Smith Greene was Jimmy's older half-brother; his son Perry,

"*P.C.*" had been on hand to witness Morgan's confession on the day of the murders.

Once Morgan and his traveling companions reached the outskirts of Walton, the Reverend Parsons slipped away to find the local justice of the peace, while Morgan went into the general store to change a $5 bill so he could pay Harper for his ride.[8] He also purchased some tobacco and a bag of peanuts.[9]

While Morgan and Harper were settling their business affairs, Bal_ Parsons was swearing out a warrant for John Morgan's arrest, "*a proceeding wholly unnecessary,*" as the *Jackson Herald* editor took pains to point out afterwards. Even though he had his eye on the reward for Morgan's arrest, the good reverend had no intention of doing the deed himself. He needed to find someone to do it for him and a local constable by the name of John Camp fit the bill nicely. Camp had just gotten back from hunting the fugitive all day and initially thought Parsons was mistaken. It made no sense for a man on the run to be hiding in plain sight this close to home. But there was no mistake. When John Camp slipped cautiously into the store, there was John Morgan, big as life, "*seated on a nail keg, and contentedly eating peanuts.*"[10]

He... said his name was Hickman and that he was a detective. At the same time he went on eating peanuts with a grin on his face as if he took it to be a huge joke.

Excerpt from the Cincinnati Enquirer, Cincinnati, OH, 07 December, 1897

It was all so anti-climactic. With the help of bystanders, Camp soon had Morgan restrained and bound. The Parkersburg paper tells the story of the arrest in an understated fashion, saying that when Camp informed Morgan he had a warrant for his arrest, Morgan "*coolly faced the officer*" and asked what for, and when Camp told him he said he was "*ready to go.*"[11] Many details of the arrest were furnished by John Morgan, who liked to portray himself as a very cool customer. This attitude of insouciance was typical during his recapture and return to jail, but is probably more accurate than accounts that described Morgan as "*greatly terrified*" and "*trembling like a leaf*" at the time of his capture.[12,13]

Several papers ran with the story the next day, reporting that Morgan had gone into the store to buy tobacco. "*His Taste For Tobacco Will Put His Neck in the Halter*" read a *Marion Daily Star* headline out of Ohio. The *Cincinnati Enquirer* seemed unwilling to give up the bloodhound angle, insisting Morgan had gone to buy a revolver in case the dogs caught up with him. Morgan admitted to Henry Deem that he *had* been concerned about bloodhounds despite the wet weather:[14]

> *He was evidently afraid of blood hounds, and this fear would seem to have influenced him from secreting himself in one of the numerous caves of which he is cognizant—keeping on the go, changing horses, etc. It was his intention, he alleges, to procure a brace of revolvers with which to defend himself from blood hounds.*

This may have been more bravado. As Deem pointed out, John could have easily gotten a weapon at his father-in-law's. And he made no attempt to buy guns at the store. Morgan was unarmed at the time of his arrest and made no effort to resist. It was all a bit of a letdown for those who'd been hoping for more exciting headlines:[15]

> *There is nothing very thrilling about the capture of Morgan whom many predicted would never be taken alive. He did not even have a weapon of any kind upon his person and made no response whatever to being arrested. If his story may be credited he had already tired of being a fugitive from justice, a hunted animal, and was ready and willing to go back and expiate the fearful crimes for which he had been condemned.*

Walton's inhabitants quickly spread word of the triple-murderer in their midst, held captive by one of their own, and their *"exultation was increased by the thought of the reward."*[16] John Camp took their congratulations in stride as he prepared his prisoner for the fifteen-mile ride to the Roane county seat in Spencer. Morgan claimed he was mounted on horseback with his feet bound and his arms strapped behind him, but the men who helped transport him told reporters a cab had been hired for the journey due to the weather. The temperature was starting to plummet and the rain was turning icy.[17,18]

Arresting Morgan was the easy part as far as Constable Camp was concerned. Holding on to him was another matter. Less than a half-hour after the arrest Deputy Wilson Slaughter tore into town and immediately realized he had missed all the action. He accosted Camp and demanded that he turn over the prisoner. A heated argument arose, but there was no contest in the end. John Camp had a sizable guard detail surrounding Morgan, whereas Wilson was alone, having out-ridden his own posse. John Morgan was going to Spencer.

And so began the jurisdictional tug-of-war over the most important prisoner anyone had seen in years. And the bickering over a nonexistent reward.

End Notes

[1] *Parkersburg Sentinel,* Parkersburg, WV, 6 December, 1897.

[2] Morrison, O. J., *The Slaughter of the Pfost-Greene Family of Jackson County, W.Va. A History of the Tragedy*, 1897.

[3] *Ibid.*

[4] *Jackson Herald*, Ripley, WV, 18 December 1897.

[5] *Parkersburg Sentinel.*

[6] Morrison.

[7] *Jackson Herald.*

[8] *Parkersburg Sentinel.*

[9] *Ibid.*

[10] *Ibid.*

[11] *Cincinnati Enquirer,* Cincinnati, OH, 7 December, 1897.

[12] *Parkersburg Sentinel.*

[13] *Evening Bulletin,* Maysville, KY, Dec 6, 1897.

[14] *Jackson Herald.*

[15] *Parkersburg Sentinel.*

[16] *Ibid.*

[17] *Cincinnati Enquirer.*

[18] *Jackson Herald.*

CONFRONTATION IN SPENCER

The inhabitants of Roane County had been on edge since news reached them of Morgan's escape. Several had participated in the manhunt and now, having missed the action in Walton, they poured into the streets of Spencer to hear all about the arrest. Someone had telephoned ahead to say that John Camp was on his way with the murderer and it was like setting a match to a powder keg.[1] Several reporters documented the dramatic nighttime events which followed.

There was a sheriff in Roane County at the time, but his official status was questionable and thus so was his authority. William Matthews had been elected to his first term at the same time as his Jackson County counterpart, but the opposing candidate had petitioned Judge Reese Blizzard to oust him from the office, citing various irregularities in the election.[2] An appeals court would eventually resolve the allegations, but

Main Street in Spencer

until then Matthews wore the badge and issued orders to his appointed deputies, though he did so in the face of a divided constituency.

The steady downpour was doing little to discourage the growing crowds and inevitably talk turned toward lynching. A worried mayor sent officials to intercept Camp's party about two miles outside of Spencer.[3] They advised him to hold his prisoner in the woods overnight and come in around daybreak. Camp adamantly refused. The rain was coming down in rivers and he didn't care if a lynch mob stood between him and a dry bed, he was determined to take his prisoner into town. The little procession continued on and then dismounted a half mile from the town limits to proceed on foot, taking a circuitous route through the open fields in hopes of avoiding detection. They made it to within a half block of the jail before being discovered. *The Evening Bulletin* out of Maysville, Kentucky provided the most detailed coverage of the evening's excitement: [4]

> *The five guards, as well as several Spencer officials, completely surrounded the prisoner as he walked through the streets, all carrying firearms of large caliber. Many citizens cried: "There goes the villain!" "Lynch him!" "Hang him tonight!" "Hang him now!"*

Once they'd managed to drag Morgan into the jail, Matthews sent out armed deputies to establish a sixty-yard perimeter, with orders to fire on anyone trying to cross it.[5]

Meanwhile, a worn-out, fuming Wilson Slaughter had been forced to turn back toward Ripley. A member of his original posse—one of the Castos—had managed to catch up with him, and the two intercepted the sheriff's party in Countsville, about four miles outside of Walton.[6]

When Shinn rode into Spencer around ten o'clock that night, Morgan was already behind bars and the town was in a frenzy. Shinn brushed aside the Roane County law enforcement officials and made a beeline for the jail where he demanded that Sheriff Matthews give him back his prisoner. Matthews refused to do so until Shinn guaranteed the reward money. The dangerous ax-murderer had simply waltzed out of the Jackson County jail. Why should they give him back?

While these tense arguments were underway, the telegraph wires were humming with the latest news account. Editors on the receiving end, however, had become a bit leery where news of John Morgan was concerned:[7]

> *Rumors of all kinds are afloat, the latest being that he was captured and*

is now being held a prisoner until the reward offered for him reaches a figure satisfactory to his captors. This story is probably as baseless as the one sent out yesterday that Morgan had shot the sheriff and the sheriff had killed the desperado.

Shinn had some skill in diplomacy, but he had run out of time and patience. There *was* no reward, he declared! It was all rumor and supposition created by the press! How can that be, the Roane County officials fired back. It had been in all the papers, and besides, there was *always* a reward! The *Cincinnati Enquirer* reported that the negotiations grew so heated, *"the Jackson County Sheriff drew his revolver and threatened to take Morgan by force. There was a hot time then for two hours."*[8]

What happened next would almost strain credulity, but for multiple sources corroborating the story. At the height of this confrontation, somebody yelled *"FIRE!"*

At first this was thought to be a ruse of the Jackson County people to gain their end but the rapid spreading of the flames in a store building close at hand soon dispelled this idea and a large part of the crowd left to attend this new scene of excitement.[9]

The fire had broken out just a few blocks from the jail in a large dry goods store belonging to C. F. Duling, located near the train depot. It was the third such conflagration in a year and flames were spreading rapidly and threatening the entire block.[10] Most of the crowd surrounding the jail rushed off to fight the fire, leaving the two county sheriffs to resolve the dispute on their own. Shinn took advantage of the situation, reiterating that there was no reward. This time, however, he offered his personal guarantee; on the chance he was mistaken, he promised to see that Roane County got its money.

At this juncture Matthews and the town officials had more trouble than they could effectively handle and so the Spencer lawmen reluctantly handed Morgan over. Shinn commandeered a four-seated spring wagon and, while his brother Reuben and Wilson Slaughter got Morgan situated, Shinn chased off a few *"obstinate reward seekers"* with the business end of his revolver.[11] By then it was nearly midnight. The rains were unrelenting and the temperature was still falling, but the sheriff refused to stay the night.[12] He'd had about all of the Roane County hospitality he could take.

Thanks to the heavy downpour, the serendipitous fire down by the train station was quickly contained. Once it was discovered the Jackson

County men had flown the coop along with their prisoner, there was
nothing left for several hundred rain-soaked, disgruntled thrill-seekers to
do but go to bed.

Shinn and his men had a brutal trip ahead of them.[13] They could
scarcely see with the rain beating in their faces, and the mud was so deep
in places they had to get out and put their shoulders to the wagon before
the horses could move again. Several of the smaller streams had become
impassable, forcing them to backtrack to find alternative fording places.
They were also unprepared for the change in temperature. It had been
unusually warm for the past several days, and now it was below freezing.
Morgan was dangerously close to hypothermia and they were forced to
make several stops to warm him up.

It took them over ten hours to cover the thirty-five miles to Ripley,
and the sheriff's bedraggled, mud-splattered little band caused quite a stir
when they arrived back in town that Sunday morning. Church services
were disrupted all over town as people came running toward the jail.

John Morgan had not fared well during the long journey. His clothes
were frozen stiff, his teeth were chattering and he was shivering violently.[14]
He was greatly relieved to be hustled back into his old accommodations,
just fifty-nine hours after he'd left them. Editor Henry Deem spoke to the
captured fugitive shortly after he arrived:[15]

*In his cage Sunday afternoon Morgan was indeed a pitiable sight. Tired,
sleepy, bespattered with mud, the only chance of escape gone, he seemed the most
miserable wretch on earth. His voice seemed the very intonation of despair, and
when during the course of a conversation his devoted wife and interesting child
were mentioned, he choked up and begged the speakers to desist.*

No one had imagined that John Morgan possessed the level of cunning
demonstrated in his escape, and no one was going to underestimate him
again. For many, the question of Morgan's sanity was now settled. Even his
attorney, when interviewed by the press, admitted, *"Morgan's wits are all
right."*[16] But it was a matter of great debate as to why Morgan hadn't made
good his escape. Despite Sheriff Shinn's assertions to the contrary, few had
expected Morgan to be found. His actions made no sense to them.

The man who was described as *"more dead than alive"* when first
dragged in, was soon, once Jenny Riley furnished him with clean, dry
clothes, a hot meal, and several cups of strong coffee, in excellent spirits.
He claimed he *"never felt better,"* and insisted repeatedly that he never

actually intended to escape—he only wanted to see *"Becca."*[17] He declared
it would have been a fine thing to be *"chased by bloodhounds."*[18] He
wanted to know if he could outrun them.[15] Once he'd had his fun, he
blithely announced, he would have returned to jail on Monday all on his
own and gone on record as the only condemned man ever to voluntarily
surrender.[19] Morgan seems to have considered the entire enterprise a fine
joke. *"The prisoner now seems livelier and brighter than at any time since his
imprisonment. His recapture does not seem to have affected his spirits in the
least."*[20]

The sheriff and his men were not laughing. Things were going to
be different, an irate Shinn decreed. From now until the hanging John
Morgan was to be confined to his cage. He was not allowed the use of the
larger cell room. New guards were going to be assigned. And the prisoner
was to have no visitors at all—except for his minister.[21] Make that two
ministers. And a good half-dozen reporters.

Morgan even sent word to O.J. Morrison that in case the storekeeper
was interested, he had a brand-new chapter for his book, contingent, of
course, on *"money up front."*[22] Morrison didn't bite. He added a detailed
version of the escape which closely followed the local newspaper's account,
but the canny merchant wasn't going to shell out any more money or
spend any more time in the unnerving presence of this wise-cracking killer.

The clever jail break, thumbing his nose at authority, and literally
flirting with danger, all were the stuff of wild-west legend. Men like
Billy the Kid and Jesse James were famous for these kinds of stunts. The
exploits of such men were romanticized by the press, their cold-blooded
killer natures white-washed and written over with heroic appeal until they
emerged as folk heroes. Center stage for the first time in his life, Morgan
had begun to strut.

Newspaper men came and went the rest of the day, as did Morgan's
spiritual advisors, but the prisoner had one other singular visitor. George
Pfost rode into town to see for himself that Morgan was indeed back
behind bars, and *"to relieve the fears"* of his sister Alice.[23]

By evening most of the hoopla was over. Earlier in nearby
Ravenswood, the weather notwithstanding, a large crowd waited
expectantly for a special train to arrive. They'd heard that the captured
fugitive was on board and they were ready for him.[24] But like so much
of what they'd been told lately this was just another rumor. In fact, most
of Jackson County had yet to hear news of Morgan's capture and several

posses were still out searching. For those who *had* heard the news there was only relief.

Wilson Slaughter was given a check for $50 for services rendered and replaced Charlie Jewell, who decided he was finished tending John Morgan.[25] Sheriff Shinn decided to give Fil Riley a second chance, and despite condemnation from the press and the community, Riley accepted Shinn's offer. In fact, the sheriff put Riley in charge of the death watch, reasoning that having lost Morgan once, he would be so anxious to reclaim his good name he would exercise more caution with their wily prisoner than anyone else.

There was just one final problem to sort out.

A constable and Preacher of Roane county are quarreling over who is entitled to the $1000 reward for the capture of murderer John Morgan.

From the Weekly Register, Point Pleasant, WV, 15 December, 1897

End Notes

[1] *Jackson Herald,* Ripley, WV, 18 December, 1897.

[2] *Reports of Cases Determined by the Supreme Court of Appeals of West Virginia,* Vol. 44, B.J.W. Printers, 1905, 372-384.

[3] *Evening Bulletin,* Maysville, KY, 6 December, 1897.

[4] *Ibid.*

[5] *Cincinnati Enquirer,* Cincinnati, OH, 6 December, 1897.

[6] *Jackson Herald.*

[7] *Pittsburgh Daily Post,* 5 December, 1897.

[8] *Parkersburg Sentinel,* Parkersburg, WV, 6 December, 1897.

[9] *Cincinnati Enquirer.*

[10] *The Morgantown Post,* Morgantown, WV, 6 December, 1897.

[11] *Parkersburg Sentinel.*

[12] *Ibid.*

[13] *Ibid.*

[13] *Cincinnati Enquirer,* 5 December, 1897.

[14] *Parkersburg Sentinel,* 04 December, 1897

[15] *Jackson Herald.*

[16] *Cincinnati Enquirer,* 7 December, 1897.

[17] *Parkersburg Sentinel.*

[18] *Jackson Herald.*

[19] *Ibid.*

[20] *Ibid.*

[21] *Parkersburg Sentinel.*

[22] *Wheeling Register,* Wheeling, WV, 8 December, 1897.

[23] *Parkersburg Sentinel.*

[24] *Parkersburg Sentinel,* 7 December, 1897.

[25] *Cincinnati Enquirer,* 6 December, 1897.

THE DEATH WATCH RESUMES

While the Jackson County Court hadn't gotten around to offering a reward for Morgan's capture, there were still other expenses entailed in the manhunt—additional man hours, for instance, and the rental of the bloodhounds. Telegrams had been sent and train tickets had been purchased. Private citizens, like Floyd Pfost, were reputedly asked to consider contributing towards these expenses. Most of them, Floyd Pfost included, were outraged and refused outright.[1]

There was tremendous public outcry after Morgan's escape, and everyone involved—the guards, the jailer, and Sheriff Shinn—had been publicly humiliated. The press clamored for a thorough investigation and castigated the two guards. One editorial was particularly scathing, describing in detail the liberties given Morgan, the negligence of his guards, their astonishment upon discovering the empty cell:[2]

What energy was then displayed! How they rode and they ran... it is a record of carelessness that cannot be surpassed. They have made themselves famous. But there are those who think this story slightly diaphanous— somewhat thin. Let the searchlight of a thorough rigorous investigation be cast upon the 'watches' who did not watch. Let the innocent be vindicated and let no guilty man escape.

The Ripley jail was not the only lockup in disrepair. Prisoner escapes, often referred to as *"jail deliveries,"* were relatively common in those days. In fact, there had been so many jailbreaks in the state during the months preceding Morgan's bid for freedom that the *Cincinnati Enquirer* was prompted to write a lengthy article on the subject:[3]

The escape of John Morgan, the notorious Jackson County murderer, from the jail of that county, has added another to the long list of mysterious jail deliveries, which have occurred in West Virginia within the past six months, and the fact that three of the parties who have been permitted to escape were under the death sentence, and being guarded by what is known as the "death watch", and nearly all the others either under conviction or awaiting trial for grave offences, is causing much speculation among the state authorities here.

There had been recent jailbreaks in eleven West Virginia counties,

and in nearly every case large rewards had been paid for the capture of
the fugitives.[4] It didn't take a genius to conclude what was behind these
occurrences. There were penalties on the books for allowing prisoners
to escape and lawmakers believed it was time for a crackdown. Those in
charge needed to be held accountable, they said, *"and it is thought that the
strict enforcement of these laws would have a very wholesome effect upon the
county jailers."*[5]

To encourage jailhouse diligence, Governor Atkinson had begun
refusing local petitions for state funding to finance rewards, and in a letter
to the editor of the *Parkersburg Sentinel* he noted that several jailbreaks
were particularly suspicious. While he didn't believe that either the
sheriffs or jailers were guilty of negligence, or worse, he didn't hesitate to
incriminate the guards.[6]

*... there is something like an organized force in our State, which has for
its object the securing of rewards offered for prisoners after they have made their
escape... If a guard discharges his duty properly, it would be utterly impossible
for a prisoner to saw his way out of iron cells, and thus secure his freedom. It is
true, some of our jails are not, by any means, secure. The fault, however, is not
so much with the jails in our state as with those who have charge of them.*

With so much attention being focused on the increasing number
of jailbreaks, West Virginia officials began to tighten security, albeit
belatedly, much to the startled dismay of inmates caught in the midst of
preparation.[7]

*Two weeks ago a revolver and two ropes were found concealed in the
jail; last week an ax and two table knives were found in one of the cells;
Monday two keys fitting the front door locks were found in the possession of the
criminals; A vigilant watch is now being kept...*

The Saturday before Morgan was to hang, the sheriff found one of the
large steel staples on Morgan's cell door nearly severed in half, and there
was evidence that work had begun on the bars of the windows. Shinn made
immediate repairs, did a complete search of Morgan's cell, had him strip-
searched, and issued a new set of clothes.[8] Nothing was found. Both Fil
Riley and Wilson Slaughter earnestly pleaded their ignorance of the matter.
The beleaguered sheriff doubled the deathwatch so that no guard was ever
left alone with Morgan, and began dropping in unannounced at all hours.[9]
Meanwhile, work was progressing out on the gallows site.

The first (and only) public execution in the county had taken place nearly a half century before in Green's Hollow, but that site was too small for the number of people expected to attend Morgan's execution, and a former Jackson County sheriff by the name of James Poling offered a spot on his farm on the outskirts of Ripley.[10] Shinn was quoted as having proudly explained to the special correspondent from the New York *Sun*:[11]

I tell you my boy, when you see that place you'll say it's made for a hanging. It was intended for a hanging from the first... The lot was a natural theater. In the center of it was an Indian mound that rose 25 feet above the surrounding land. On the very top of this land, the sheriff built himself a gallows and invited the populace to gather.

Locals had always supposed the knoll to be an Adena burial mound, although when it was eventually bulldozed in the 1970s to make way for progress nothing was found to support that theory. Today a baseball diamond and a parking lot next to the Jackson County Board of Education mark the site of the last public hanging in West Virginia.

Shinn had been meticulous in his preparations. The week after Morgan was sentenced to hang the sheriff traveled to Fayette County to witness the execution of Albert Voiers, a convicted murderer whose recent escape had disrupted the town's enthusiastic plans for a triple hanging, and there he met Milton Koontz, a master builder of scaffolds.[12] Hangmen like Milton Koontz were the last of a dying breed, their expertise a rare and painstaking art. Shinn so admired Koontz's latest masterpiece—a huge triple scaffold—that he asked him to serve as a consultant for his own gallows.[13] He'd then employed local woodworker and builder, Charles Progler, to put Koontz's design to work.

Major Progler was a dignified old gentleman of 68 years when Sheriff Shinn asked him to construct his first instrument of destruction. The entire project was pre-fabricated in Progler's factory in such a way that it could be easily dismantled and rebuilt on site. Fully assembled, it provided a 10 x 12-foot platform rising 8 foot, 4 inches off the ground.[14] The factory construction had proved to be a popular attraction. By the time the scaffold was completed on the Saturday before the hanging, hundreds of people had already stopped by to admire the work.

On the eve of the execution Progler's men loaded the sections on freight wagons, hauled them out to Poling's farm, and reassembled them on top of the mound.[15] A barbed-wire fence was erected around the scaffold to keep the crowds back; only reporters and other dignitaries were to be admitted within the enclosure. Shinn received several letters from out-of-state lawmen requesting to be allowed on the scaffold, but there wasn't room for everyone and they were left standing inside the barbed-wire perimeter when the time came.

By 1897, the science of hanging had evolved, allowing the practice to become somewhat more efficient and humane.[16] Gallows were generally built eighteen to twenty feet in height from ground to brace. The platform stood several feet off the ground and was reached by a traditional set of thirteen steps. A trap door could be sprung through the release of a rope thrown over a cross brace or by means of a lever mechanism. Sometimes *jerker* weights were used and when released, the prisoner was jerked upwards instead of falling though the trap door. Progler's gallows employed what was known as the *standard drop*. This scientific approach to hanging involved dropping the condemned man four to six feet and was used well into the 1920s. The idea was to create enough weight and momentum to break the neck of an average individual relatively quickly. This was small consolation to those individuals who were not of average height and weight, and botched executions continued to occur with alarming regularity.

Several years after the hanging of John Morgan, the West Virginia Penitentiary in Moundsville began using the *long drop*.[17] The individual's height and weight were taken into careful consideration in a mathematical formula that determined how much slack was needed. The prisoner was then dropped a precisely measured length to ensure a painless death. Most hangmen, however, did not perform these duties often enough to gain any real proficiency, and there remained considerable margin for error. Not enough force and the prisoner died by agonizing degrees in slow strangulation; too much force and he was decapitated, which happened on more than one occasion at Moundsville.

The noose and its exact placement was another essential element for a successful execution.[18] The traditional hangman's rope was thirty feet long and made of corded Manila hemp between three-quarters and an inch in diameter that had been boiled to reduce stretch and coil. The knot had six to thirteen coils—thirteen was customary—and was well lubricated with soap, wax or oil so it would slide easily to its proper placement just under or behind the left ear. Placement of the heavy knot was crucial to a favorable outcome.

A hood, usually black, was placed over the prisoner's head before the noose. This prevented the condemned man from seeing the hangman initiate the drop, and kept him from moving reflexively at the last minute. Just as importantly, it preserved the individual's dignity and offered some protection for the audience. The hands were cuffed behind the back or in front, and leather straps or sometimes cloth strips were used to bind the legs at the knees and ankles to prevent the condemned from trying to straddle the trap when it opened.

The year before Morgan's execution, Fort Smith, Arkansas gained national notoriety for having the highest number of hangings in the nation. Judge Isaac Parker, famously known as "The Hanging Judge", sentenced 160 people and one hangman in particular had carried out the majority of these executions. He'd begun to brag about his prowess and the exacting calculations he performed to ensure a speedy demise. The town officials took exception and believing that this noticeable lack of humility was unbecoming, they voted to replace him. Sadly, their new hangman got off to an exceptionally bad start:[19]

The victim was a slight young fellow, weighing less than 100 pounds, and the drop was not long enough to break his neck....the knot slipped around under his chin, so that the windpipe was left partially open. The unfortunate wretch hanged for over an hour before death relieved him.

Learning a lesson by this, the hangman dropped his next man eight feet. This time the victim was a heavy man, and the long drop not only broke the neck, but jerked the head almost off the shoulders, the blood drenching the corpse and the physicians who were witnesses of the execution.

It is not known whether this learning curve was permitted to continue.

End Notes

[1] *The Jackson Herald,* Ripley, WV, 18 December, 1897.

[2] *Parkersburg Sunday News,* Parkersburg, WV, 12 December, 1897.

[3] *Cincinnati Enquirer,* Cincinnati, OH, 6 December, 1897.

[4] *Pittsburgh Daily Post,* Pittsburgh, PA, 7 November, 1897.

[5] *Ibid.*

[6] *Parkersburg Sentinel,* Parkersburg, WV, 7 December, 1897.

[7] *Charleston Dailey Mail,* Charleston, WV, 24 December, 1897.

[8] *The Evening Bulletin,* Maysville, KY, 13 December, 1897.

[9] *Parkersburg Sentinel.*

[10] *Wheeling Register,* Wheeling, WV, 25 November, 1897.

[11] *New York Sun,* New York, NY, 19, December, 1897.

[12] *Cincinnati Post,* Cincinnati, OH, 24 June 1897.

[13] *Clarksburg Telegram,* Clarksburg, WV, 26 November, 1897.

[14] *Jackson Herald,* Ripley, WV, 18 December, 1897.

[15] *Ibid.*

[16] *Capital Punishment UK; The death penalty in the U.S.* Retrieved from the World Wide Web 08-23-2015, http://www.capitalpunishmentuk.org/hanging.html

[17] Blake, Sherry, *The Haunted History of the West Virginia Penitentiary,* CreateSpace Independent Publishing: 2011.

[18] Brandon, Craig. *The electric chair: an unnatural American history.* Jefferson, NC: McFarland & Co, 1999, p. 35.

[19] *The Daily Inter Ocean,* Chicago, IL, 10 February, 1896.

WHAT ABOUT BEN ANDERSON?

Earlier when the sheriff was on his way to Fayette County to witness the hanging of Albert Voiers, pick up pointers and borrow a rope, he passed through Parkersburg where he was interviewed about the upcoming execution. He remarked that this was not the first time a man had been hanged in Jackson County and recounted the story of Charlie Green. Both Green and his victim, fellow steamboat worker Timothy Fox, were strangers to the area, and the wheels of justice had turned smoothly and objectively without the complications of communal horror and grief. Green was convicted of *"Murder in the direst degree"* and sentenced to hang on July 1, 1850;[1] his hanging set a benchmark of sorts for the young county's legal system.

The hanging of John Morgan would be different. Morgan had grown up in their midst, had bantered and bartered with them, rocked their babies, and plowed their fields. This execution would be intensely personal. The young murderer and his three victims were home-grown, and John Morgan's very presence on the scaffold spoke of the deep betrayal of his community. On an emotional level, if not in the bloodline, they had all been kin.

On December 13th, just three days before he was to hang, John Morgan announced that he wanted to make his last confession and *this* time he would tell all the facts of the matter. *"I had intended dying with this secret locked in my breast, but concluded to ease my mind…"*[2] He admitted that all his previous statements had been false and he was now ready to set the record straight:[3]

I am going to tell it, it is just this way now. I put it off and never intended to tell at all, but I saw that I could not afford to die this way, and I have put it off until the last moment.

This was to be his sixth and final confession and it was a doozy. Not only did he detail the actions of an accomplice, he implicated one of his victims in the planning.[4]

The whole instigation of this thing was that girl Alice Pfost. She has done everything in her power to separate me and my wife; she throwed herself in my way and offered every inducement for me to leave my wife ever since we have been married. The day before we were married, I went back to their place for some of my clothes, and she followed me up stairs and got down on her knees to me and begged me to burn up the license that I had got to marry Becca and get one to marry her. I told her that it was nonsense, that her mother would not permit her to wed me, but she said she would ask her mother, so she did, and came back to me and said that her mother said that the other girls had had their choice and there was no reason why she should not marry her choice. I told her there was no use of fooling; I told her that time and again. I left their house six months before I was married to get rid of her and after I got married then she tormented me to leave Becca and go with her. She proposed to put the family out of the way, and that she would have enough to keep us both, after affairs were settled up, if I would go away with her. I told her I would not do any such a thing; she said then if she would have it done, would I promise to leave with her after the matter was settled up. I made her no promise whatever. I never had any intention of leaving my wife, but she got this other man that is living there now, right there in their house, as was planned upon and agreed to do this thing, and I went there that night.

He was to come in the night, but he did not come till 4 o'clock and when he come it was after they got up. He whistled a low soft whistle. They had at that time been to the smokehouse for milk, and he come right in there and killed that old woman and Tillie Pfost, the daughter with the axe. I never struck but one lick, that was what I struck with the rock.

Alice Pfost was never touched or struck at all. She run out to where there was a pile of boards. I met her and after it was all over, she turned to me and said, "What are you going to do, now?" I said, "I am going home; going to do nothing at all." She says, "You are not going to treat me that way, are you?" I said, "I am going home."

She screamed and started to run towards John Chauncey's, and Anderson came up then and says, "Where has she gone." I said, "I don't know, but I guess she has gone to Chauncey's, she has gone in that direction." He says, '____ ____ her soul to ____of her. I will kill her." And he started after her as fast as he could go. How far he followed I do not know as I went the other direction toward home. And that is the way it was. It has proved out on me, yet I did not do the killing. The courtship between myself and Alice Pfost existed ever since three weeks after going there to live until six months before I was married.

…And to think that she was wicked enough to propose to destroy her own mother, brother, and sister. She said if I would just make her a promise,

that in the future we would go away together, that she would give me what money there was about, which was $200 or $300, and after she got matters straightened up and her real estate turned into money, she would have enough to keep both of us.

How things have proved out on me you all know. You people may not believe this is true, but it is, and I know I have to die in a short time. When I left there, the girl was going to Chancey's; this man Ben Anderson was in the house. What he done I don't know; if there is anything missing, he got it. I did not. I never taken anything from them. My mind is more at ease. I intended to die with the secret in my breast. Alice Pfost knew that the deed was to be done at the time that it was, when I went there that evening, she says, "Does it have to be done tonight?" I told her that was the plan, and she said, "All right, the sooner, the better." It was to have been done that night in the night. Ben Anderson did not come until 4 o'clock in the morning. Anderson has approached me, I should say, fifty times about it; she got him to do that thing, she said she wanted me to promise to go with her some time in the future, but I did not promise, and after it was done I told her I was going to do nothing and away she went to Chauncey's and gave the alarm and this is the way it has proved out on me, while I did not do it.

This wasn't the first time Ben Anderson's name had come up. Morgan had blamed him before, though not in so well organized a fashion. At the time of his sentencing Morgan denied committing the crimes, but intimated there was another man likely to have done so:[5]

I am not the man that did the crime; I know this about it that death will be my portion, I suppose, but I hain't the man that done the murder; just give me a little time, and I will tell you all about it.

He then added, *"a man living there on their place got into a little dispute about the crop"* and went to say, *"He come to me four times to get me to help destroy this family…"*

At the time of the sentencing, Morgan's rambling and incoherent description of events seemed little more than a desperate attempt to escape the consequences of his own actions by shifting the blame to someone else. Despite this, Owen Shinn had not completely discounted his assertions. From the beginning, he seems to have had reservations about whether Morgan had acted alone, and he had been conducting further investigations.[6]

Shinn is reported to have made some startling disclosures to the press regarding his theories about the motive during his Parkersburg stopover while in route to Fayetteville. According to the *Pittsburgh Post-Gazette,* the sheriff believed that Morgan committed the murders *"solely for love of Miss Alice Pfost,"* and that *"Morgan's passion was returned."*[7] This interview was published under the titillating headline, *"Love and Not Robbery the Alleged Motive."* Shinn was quoted as saying the family objected to their relationship because Morgan was a married man, and so the two made contingency plans.

Later, the sheriff reported that Ben Anderson had spent the night before the murders away from his home, and was giving conflicting information regarding his whereabouts that evening.[8]

Just before Morgan made his last confession, Shinn questioned him again:[9]

> *"How was Jimmy Green killed?"* he asked.
> *"I struck him first and then Ben Anderson hit him with a mattock."*
> *"Did you kill Alice's sister?"*
> *"Yes I did that."*
> *"Who killed old Mrs. Chloe Green?"*
> *"Ben Anderson hit her on the head with an ax."*

These earlier responses do not match the information Morgan gave in his final confession. He claimed responsibility for Tillie's murder, according to the *Cincinnati Enquirer,* although he later said Anderson killed her. The *Enquirer* also emphasized that during this interview Morgan told Shinn that Alice's wounding had been an accident. Yet when he made his last confession this aspect is left open to speculation, since Morgan claimed Alice had been unharmed when he last saw her running toward John Chancey's. He said Ben Anderson threatened to kill her and went running after her, leaving us to conclude that it might have been Anderson who struck Alice. Finally we have Chancey's testimony about the tracks he found in the cornfield. *Someone* had been following Alice.

Three days before he was to hang Morgan unequivocally pointed the finger at Ben Anderson, and his earlier disjointed comments began to make more sense. Court reporter Anna McVay transcribed the final confession, and Owen Shinn and Rebekah Morgan both witnessed it. It was printed in its entirety in several major newspapers and the hometown *Jackson Herald.* Morrison was already on his way to the Cincinnati publishers with his manuscript and so did not include it, although souvenir copies were made available at the hanging for the price of 25 cents apiece and reportedly the proceeds were given to Rebekah and Albert.[10]

When news of this latest confession hit the streets, the reaction was shock and disbelief. How had things spiraled into this bizarre standoff between John Morgan—reputed liar, thief, and murderer—and Alice Pfost, the tragic heroine who ran for help despite her terrible wound? There was no doubt who most people wanted to believe. Nonetheless, the papers printed every word and reporters pounced on this latest opportunity, chasing down any lead they could find on Ben Anderson. Few people were willing to entertain the notion that a member of the Pfost family could have been involved, but many began to consider the possibility that Anderson was somehow complicit in the crimes.

Ben was known to work for the Pfost-Greenes, and he and his family lived on or very near their property. In fact, on the Saturday following the murders, Chloe's son George Pfost asked Anderson to move into the family's deserted farmhouse to take care of the property and the livestock.[11] Thirty-three-year-old Anderson, his wife Ann and their three young children had been living there ever since.

Ben Anderson moved into the Green house, in which John Morgan committed the triple murder, on Saturday, the same day on which Morgan was sentenced. The house had not even been cleaned, and blood was bespattered over everything. He worked for three days, and has never been able to do a day's work since he cleaned the blood off the floor. He was a strong and robust man and was never known to be seriously ill before.[12]

Mary Chancey also remembered the Andersons moving into the property following the murders:[13] *They stayed there and took care of the stock, but they were too afraid to live in the main part of the house. So they lived in the great big kitchen.*

Speculation regarding Ben Anderson's possible collusion in the crimes, at least according to newspaper accounts, went something like this. Ben Anderson was known to have quarreled with the family over a field that he had sown with wheat and wasn't being allowed to use. When he was asked to move into the family farm after the murders and was then nominally in position to oversee the use of the property, it was argued that this had been his intent all along.[14] In addition, the *Parkersburg Sentinel* alluded to rumors that Anderson had been heard making cryptic comments two weeks prior that a mysterious murder would be occurring in the county before very long.[15]

When questioned, Anderson told authorities that he had spent the night before the murders at a neighbor's home. The neighbor denied ever seeing him on his property.[16] This last mystery may have been addressed during an interview that took place in the 1990s. It seems as if there may have been at least one individual for whom Morgan's accusations came as no surprise. Ben Raines, Morgan's first cousin, supposedly concluded that Anderson might have been involved as soon as he heard the news of the murders. Nearly a century later, his son would tell a reporter that his father had gone to visit Morgan in jail shortly after he was captured:[17]

He said Morgan was irrational, but told him someone was supposed to help him with the killings but backed out and never answered his whistle signal. Morgan told him it would do no good to implicate anyone else and that he would pay the price for the murders alone.

If this story is true, Morgan apparently admitted to his cousin that he committed the murders, and made yet another reference to the supposed *"signal"*—the whistling on the back porch. Alice, during her first deposition with David Brown, clearly remembered hearing Morgan whistling, and afterwards in her panicked state she assumed he'd been signaling someone: *"I was afraid that someone else might come, for the reason that Morgan went out on the porch before that and whistled."*[18]

Why did Ben Raines assume Ben Anderson was involved? According to his son, he and Anderson had been with John Morgan at the Pfost-Greene farm the evening before the murders. After which, Raines recalled Morgan and Anderson falling behind to talk, then Morgan made the decision to return to the Pfost-Greene farm alone. Raines told his son that Anderson left him shortly afterwards saying that he had decided to stay the night in a nearby barn belonging to one of the Pfost neighbors. Ben Raines allegedly told his family that he believed he might have prevented the killings if only he had stayed with Morgan or talked him out of returning to the farm that night.

In Morgan's own account of the night he escaped from jail, he went by the Pfost-Greene farm in the early hours of the morning and broke into the winter store of apples. He was undoubtedly aware that Anderson was living there by then. He arrived at a time when he might have expected to see the hired man out feeding the livestock, and he appears to have lingered for a considerable amount of time. Did he confront Anderson that morning? If so, what did the two men talk about?

Sheriff Shinn, for one, is firmly impressed with the idea that Anderson, at least had a guilty knowledge of what was about to happen, and perhaps as Morgan says, took a hand in the bloody work.[19]

On the day following Morgan's latest formal confession, a warrant was issued for Anderson's arrest. This came as no surprise to Anderson who had heard rumors to that effect. The prosecutor sent word that he should come into town as part of an immediate investigation, but George Pfost advised him to stay at home.[20]

When Shinn arrived at the property he was unable to serve the warrant. He found Ben Anderson in bed and so agitated, according to several sources, that he was literally speechless.[21,22] The sheriff left a constable behind to monitor the situation and sent a physician out to ensure the man was not malingering. The physician evaluated the situation and reported that Anderson was severely ill with some form of fever and was in no condition to be moved. The news accounts offered various diagnoses claiming that Anderson was suffering from a bout of either typhoid or malaria, or as one reporter referred to it, "a *fit of nervous prostration.*"[23,24,25]

Anderson's condition continued to deteriorate, "*He has broken down both physically and mentally and is a wreck of his former self,*"[26] and within a few days it was announced that he was on his deathbed.[27]

Shinn had informed both David Brown and James Seaman about the latest implications and Brown immediately began campaigning for a stay of execution.[28] If he hoped for support in postponing matters until Anderson could be brought to trial and Morgan could testify against him, he was to be disappointed. Seaman refused to go along with this suggestion, and although Shinn may have felt the idea had merit, he also had a healthy regard for mob mentality. Morgan's execution was only three days away and already the town was starting to fill with outsiders. The consequences of trying to halt the proceedings, even if only temporarily, did not bear thinking about.

Brown was left to act on his own. He fired off a telegram to Governor Atkinson requesting a brief respite since evidence was emerging which implicated others.[29] Re-energized by the opportunity to see justice done, Brown would carry this new offensive well into the New Year, only this time it would be in his new role as the prosecuting attorney assigned to the case, and without the benefit of testimony from the primary accuser. As for the general populace, there was plenty of confusion and dismay to go around.

STAY For Morgan Favored by Many
His Confession Implicating Anderson Changes Public Opinion

Everybody is talking about Morgan, his crime, and his fixed execution. Many people say that if what he says is true he should be respited and given a chance to give his testimony as to what part he claims Ben Anderson took in the murder.

Excerpt from Cincinnati Post, 15 December, 1897.

All along Morgan had been telling everyone he wouldn't hang. He had thought he had a good chance of escaping, but he'd been foiled twice. His lawyer's efforts had failed as well. Now that he was almost out of time, he realized that he might not avoid the noose after all.

Morgan informed the sheriff today that he would never hang, as he had been praying to God, and that God had answered his prayers, and when the Sheriff comes after him he will find him dead in his cell. Last evening, when Sheriff Shinn handed Morgan the picture of Morgan's wife and baby he cried like a child. He continued crying and sobbing for two hours, occasionally calling his wife's and baby's names. [30]

John Morgan in his final hours seems a pathetic creature. Whether the allegations against Ben Anderson and Alice contained any kernel of truth, were a last-ditch effort to gain a respite, or were born of Morgan's fevered imagination will never be known. If nothing else, this latest public disclosure was meant to destroy lives in the only way left to him.

Neither Ben Anderson nor Alice Pfost are here to defend themselves, and whatever secrets they may have known were carried to the grave long ago. All that remains are a few bare facts and some tantalizing clues in faded newsprint. And the words of a man whose words could not be trusted.

End Notes

[1] Author's Note: Information about Charles Green can be found in Hardesty's *History of Jackson County* and there is a scant paragraph in U.S. Marshal Dan Cunningham's memoirs, but it is John House, that ubiquitous writer of Jackson County histories, that provides details of Green's childhood and early criminal activities quoted here, and House claims this information was original to Green's own autobiographical publication. The *Wheeling Register* Nov 17, 1897 also provided a full account of the *"First Execution"* as reprinted from the Ravenswood News.

[2] *Pittsburgh Post-Gazette*, Pittsburgh, PA, 17 December, 1897.

[3] *Wheeling Register,* Wheeling, WV, 13 December, 1897.

[4] *Jackson Herald,* Ripley, WV, 18 December, 1897.

[5] Morrison, O. J., *The Slaughter of the Pfost-Greene Family of Jackson County, W.Va. A History of the Tragedy,* 1897.

[6] *Wheeling Register,* Wheeling, WV, 22 December, 1897.

[7] *Pittsburgh Post-Gazette,* Pittsburgh, PA, 12 November, 1897.

[8] *Cincinnati Enquirer,* Cincinnati, OH, 15 December, 1897.

[9] *Ibid.*

[10] *Jackson Herald,* Ripley, WV, 18 December, 1897.

[11] *Cincinnati Enquirer,* Cincinnati, OH, 16 December, 1897.

[12] *Ibid.*

[13] "Last Public Hanging," *Goldenseal Magazine,* Spring 1990.

[14] *Parkersburg Sentinel,* Parkersburg, WV, 16, December, 1897.

[15] *Ibid.*

[16] *Ibid.*

[17] *Ripley Star News,* "Could One Man Have Stopped John Morgan?," by Greg Matics, (newspaper clipping, undated except for the year 1993).

[18] Morrison.

[19] *Parkersburg Sentinel,* 17 December, 1897.

[20] *Wheeling Register,* Wheeling, WV, 22 December, 1897.

[21] *Pittsburgh Daily Post,* Pittsburgh, PA, 15 December, 1897.

[22] *The Evening Edition.*

[23] *Ibid.*

[24] *Parkersburg Sentinel.*

[25] *Evening Bulletin,* Maysville, KY, 18 December, 1897.

[26] *Wheeling Register.*

[27] *Cincinnati Enquirer.*

[28] *Ibid.*

[29] *Wheeling Register,* Wheeling, WV, 16 December, 1897. [30] *Parkersburg Sentinel,* Parkersburg, WV, 13 December, 1897.

174

TALES OF THE HANGMAN

People began arriving in Ripley at the beginning of the week, many of them having journeyed over a hundred miles. The *Cincinnati Enquirer,* whose own reporter reserved a room early on, said the town was so packed, "*Only those who had engaged rooms weeks in advance could go near enough to a hotel to hail a landlord.*"₁ The largest hotel in town, the McGuire House, received a letter from Fayetteville, which had already seen its fair share of hangings for the year, requesting accommodations for 40 people.₂ It had been mailed the day after Morgan was sentenced. Enterprising townspeople were renting out spare rooms, barns, hay mows and back yards. Those arriving without reservations were camped in the public square and in the fields outside of town, and several asked for permission to bed down in Major Progler's old hotel that was now the high school.₃

Folks in outlying areas sat on their front porches and watched hour after hour as the endless procession passed by on the muddy roads. Wagons lumbered past, some covered in canvas to improve camping conditions, and loaded with women and children gaily waving and smiling. Men rode on horseback or walked.

With the holiday fast approaching—there were just ten shopping days left before Christmas—the gathering crowds gave Ripley a welcome boost to its economy. Merchants like O. J. Morrison laid in extra supplies for the occasion and an ad for A. M. Carson's read:₄

A GREAT XMAS SHOWING!
On account of the Great Crowd and Jam Expected on the 16ᵗʰ and the great demand for other lines, we will not show the MORE BREAKBLE ARTICLES of Xmas goods until Friday December 17ᵗʰ. Yes we will have enough to select from.

More Wonderful Than Ever are the offerings of this store for the great crowds that fill the aisles in search of Holiday collectibles for both friends and relatives.

The Mill Creek and Ripley Railroad was also doing a bang-up business. Trains arrived daily, their lone passenger car loaded to capacity. When the little train arrived at 7 o'clock on the eve of the hanging, it carried the biggest load of passengers in its history—well over 100.₅ *"They were packed in box cars, on coal cars, on the engine, and the single passenger car was jammed to the point of suffocation."*[6]

The area's largest railroad, the Ohio River line was asked to run special *"excursion"* trains and reduce their rates, but railway officials refused to be a party to these proceedings and their response was hugely applauded in some quarters:[7]

The regular trains will be run and regular fare charged, as the management are adverse to catering to the morbid curiosity of people who desire to see a man expiate his crimes on a scaffold.

Anyone traveling by train to see John Morgan hang would be paying full fare, and over-crowding assured that the railway made substantial profit. The riverboat lines followed suit.

There will be a hilarious time in the old town of Ripley today, at the execution of Morgan. For a week or more the trains and boats have been freighted with what is commonly called "Undertakers Delight."

Excerpt from Point Pleasant Weekly Register, 17 December, 1897.

Several editors soundly denounced the gathering spectators and took the opportunity to speak out against public hangings and the death penalty. *"This all goes to prove that public executions should not be permitted in this State. The hanging of this one man will only result in more crime, in the end."*[8] While thousands were turning out for what would prove to be the last public hanging in the state, there were many who found the practice archaic and barbaric. Mrs. B. M. Pollack, a resident of Morgantown, was so disturbed by the headlines she was moved to write the following letter to the editor of her hometown paper:[9]

In looking over the columns of a daily paper recently I saw this astonishing headline: "Excursion to a Hanging." I held the paper a moment and pondered. Is this the nineteenth century, and are we a civilized people?

The word was out, however, that West Virginia would soon be joining the ranks of those states that had abolished public executions. They'd been banned in Ohio for many years now, and Ohioans, nostalgic for the good old days and this lost form of entertainment, were streaming across the river into Jackson County.

In most states, executions had been the responsibility of the county sheriff up until the 1880s, and they had taken place in public as a kind

of morality play. A public hanging involved a good deal of ceremony
and ritual. First there was the procession to the hanging grounds, during
which the condemned man might ride on his coffin. On the way, ministers
led the prisoner and the accompanying multitudes in prayers and hymn
singing, and once on the scaffold they exhorted the spectators to take note
of the wages of sin, and prayed long and hard for the soul of the doomed
man and anyone in the audience traveling the same path.

The victim was encouraged to make a speech before the trap was sprung
in hopes that he would make one final heart-wrenching confession. And
once death was pronounced, the crowd was given an opportunity for a
look-see before the body was handed over to the family or local undertaker
for burial, usually in an unmarked grave in unconsecrated ground.

Such spectacles attracted huge turnouts. One of the largest on record
occurred in 1827, when an estimated 30,000 to 40,000 attendees gathered
to witness the hanging of murderer Jesse Strang in Albany, New York.[10]
Because the carnival-like atmosphere associated with hangings provided an
economic boost to small towns, festivities might be prolonged for several
days. Merchants set up booths to sell food and drink, and street vendors
hawked all manner of souvenirs, including relics from the crime scene,
photographs, murder pamphlets, and copies of confessions. Large amounts
of whiskey were consumed, even in so-called *dry* towns.

By the turn of the century public hangings were becoming less
common. An anti-gallows movement emerged as ministers and
philanthropists allied with newspaper editors, and the movement gained
nationwide momentum in tandem with women's rights and temperance.[11]
Several states had moved executions away from the public eye. Some,
like Michigan, had dismissed the death penalty altogether in favor of life
imprisonment.

But even when executions were conducted behind the walls of a
prison, small numbers of the public might be permitted to attend, and
such opportunities were highly sought after. Tickets were often sold as a
means of defraying court costs.

Such was the case when "Terrible Pete" Wassel was scheduled to hang
in Pennsylvania a few months before John Morgan. Sheriff Martin received
over 500 letters requesting tickets, some of them rather surprising:[12]

Dear Mr. Martin:
I am a student of human nature…and for that reason desire very much
to secure a pass for the execution of "Terrible Pete" Wassel…Of course I would

not like to stand in the jail yard to be stared at by the men and possibly hear by sex condemned, but I thought it possible for you to provide a window through which I could see without being seen. If you can do this I will bring three other ladies. Kindly let me hear from you at once.

> *Dear Sheriff:*
> *Do you give rain checks to hangings like they do at ball games. When the game does not take place they give tickets to the next one. I had a ticket to Eckert's execution and it failed to materialize. You owe me a ticket to this one.*

Among them he found one especially deserving of a pass. It was from a widow who had reached her wits end trying to reform her wayward son. She thought perhaps seeing a man hanged for his crimes might prove more transformational that all her efforts thus far.

The press had always reported executions, but during the latter part of the 19th century when rival publishers used attention-grabbing headlines to vie for readership, public hangings proved a particularly rich vein. Everyone, even thousands of miles or a world away, could have a ringside seat at a hanging via the correspondent's faithful renditions.

Americans across the nation, many of whom would never have considered attending a hanging, found themselves confronted with these horrific accounts on a regular basis within the sacred confines of their own homes. While some derived immense satisfaction from this evidence of justice served, the more reform-minded became determined to put a stop to such brutality.

In a parallel development, a celebrity inventor whose fame and fortune allowed him to pursue his own private and audacious agenda was championing an alternative to the gallows. Thanks to this man, a New York ax-murderer by the name of William Kemmler drew national attention in 1890 as the first person to be put to death by means of the electric chair.[13] Kemmler, a vegetable peddler, picked up a hatchet during a bitter argument with his common-law wife and killed her, after which he went straight to his neighbor and confessed. To say that Kemmler died hard is an understatement—one of the attending physicians declared, *"there'll never be another execution by this means."*[14] It was, as witnesses described it, *"worse than hanging."*[15]

William Kemmler owed this inaugural debut to none other than Thomas Edison. The electric chair was part of Edison's opening salvo in a clash with industrial giant George Westinghouse which came to be known as the *War of the Currents*. It essentially boiled down to which type of electrical current—DC or AC—was safest and most efficient. Edison was a pioneer in electricity, specifically direct current electricity known as *DC*. Unfortunately, direct current, which flows in only one direction, was proving to be impractical for use over great distances since it required proximity to large central power stations. By contrast, Westinghouse's *AC*, or alternating current, could reverse direction in a circuit at regular intervals and be transported over thousands of miles, being stepped up for sending and stepped down for actual usage.

Edison had a lot riding on his *DC* current, as impractical as it was, and was determined to put Westinghouse out of business. As part of a smear campaign he arranged for public demonstrations, electrocuting dogs, old horses, even Topsy the elephant, all designed to showcase the dangers of Westinghouse current. In 1889, following the abolishment of hanging in the State of New York, he went a step further, advocating death by electricity using Westinghouse's dynamos.[16] Legislation was passed to this end.

George Westinghouse wanted no part of capital punishment. He fought tooth and nail in the courts to forbid the use of his equipment, claiming that death by electricity was *"cruel and unusual punishment."*[17] And when this failed he turned his attention to funding appeals for prisoners like William Kemmler who had been sentenced to die in the new electric chair. Westinghouse lost this battle as well.

In the end, Kemmler had to be shocked twice in quick succession because he was not killed outright. Blood and smoke appeared, Kemmler groaned like a dying beast throughout, panicked officials screamed at one another to try another round, and one of the reporters fainted dead away.[17] Afterwards, when the press cornered Westinghouse to get his response, he said:[18] *"It has been a brutal affair. They would have done better using an axe."* Edison stoutly maintained that the man died painlessly within seconds, and spread the word that Kemmler had been *"Westinghoused."*[19]

The press had a field day. But Edison's efforts to encourage the use of the term Westinghousing, to the detriment of his rival, failed to excite the press. Instead the newspapers invented their own neologism. The word *"electrocute"* did not exist at the time of Kemmler's demise, yet almost overnight it began to appear in one newspaper after the other. Ultimately several reporters took credit for coining the name for this horrific new form of capital punishment.

Despite the discouraging setback and all the bad publicity, George Westinghouse went on to win the bid for illuminating Chicago's

1893 World's Fair. He managed to undercut Edison's bid by half since alternating current did not require nearly the amount of copper wiring, and on May 1st of that year President Grover Cleveland, himself a former hangman, pulled the switch that illuminated a hundred thousand incandescent light bulbs.

The rest is history.

End Notes

[1] *Cincinnati Enquirer,* Cincinnati, OH, 17 December, 1897.

[2] *Wheeling Register,* Wheeling, WV, 8 November, 1897

[3] *The Breckenridge News,* Cloverport, KY, 15 December,1897.

[4] *The Jackson Herald,* Ripley, WV, 18 December, 1897.

[5] *Cincinnati Enquirer,* Cincinnati, OH, 17 December, 1897.

[6] *New York Sun,* New York, NY, 19 December, 1897.

[7] *Wheeling Register,* Wheeling⁴, WV, 12 December, 1897.

[8] *Clarksburg Telegram,* Clarksburg, WV, 15 December, 1897.

[9] *Morgantown Post,* Morgantown, WV, 9 December, 1897.

[10] Brandon, Craig. *The electric chair: an unnatural American history.* Jefferson, NC: McFarland & Co, 1999, p. 26.

[11] Flanders, Judith, *How the Victorians Invented Murder: How the Victorians Revelled in Death and Detection and Created Modern Crime,* St. Martin's Griffin, 2014.

[12] *Sunday Leader,* Wilkes-Barre, PA, 1897.

[13] Brandon, p. 62.

[14] *Evening World,* New York, NY, 6 August, 1890.

[15] *Ibid.*

[16] McNichol, Tom. *AC/DC: the savage tale of the first standards war,* San Francisco, CA: John Wiley and Sons, 2006 p. 123.

[17] *Ibid.*

[18] McNichol, p. 125.

[19] *Ibid.*

A LADY PHOTOGRAPHER

A professional photographer was hired to take Morgan's photograph a few days before his execution. This was undoubtedly Miss Susan King, referred to in contemporary accounts as "the only photographer in Ripley" or "the Ripley photographer". [1,2] Susan had been in business since the late 1880s and it is her slender "Gibson Girl" figure that is so prominent in the foreground of the photograph taken to mark the occasion of the grand opening of the railroad line in Ripley in 1888. It is a remarkable image. There she stands, front and center in the middle of the track,

Photograph of Susan King courtesy of Vicky King.

very much the focal point as the eye is drawn first to her and her camera, then to the crowd facing her and finally to the flag-festooned locomotive in the background. In an age when women were cautioned to remain understated and to refrain from drawing attention to themselves, Susan King commanded it.

She owned a well-established studio in town, but the prisoner was not taken there. No effort was made to arrange the elaborately painted backgrounds, furnishings, and props so typical of the period. Instead, Morgan was photographed in the jail with simple duck canvas as a backdrop. He dressed in his new suit and tie and posed solemnly for what may have been both the first and last portrait of is life. Though taken as a full body photograph, O. J. Morrison chose to crop Morgan's head and shoulders for his publication. Copies of this portrait, along with the murder pamphlet and Morgan's numerous confessions, were sold as souvenirs. A photograph of Rebekah and Albert was taken at roughly the same time, and John was given a copy to keep in his cell.

What was he thinking as he held his breath and his pose for the camera? He gazes somewhere into the middle distance without expression, and it is tempting to view this as the carefully cultivated study of *"careless indifference"* so remarked upon by the press. Most likely it was simply the traditional pose adopted to keep the image from blurring. When he was shown his portrait, Morgan studied it closely and said, *"I am a nice looking man, and had I only done right I would have my liberty today".*₃

Susan's accomplishments should not be taken lightly. Like the widow McVay, who braved the male bastion of court reporting to make her living, the unmarried Susan King seems daring and out-of-the-ordinary. Her father, John King,

Cropped portrait of John Morgan sold as souvenirs at his execution

argued against her decision to photograph the execution, but Susan was determined, and ultimately he agreed to help her under two conditions: she would take her photos from the periphery of the crowd to avoid its crushing confines; and she would take no photos once the trap had sprung.

Anna McVay attracted nearly as much attention as the condemned man when she was asked to be present on the scaffold to record Morgan's last words. Her appearance *"produced quite a little flurry of comment"*, according to the *Parkersburg Sentinel,* and drew mixed reviews from the press.₄ At least one third of the crowd was female, and several of the women crowded around the scaffold

One of King's cartes d'visite, popular Victorian photographs mounted on cardboard and collected by family and friends. It is thought that Susan herself is included in this one, third from the left. Photo courtesy of Dallas Skeen.

reportedly fainted when the trap was sprung. Yet the *New York Sun* wrote of Anna McVay, who was standing just a few feet from Morgan when the fatal moment came, *"She did not flinch."*

All eyes were on that scaffold on the day Morgan was hanged. Not a single newsman, not even the Sun correspondent who was unfailingly observant in all else, remarked upon the lady photographer moving carefully along the fringes of the crowd. Surprisingly, Rebekah Morgan chose to keep one of Susan's original 8 x 10s showing her husband standing at the edge of the scaffold with his head bowed in prayer. It has been passed down to their great grandson.

End Notes

[1] King, W.M. *History of the first Settlers of Cow Run*, January 30, 1953) West Virginia Archives Call number 975.431 K54.

[2] Undated contemporary newspaper clipping from the archives of the Jackson County Historical Society.

[3] *Cincinnati Post*, Cincinnati, OH 17 December, 1897

[4] *Parkersburg Sentinel*, Parkersburg, WV, 17 December, 1897.

A HOT TIME IN THE OLD TOWN

John Morgan began his last full day on earth in much the same way as the days before. By now he'd begun to have radical mood swings. He continued his avowals that he wouldn't hang, but vacillated between whether to pin his hopes on Governor Atkinson, who was once again being petitioned by his attorney, or the angel of death. He had asked the Almighty to deliver him safely to heaven straight from his cell so he could skip the unsavory bits, and it was feared he would do away with himself if given the opportunity. *"He insists that when Sheriff Shinn comes after him the day of the execution, he will find him dead in his cell."*[1]

His jailbreak escapade of two weeks before had left him in ebullient spirits initially, and the telling and retelling of those adventures to anyone who would sit still long enough had kept him aloft for days. But when his second attempt failed he had finally wound down:[2]

Morgan appears to be much concerned about his terrible predicament and his indifferent manner has disappeared. He sits for hours and says nothing to his guards, his former days of confinement being days of conversation and funny story telling on his part.

The morning before the execution Rebekah brought Albert to see his father. It was the last time they saw him alive. As soon as he saw his family Morgan broke down and wept bitterly, and several reporters commented upon the *"very touching scene when they met."*[3] They were not afforded any privacy and Morgan was not allowed outside of his cage to embrace his wife, though he pleaded to do so. Owen Shinn was present during this last meeting and allowed John to hold Albert for a few minutes inside the cage. Morgan begged Rebekah to raise him *"right"* and do her best to *"keep him out of bad company."*[4]

Finally, he spoke to her about his burial. He had a nice place picked out, he said, on her father's property near some large oak trees. He claimed to have visited the spot when he stopped off to see her on the night of his escape.[5,6] No plans had been finalized for the disposition of John's body following the hanging, and though many had assumed Rebekah Morgan would be stepping forward to receive it, this was the first time she agreed to do so. John's sisters had both refused.[7]

Just in case, Shinn had made contingency plans. Several individuals offered the use of their property and Shinn had already paid former sheriff James Poling, who owned the gallows site, to allow Morgan to be buried nearby.[8] The rest of the funeral expenses would be paid for by the county. The undertaker, Isaiah Vail, was standing by with the coffin, a plain pauper's box.[9]

The sheriff continued to tick through his mental checklist. The gallows stood ready, and Major Progler and his team assured him the rope was securely in place and the trap had been fully tested; everything was working perfectly. Shinn had arranged for guards to stay on site around the clock to make sure no one tried to tamper with or destroy the mechanism.[10] He had chosen two physicians, Dennis Casto from Ripley, and Benjamin Early Harrison from Cottageville, to be on hand to pronounce the time of death.[11] Harrison was an uncle to Matilda and Alice Pfost. A death panel composed of twelve men had also been appointed to attest to the prisoner's time of death.[12]

The Reverends Curtis Robinson and J. J. White had taken turns offering comfort and religious instruction to Morgan during his incarceration. Morgan professed salvation, but while he appeared as contrite and beatific as a choirboy in the presence of his ministers, the journalists noted that he quickly reverted to his profane habits once they'd left and was soon *"joking and swearing like a trooper."*[13] White, along with the Reverend Thomas Rymer from the Methodist Episcopal Church in Fairplain, had agreed to accompany Morgan onto the scaffold.[14]

Several people had approached Shinn with special requests to be on the gallows, but he had turned them all down. He needed his deputies— he'd asked his brother Reuben for moral support, and a couple of the others—as well as the two ministers. And he wanted court stenographer Anna McVay to be there as well. He realized that was going to shock some people, but since Morgan had requested ten minutes to speak to the crowd Shinn wanted to be prepared.

Rebekah remained with her husband for some time. Little Albert, an *"interesting,"* *"bright child of ten months,"* had charmed everyone at the jail and his mother proudly informed them he had just said his first word—*"Papa"*—and had been saying it over and over again.[15] John tried repeatedly to get Albert to say it for him, but Albert, suddenly shy, refused to perform on cue. As Rebekah rose to leave, Morgan again insisted she was not to worry about him; he would not hang the next day. God, he assured her, had promised to take him in his sleep.[16] It was a painful moment for everyone:[17]

The final leave taking of the husband and wife was most pathetic and was not witnessed by a single dry eye... the door of the cage was left slightly opened, as quick as thought he stepped from his cage, grasped the wife and boy in loving lingering embrace—as quietly he stepped back and the door swung to...

Shinn spoke with Rebekah on her way out and gave her what remained of O. J. Morrison's payment, which amounted to $23.60, along with John's pocketknife. He also promised that he would escort John's body to the Hall property on Friday morning and bring along his old set of clothes.[18]

Morgan's continuing assertions that he wouldn't hang were troubling. Shinn was practically living at the jail now and the deathwatch was on full alert. Tensions were running high as more people arrived in town and every hour brought new rumors. Morgan's latest and nearly successful escape attempt had left Shinn on edge and the citizenry were righteously indignant. The sheriff still didn't know how Morgan had managed the second attempt, though he had his suspicions. Then too, there was the matter of Brown's last telegram to the Governor to worry about.

He knew David Brown had wired the Governor to plead for a stay of execution, and respites had been granted often enough in similar cases. Word was on the street that the hanging might be called off, and some of the crowd was starting to make contingency plans. Shinn couldn't tolerate that. He made up his mind to hang Morgan at the earliest possible moment. Postponement might be a moot point anyway. If the rumors about Ben Anderson were true, the man was in critical condition and unlikely to recover. There might be nothing more to settle on that score. But just in case he sent Constable Dunlap back out with the warrant to check on things first-hand.[19]

Shinn didn't have long to worry over Governor Atkinson's response at least. Brown received his answer that very morning. The Governor refused to intervene; he had no faith in anything John Morgan had to say.[20]

The next few hours progressed calmly enough. Reporters came and went, though a few seemed to have taken up permanent residence inside the jail, and who could blame them? It was utter chaos in the streets and by contrast the cellblock was almost peaceful.

A local barber was allowed in as well, and Morgan's hands and feet were strapped so he could be shaved safely with the straight razor and have his hair trimmed.[21] Morgan joked that he wanted to be remembered looking his best. Then he asked for a tub of hot water so he could leave the world a clean man.

Constable Dunlap rode back into town that afternoon and informed Shinn that Ben Anderson didn't strike him as a very sick man. Still, he wasn't comfortable making an arrest until the doctor verified that it was safe to move him. Dunlap said he felt sorry for the family and told Shinn that Anderson's wife and children were all hovering around the bed crying while Anderson did his best to reassure them. *"Don't cry. Papa is not guilty, and will have no trouble."*[22]

As the afternoon began to wane, Morgan grew more restless. He'd had his bath and a light meal and now he didn't know what to do. By the time the sun went down Bill Taylor from the *Cincinnati Enquirer* noted that, *"he had utterly collapsed."*[23]

For an hour or so he attempted to write, but soon gave that up. He seemed to realize his rapidly approaching doom and broke down and cried in a heartbroken manner. When spoken to he asked to be left to himself. About dark his spiritual advisers spent an hour with him, but their efforts to compose him were unavailing. He prayed and wept as they talked to him. He was unable to stand on his feet.

Owen Shinn was alarmed by the prospect that Morgan might not be able to climb the scaffold or stand unassisted. He made plans to have him carried up the steps if necessary, and then had a couple of crude crutches fashioned, just in case.[24]

Finally, having spent himself during his emotional storm, John Morgan fell into an exhausted sleep and Shinn thought it safe to leave the building. Outside it was near pandemonium—as though a dozen carnivals had all come to town at once. The boardwalks were lined with street vendors and everywhere he looked hucksters worked the crowds, selling everything from home remedies to peanuts and cheap trinkets. The newsboys were busy as well, selling Morrison's *Slaughter of the Pfost-Greene Family,* along with copies of John Morgan's portrait and his various confessions. The shorter ones were the cheapest and could be had for a dime, but the last and longest involving Ben Anderson and Alice cost a quarter.

A Punch and Judy show had drawn a good-sized gathering and puppets chased one another waving hatchets. Large crowds gathered

outside the opera hall to view a theatrical performance, and Shinn went in
to see for himself. There were three actors—two men and a woman—*"they
had it full of killing, and they would wind up by hanging a man on the stage,
to the unquestionable delight of everyone who would get in the hall, including
the Sheriff."* [25]

It was a rough and rowdy bunch in town, but precautions had been
taken against any serious criminal element. Most of the merchants had
hired their own watchmen, and both banks had armed guards stationed
out front. In those days, Ripley was known as a prohibition or *temperance*
town. Liquor sales were illegal, which did nothing to stop the town from
being awash in whiskey on the eve of John Morgan's hanging. Every train
coming into town brought in jugs of liquor for the occasion and although
the lawmen had intercepted some of it, it was impossible to stem the tide.

Shinn's deputies were out in force trying to keep law and order, but it
was mostly a losing proposition and John Morgan had plenty of company
in the cages. One of these was an out-of-towner caught selling whiskey
out of the back of Granderson Statt's store. He'd been doing a booming
business selling pint flasks at 25 cents apiece—the same price as Morgan's
best confession—and still had several hundred pints to go when the law
arrived. [26]

While there may have been laws against selling whiskey, there was no
law against drinking it. There were very few teetotalers in Ripley that night
and the sheriff wasn't one of them. Everywhere he looked there were clusters
of men passing around five-gallon jugs and having a high old time. But as
far as he knew nobody had died yet. That is, nobody except *"Uncle Billy."*

Old William Fletcher, known to everyone as *"Uncle Billy"* had been
looking forward to what, for him, would be the second chance of a
lifetime. He was locally famous as the man who'd tied the noose around
Charlie Green's neck nearly fifty years before. Sadly, the excitement of this
second coming attraction proved too much for him. He'd fallen over dead
toward evening, and people said it was a shame he couldn't have lasted
another twenty-four hours. [27]

By most accounts the town of Ripley was partying well into the night
on Wednesday, December 15th. Of all the merry revelers, it was the press
gang who had the most fun, gathering in a semi-secret, by-invitation-only
enclave in an upstairs room at the Maguire House across the street from
the jail. There were twenty or more newspaper men on hand to witness
the hanging and they were more or less hosted by Henry Deem from the

Jackson Herald. Thanks to Charles Hartley, a writer for Pomeroy, Ohio's *Tribune Telegraph,* we have an amusing glimpse into the smoke-filled, whiskey-doused world of these hard-boiled newspapermen. His description was later republished by Henry Deem on the one-year anniversary of the hanging under the headline of *"Night Before the Hanging: What a New York Reporter et al Did to a 2-Gallon Jug and a 10-Gallon Keg a Year Ago Last Night:"* [28]

It was the night before John Morgan was hanged at Ripley, W.Va, and we were in an upstairs room in the Maguire House. Taylor, of the Cincinnati Post, was there—a fat, chubby fellow; Anthony, of the Times Star, a dudish sort of chap who did not quit smoking to go to bed; Israel, of the Pittsburg Dispatch, a keen-eyed, sharp natured man, who probably was never still a moment in his life unless hypnotized; Boyd, a Parkersburg man, who had a string of Eastern papers so long as the moral law and who would wake up nights to tell war stories, and others, probably aggregating 20 in all, including the sheriff of the county and …a few convivial spirits who were known for their flow of wit and consuming desire for cigars and a certain fluid which is mostly conveyed to Ripley in earthenware vessels… What happened in that smoke bedimmed room did not appear in connection with the account of the hanging the next day. At an extremely late hour the guests of the house complained that their peaceful dreams were disturbed by the hilarity of the press gang, which by some means had consumed the contents of a two gallon molasses jug and burned enough tobacco to paralyze all the insects in two country hotels. The men who didn't smoke like a furnace, sing or make speeches had rough sledding in that aggregation of merry spirits. All this went on while the poor devil of a victim of his own crimes was getting ready just across the street to pay the earthly price of his sins…

Despite Mr. Deem's pointed use of the *"New York reporter"* in his headline, neither he nor Hartley ever named the man whose article became synonymous with the last public hanging in the state.

Across the street from the press party John Morgan was awake again. Recovered from his earlier collapse, he now paced back and forth in the confines of his cage, weeping one minute, laughing the next. [29] Finally, around 9:30 he dropped off to sleep again.

At one o'clock in the morning he woke up complaining of a headache and Shinn returned from Maguire's with a physician in tow who gave the prisoner some headache powders. [30] He slept intermittently, waking up every hour to ask anxiously if it was time yet. He'd pace a bit and then lay back down.[31]

This was a grim time for his deathwatch guards who wished the man could find oblivion in sleep. When Morgan woke again at four he talked about his escape, laughing ruefully, and saying he'd give a great deal to have that *"same chance again."*[32] He woke again at five, but upon being told it was still too early, went back to sleep and slept soundly for the next hour. Finally, around six o'clock he got up and *"appeared to be in a good humor and displayed very little nervousness."*[33]

It was almost time.

End Notes

[1] *Huntington Advertiser*, Huntington, WV, 15 December, 1897.

[2] *Wheeling Register*, Wheeling, WV, 15 December, 1897.

[3] *Evening Bulletin*, Maysville KY, 15 December, 1897.

[4] *Ibid.*

[5] *Evening Bulletin*, Maysville, KY, 18 December, 1897.

[6] *Cincinnati Post*, Cincinnati, Oh, 17 December, 1897.

[7] *Clarksburg Telegram*, Clarksburg, WV, 3 December, 1897.

[8] *Cincinnati Enquirer*, Cincinnati, OH, 19 December, 1897.

[9] "The Last Public Execution in West Virginia," *The West Virginia State Prison Magazine*, Moundsville West Virginia, July 1926.

[10] *Cincinnati Enquirer*, Cincinnati, OH, 16 December, 1897.

[11] *Cincinnati Enquirer*, Cincinnati, OH, 17 December, 1887.

[12] *Wheeling Register*, 17 December, 1897 names these: W. H. O'Brien, foreman; James Harpold; D. K. Hood, Jr; G. W Harpold; John Taber; J. M. Booth; J. P. Kiser; C. P. Shinn; Samuel H. MaGuire (owner of the MaGuire House in Ripley) ; L. Maddox of Kenna (O. J. Morrison's former business partner and brother-in-law; R. T. Wetzel of Ravenswood; and W. S. King. (one name is missing.)

[13] *Wheeling Register*, Wheeling, WV, 17 December, 1897.

[14] *Cincinnati Enquirer*, Cincinnati, OH, 15 December, 1897.

[15] *Jackson Herald*, Ripley, WV, 17 December, 1897.

[16] *Huntington Advertiser*.

[17] *Jackson Herald*.

[18] *Ibid.*

[19] *Cincinnati Enquirer*, 17 December, 1897.

[20] *Parkersburg Sentinel*, Parkersburg, WV, 17 December, 1897.

[21] *Cincinnati Enquirer*, Cincinnati, OH, 15 December, 1897.

22 *Cincinnati Post,* Cincinnati, OH, 16 December, 1897.

23 *Cincinnati Enquirer.*

24 *Pittsburgh Daily Post,* Pittsburgh, PA, 16 December, 1897.

25 *New York Sun,* New York, NY, 19 December, 1897.

26 *Jackson Herald.*

27 *Evening Bulletin,* Maysville, KY, 15 December, 1897.

28 *The Jackson Herald,* Ripley, WV, 17 December, 1897.

29 *Evening Bulletin,* Maysville, KY, 20 December, 1897.

30 *Clarksburg Telegram,* Clarksburg, WV, 24 December, 1897.

31 *Parkersburg Sentinel.*

32 *Clarksburg Telegram,* Clarksburg, WV, 17 December, 1897.

33 *Cincinnati Post.*

HAD I ONLY DONE RIGHT

Let the reader imagine a town built around a public square covering perhaps five acres. In the middle of this square is a brick building two stories high, 75 feet deep and 50 feet wide. Fill the square with people on foot, with men, women and children in every imaginable kind of country vehicle, and with men and women on horseback, some of the women with babies in their arms, put here and there in the crowd a black or white fakir, with a stand in front of him, loaded down with imitation silverware, gold watch chains, diamonds and every conceivable kind of spurious jewelry—imagine them all yelling at once, or singing or shouting and punctuate that part of the turmoil with the loud shrieks of a hundred or more youthful fakirs on foot, each with a bundle of printed matter in his arms and each shouting, "Last and only true confession of John F. Morgan." "Here you are, only 5, 10, 15 cents, as the case might be. The first confessions were the cheapest, the last cost a quarter. Just lay out this scene in your mind and you have a picture of the town of Ripley as viewed from the Court House steps at daylight Thursday. The man who was to provide the days pleasure for this crowd was shivering in his cell praying and singing alternately." [1]

Morgan woke up around six o'clock and donned his new suit along with his crush hat. The suit had taken quite a beating during his adventurous escape, but it had been sponged and pressed and the prisoner seemed oddly pleased with his appearance. The jailhouse was packed with people—several lawmen, the jailer and his wife, the prosecutor and various other officials, numerous newshounds—all milling around and conversing in hushed tones. One of the constables was asked how he thought Morgan would die. *"Game,"* he said, without hesitation. [2] At one point Morgan demanded that people stop whispering about him.

He was given a hearty breakfast and ate well, quipping that since this was his last meal he wanted to see just how much he could eat. Someone offered him a cigar afterwards, but not being used to them, he was *"not very successful."* [3]

Well before daylight the street vendors were setting up and people started gathering. Morgan could hear the harangue of the hawkers and the laughter of the crowd. The noise disturbed him and at one point he asked, *"Why do so many people come to see a poor wretch like me hang?"*[4] He was quiet for a spell and seemed very melancholy, but then roused himself enough to begin telling his fellow prisoners about his escape. Only his heart wasn't in it. Someone handed him a copy of O. J. Morrison's *Slaughter of the Pfost-Greene Family* and he read for several minutes before throwing it aside. Morrison got it all wrong he said disgustedly.[5]

Around nine o'clock he asked one of his guards to address a letter for him. He wanted to send it with a box of candy to his little boy. He also arranged for copies of his new photograph to be sent to Rebekah and his sisters, Ida and Florence. None of this took very long and when he was finished he sat down, put his head in his hands, and declaring that he'd just completed his last work on earth, began to weep softly.[6]

It was uncomfortably quiet inside the jail. It had been an odd sort of business guarding John Morgan for the past several weeks and the last few days had not been easy for any of them, particularly men like Wilson Slaughter who had known John for years. All of them were moved by his plight. Suddenly, as the raised voices of the confession sellers became louder, Morgan broke completely under the strain, throwing himself down on his cot, sobbing and moaning and begging for someone to do something for him. One of the guards asked the sheriff if he could give Morgan a little whiskey, but Shinn was adamant: *"No, Sir!,"* he said, *"He will have to go through the ordeal on cold water."*[7]

The reverends Rymer and White arrived around ten o'clock and began their last valiant efforts to wrest Morgan's soul from eternal torment:[8]

The scene in the jail this morning beggars description. His spiritual advisors were praying, singing, and pleading with the doomed man to surrender his soul to its Maker, while Morgan was a pitching, crying, agonizing man.

The preachers had spent their entire lives in spiritual warfare and were determined that John Morgan would die repentant and redeemed. As they raised their considerable voices in *"Praise God from Whom All Blessings Flow,"* John began to rally and joined in, but soon halted again and cried out, *"God save me! Oh Jesus save me and forgive me."* Reverend J. J. White attempted to sooth him with prayer and then began belting out, *"Oh Bear me away on thy snowy white wings to my eternal home."* Morgan became completely unstrung and the crusade continued.[9]

Those outside the jail could hear the raised oratory of the pastors as well as Morgan's pathetic appeals for mercy and deliverance— *"they were the harrowing cries of a condemned man in deepest distress and despair and without hope."*[10]

The evangelical duo assured everyone that they sensed a *"big change"* in Morgan and fervently believed he had seen the light.[11] Ballard Parsons might have told them he'd been disappointed in a similar conclusion some years back, but then he'd not employed so powerful an incentive. This time around there would be no room for backsliding.

At 10:40 Owen Shinn appeared on the courthouse steps and ordered the remaining on-lookers to ride on out to the scaffold if they wanted to find a suitable location to view the hanging. He'd made several attempts over the past hour to break up the crowd and was no more successful this time. At a quarter to the hour he collected Dr. Harrison and stepped back inside to read the death warrant aloud. He found the mercurial prisoner once again fully composed and attentive.[12]

"...thereupon it is considered by the court, that he be hanged by the neck until he be dead, and that execution of this judgment be made and done upon him, the said John Morgan..."

Shinn had originally planned to wait until closer to two o'clock before proceeding to give anyone arriving on the afternoon trains an opportunity to attend the hanging. However, rumors that Morgan's supporters were trying to obtain a last-minute reprieve had changed his mind, since any such communication would come by dispatch on the afternoon train. Deciding not to risk it, the sheriff told Morgan to be ready in twenty minutes. Morgan asked to be baptized first and Shinn allowed Reverend Rymer to perform the ritual.[13]

At 11:20 John Morgan was handcuffed and led outside to a surrey hitched to a pair of matching black horses and driven by Alonzo Bowman, a young man from Spencer.[14] Deputy Jim Weas and the sheriff's brother, Reuben, mounted and rode point, followed by the surrey containing Shinn and his prisoner, looking *"cool and collected,"* and the ministers.[15] Next in line was a buggy containing Dr. Harrison and Attorney James Seaman, followed by two large farm wagons, the first transporting approximately two dozen reporters, and the second, members of the death panel and the coffin.[16] The men in the last wagon would have a difficult trip. After some debate they had decided it wouldn't be proper to sit on Morgan's coffin, and so they ended up standing, at some risk to life and limb, throughout the journey.[17]

At first it was utter chaos. The crowd surged around the official vehicles as every man, woman, and child jostled one another to gain proximity to the condemned man. Then slowly, after much shouting and swearing from the deputies, the lead officials and their parties got underway at about 11:30. *"And following them came hurrying scurrying, helter skelter a mob of people afoot, in wagons, and buggies and upon horses."*[18]

It was warm for December, with just enough coolness in the air to be *"bracing."*[19] It was comfortable enough that some, whose feet were pinched and bruised from their long trek to Ripley, went barefoot, cooling their blisters in the soothing balm of the mud-slick roadway.[20] Although the sun was shining, there had been heavy downpours the week before and the road was a morass of mud, well over a foot deep in places, and those drivers not wary enough to avoid the swampy areas found themselves left by the wayside.[21] It was usually about a fifteen-minute ride from the jail to the site of the scaffold on Poling's farm on the outskirts of town, but it was a rough slough the entire way, and the addition of an intemperate crush of riders, conveyances and pedestrians made for a lengthier, somewhat perilous journey. Most of the crowd were already at the gallows, but a large number had stayed in town to join what a reporter from Baltimore described as a *"Sensational March:"*[22]

The march to the scaffold nearly a mile away, was sensational, from the start until the drop fell. …Fully two thousand men, women, boys and girls pitched, tumbled and fell over each other to go along with the Morgan procession. Men were hurt and women fainted in the crowd, which would not keep back.

Given the circumstances, John Morgan withstood his journey to the gallows very well, and, in fact, displayed a keen interest in the tumult around him. He searched constantly for familiar faces, occasionally turning in his seat to peer behind him. At times, he nodded and smiled at someone he knew. The ministers tried admirably to lead their free-wheeling congregation in a hymn-sing, and as soon as one wound down they would commence another.[23] They began with the poignant *Jesus Lover of My Soul*, and Morgan appeared contemplative as his ministers crooned beside him, *"Hangs my helpless soul on thee."* But the crowd picked up the pace with the old gospel favorite, *Lead Me On*, and the voices swelled:

Traveling to a better land
Over the desert's scorching sand
Father let me grasp thy hand.
Lead me on, lead me on!

Granted they were ankle deep in mud—a world away from *"scorching sand,"* but they were all joined in the same struggle. Even Morgan joined in on this one, his voice growing in strength and assurance:

When I stand on Jordan's brink
Never let me fear or shrink;
Hold me Father lest I sink;
Lead me on, lead me on!

Onward they forged, this odd cavalcade, weaving its way among the hills, their voices rising and falling in unison as they approached the end of their journey. Those waiting at the gallows mound could see and hear them well before they arrived. *"Oh Beulah Land, sweet Beulah Land, as on the highest mount I stand,"* sang Morgan. And there rising before him stood the gallows outlined against the bright blue of the sky, the hangman's noose *"dangling to and fro as if impatient at the slowness of the process."*[24] It was an overwhelming sight:[25]

The hillsides sloping up and away from it on all sides were black with people and the skeleton-like scaffold stood out and above them all, its newly planed oaken timbers gleaming in the sunlight of a beautiful day.

So many people! John had never seen so many in one place—and all of them there because of him. In all his imaginings, it had never been like this. Never had he been so awe-struck…so terror-stricken… so strangely proud and determined to see a thing through. All his life he had sought the attention of those around him. He had played the part of the fool, the court jester, the swaggering braggart. He had lost both his nerve and his self-respect so many times he couldn't count. But now, as a hundred shouting men on horseback made a way though the crowds like Moses parting the Red Sea, Morgan squared his shoulders and assumed his final role.

Owen Shinn had feared that Morgan would have to be carried up the scaffold wailing and sobbing, but when they arrived just before noon Morgan got out of the carriage unaided, stepped in front of the sheriff, and boldly led the way. Without hesitation he ascended the thirteen steps to the top of the platform. Once there he stood tall and, with an air of solemn dignity, surveyed the tremendous throng of men, women and children gathered on his behalf, and then he removed his new hat and bowed.

End Notes

[1] *New York Sun,* New York, NY, 19 December, 1897.

[2] *Cincinnati Post,* Cincinnati, OH, 17 December, 1897.

[3] *Ibid.*

[4] *Clarksburg Telegram,* 24 December, 1897.

[5] *Cincinnati Post,* 17 December, 1897.

[6] *Ibid.*

[7] *Ibid.*

[8] *Baltimore Sun,* Baltimore, MD, 17 December, 1897.

[9] *The Parkersburg Sentinel,* Parkersburg, WV, 17 December, 1897.

[10] *Clarksburg Telegram,* Clarksburg, WV, 24 December, 1897.

[11] *Cincinnati Post.*

[12] *Parkersburg Sentinel.*

[13] *Ibid.*

[14] *Ibid.*

[15] "The Last Public Execution in West Virginia," *The West Virginia State Prison Magazine,* Moundsville, WV, July, 1926.

[16] *Ibid.*

[17] *New York Sun,* New York, NY, 17 December, 1897.

[18] *Clarksburg Telegram.*

[19] *Cincinnati Enquirer,* Cincinnati, OH, 17 December, 1897.

[20] Undated newspaper clipping: Charles Conner's "Roving the Valley" column from the *Charleston Gazette,* Charleston, WV.

[21] *Morgantown Post,* Morgantown, WV, 17 December, 1897.

[22] *Baltimore Sun,* 17 December, 1897.

[23] *Wheeling Intelligencer,* Wheeling, WV, 17 December, 1897.

[24] *Morgantown Post.*

[25] *Clarksburg Telegram,* 17 December, 1897.

UNTIL YOU ARE DEAD, DEAD, DEAD

Opinions differed regarding the size of the crowd that day. The reporter for the *Wheeling Register* was convinced there were *"fully 15,000, one third of whom were women"*[1] and while this estimation was greatly inflated, his observation concerning the high percentage of women in the crowd tallied with that of his colleagues.[2] The *Baltimore Sun* journalist declared that there were *"between ten and twelve thousand people,"* but said that some of his fellows had argued for upwards of 20,000.[3] The *Cincinnati Enquirer* reported 8,000 to 10,000, leaning toward the higher number,[4] and the *Parkersburg Sentinel* concurred.[5] The *New York Sun* reporter's appraisal, for all his other exaggerations, was the lowest at half that amount and probably much closer to the mark.[6]

But regardless of the size of the crowd, everyone agreed Owen Shinn had chosen the perfect setting. The scaffold stood atop a large knoll that rose twenty-five to thirty-five feet in the center of a ten-acre lot at the foot of a hillside. The natural amphitheater surrounding it would have easily accommodated several times the actual number of witnesses and still given everyone a clear view of the action. As the New York observer put it, *"Any spot in the neighborhood was a good spot to see the hanging."*[7]

Photograph of the hanging taken by Susan King. There were several photographs taken of the execution; this particular copy, courtesy of the family, was kept by Rebekah Morgan.

When the New Yorker scanned the crowd, he was surprised to
find that the majority had complied with the warnings to leave their
weapons at home and were mostly unarmed.[8] While there were no overt
demonstrations, there was little in the way of support or regard for the
condemned—*"there was not one outward display of sympathy for Morgan.
On the contrary all present seemed to delight in the affair."*[9]

Morgan stood on the platform with the sheriff and his deputies,
Reuben Shinn and Jim Weas. Joining them were the two ministers,
Prosecutor James Seaman, and the clerk of the court, Marshall Archer.
Visiting dignitaries, members of the death jury, the physicians, and
newspaper men all crowded into the barbed-wire enclosure surrounding
the gallows.

To everyone's amazement a woman began ascending the steps of the
gallows. She stopped just before the platform and took a seat on the top
step with her back to the men. A low murmur swept through the crowd
along with a name. *"Pretty widow McVey,"* the *Cincinnati Post* reporter
wrote, proved a distraction and attention was divided between her and
the condemned man. No one had ever heard of a woman on the gallows
who wasn't there to be hanged, and some found it distasteful. But the *Post*
reporter, who was obviously a fan, admired her bravery and remarked that
she conducted herself in a dignified fashion, *"as though reporting hangings
was an ordinary affair."*[10]

Morgan stood above it all with his hands crossed and shackled in front
of him. He had removed his hat and was bowing to the crowd, gazing out
over the sea of onlookers in search of familiar faces. It wasn't quite true
that the man had no support that day. Rebekah wasn't there of course and
neither were his sisters, but old friends and neighbors stood below, as well
as in-laws and relatives. John and Billy Chancey were there to bear witness,
as were Ed and Charlie Southall.[11] They did not understand or condone
what he had done, but many were not without compassion as he stood
before them on this, his last day on earth. *"He found one and more than
one, for he nodded a number of times to persons whom he recognized and to
those who waived adieu to him."*[12]

It was just before noon when the little group climbed the steps to the
platform and once everyone assumed their places, Owen Shinn called out
"Silence!," and a hush fell over the crowd. Reverend J. J. White stepped
forward and began to read from the 90th Psalm. Morgan looked over his
shoulder to follow along:[13]

...For we are consumed by thine anger, and by thy wrath we are
troubled.
Thou hast set our iniquities before thee, our secret sins in the light
of thy countenance.
For all our days are passed away in thy wrath, we spend our years
as a tale that is told...

Reverend Rymer followed with a prayer, which, as Henry Deem would
point out, was *"a rather lengthy exhortation under the circumstance, but one*
which was perfectly agreeable to the condemned man."[14]

Almighty God, our Heavenly Father, Thou, who art the creator of the
heavens above and the earth beneath, Thou, who holdeth the destiny of angels
and men in thine hands, Thou seest and understandeth the secrets of all hearts;
it is before thee and in Thy presence that we stand here today on this sad and
awful occasion to witness the execution of the law on one of our citizens—one
of our number—who has been charged with crime, has been tried by the law of
our State and sentenced to die.

In this close-up from the previous photo it is clear that this was taken during
the prayer. In the front J.O. Shinn stands on the right with his head bowed and
next to him is Rev. Rymer. Morgan stands to his left. Rev. White leans against
the railing near Mrs McVay who is seated on the top step. Reuben "Dug" Shinn
stands in the rear along with the prosecutor, James Seaman, and Deputy Weas.

He prayed with earnest eloquence for several minutes, sending many a plea for mercy heavenward, and then with one last request the loquacious pastor turned John Morgan over to his Maker: *"Father in heaven, we commend the soul of this man into thine hand. Lord Jesus, receive his spirit into the habitation of the blessed. Amen."*[15]

As soon as Rymer struck the *"Amen!,"* Sheriff Shinn turned to Morgan and asked, *"John, do you want to make a speech? I will give you ten minutes if you want to do it."*[16] Morgan, who had planned to do that very thing found himself suddenly tongue-tied and replied, *"I'd like to say a lot, but I guess I won't. I'm afraid I might break down."*[17] But then he gathered himself, held up his manacled hands and stepped forward to the edge of the platform. He was in full view of the crowd, and the newsmen standing just below him strove to capture every word, every quaver in his voice, every tremble of his limbs:[18]

Morgan's incarceration, although of less than fifty day's duration, had told plainly upon him, and his rugged appearance when arrested Nov 3rd, had all left the man... he appeared not the strong, healthy farm hand of a few weeks before, but a pale, nervous creature...

And yet all agreed that the man was remarkably cool. Indeed, he seemed more composed than anyone on the scaffold and there was nothing about him that looked the part of dangerous triple murderer:[19]

Morgan in his new clothes looked rather handsome and his large eyes were luminous and sad and hopeless. To some the man looked all eyes. No tears stood in them, but it might be said, there were tears in his voice—soft, emotional and tender. He looked not over twenty-two years of age and appeared not the low, depraved wretch, the butcherous murderer that he was.[19]

And then he spoke, *"Good people, all farewell. I bid you all goodbye."*[20]

Morgan walked around the platform taking his leave of everyone there, shaking hands and saying, *"Goodbye gentlemen. Meet me in Heaven."*[21] Then he walked to the middle of the platform and took his stand upon the trap saying in a clear, firm voice, *"Gentlemen this is a warning to all young men. Don't do as I have done. God forbid that any of you ever go astray as I have done. Good bye."*[22] And once again he waved his hands in the air.

This time around several voices called out in response, *"Goodbye John! Goodbye."* When Shinn removed his handcuffs, Morgan placed his hands behind his back to have them strapped, and in that instant a man climbed up into a wagon bed and shouted, *"John, Ida sends goodbye to you."* John

In this photo a man with a hat partially obscures the scaffold as Sheriff Shinn places the noose around Morgan's neck.

turned toward him, nodded once, but said nothing. As the deputies strapped Morgan's legs together, James Seaman whispered to him, *"Bear up!"* And Morgan muttered, *"I'm trying."*[23]

As Owen Shinn pulled the black cap from his pocket, Morgan whispered to him quietly and urgently. Then the sheriff nodded brusquely and things moved quickly after that. Shinn pulled the silken cap over Morgan's head as John begged, *"Tell me when you're going to do it."* And Shinn replied, *"All right, John, draw a long breath."* Then just as Shinn slipped the noose around his neck, came Morgan's last words, *"Don't make it too tight."*[24]

In the end, it happened so fast that many were caught off guard. Shinn stepped behind Morgan to adjust the noose, then in one quick move pulled the lever and sprang the trap. Morgan appeared to shoot upwards as the rope pulled taut and then he dropped like a stone. In a flash, he hung suspended between heaven and earth. Reporters noted a slight quivering of his feet and that was all.

Some, including John Chancey, had turned their heads away as soon as the black hood was put in place. Chancey later told his family he found it all *"too cruel"*— he couldn't bear to watch *"the life crushed out of someone he had known for so long."*[25] There were several who felt that way, but others, like Ed Southall who stood with John Chancey in the crowd, no longer counted those years of friendship. Those boyhood memories had been driven out by the horror of that November morning. *"[I]t was half of what he deserved for what he'd done,"* he said.[26] Twenty-five-year-old George Wallace Casto, known as *"Wall,"* was in the crowd as well. The son of Permelia Shinn Casto was proud of both his uncles up there on the platform and awed by the way they handled their difficult responsibilities. Yet, years later, he too admitted that he couldn't watch Morgan's final moments:[27]

It was too brutal, too public. I stood not 20 feet away, with a clear view of the gallows, but I think I shut my eyes when my uncle…sprung that trap. Women fainted as far as a 100 yards behind me.

Yet there were women who did not faint or shy away from the drop. When it was obvious that John Morgan had finished his speech, Anna McVay stood up and turned to watch the condemned man meet his death, and as the *New York Sun* reporter remarked, *"She did not flinch."*[28] At the same time, Susan King moved purposefully around the edges of the crowd. With her tripod and camera, she recorded the occasion from every angle, her father dogging her heels to assist her and ensure she kept her promises. She, too, may have watched Morgan's final moments as the trap was sprung, but if so, she didn't press the shutter.

Less than fifteen minutes had elapsed from the time Morgan reached the top of the platform until the trap was sprung. It took slightly longer than that for him to die. The trap dropped at 12:09. And just as they had in the courtroom while waiting for the jury to render its verdict, men had their pocket watches in hand. They watched the minute hand sweep by, counting down the final moments of a man's life. Below the trap, the physicians stood by the gently swaying body. Surrounded by members of the death jury and the press, they began calling out minute-by-minute fluctuations in John Morgan's vital signs.

At 12:11 his pulse rate was 120; at 12:12 it was 102; at 12:13 it had dropped to 72. By 12:16 it had climbed to a rate of 114 where it remained for several minutes before dropping back down again. Finally, at 12:24, a full fifteen minutes after the trap had dropped, came the pronouncement that John Morgan was dead.[29,30] The Parkersburg reporter and Bill Taylor from the *Cincinnati Enquirer* carefully jotted down these macabre details for the benefit of their readers, and Taylor noted, *"the man was dying so long that it was believed he had been strangled, but an examination showed that his neck had been broken."*[31]

The body was left hanging for another half hour as witnesses moved in for a closer look and then Shinn untied the rope from the brace and Morgan was lowered into the arms of the undertaker, Isaiah Vail, and his assistant John Connelly.[32] The two physicians stepped forward to examine the body and determined that the noose, although it had been meticulously placed just behind the left ear, had slipped a bit when the body plunged through the trap. Still, the hangman's knot had done an efficient job and broken the neck. Both doctors were of the opinion that Morgan's death had been painless and *"practically instantaneous,"* as there was a two-inch separation in the vertebrae.[33] In all, the *"execution was a success in every way."*[34]

   Considering all the things that could have gone wrong, and often did when a man was hanged, Sheriff Shinn had every right to feel a certain sense of victory. Congratulations were being shouted at him from every direction, accompanied by hearty back-slapping and hand-shaking. He was polite as always, but certainly in no mood to celebrate. He had done his duty, but it had taken its toll. *"You have no idea the relief I feel since this bad work is over,"* he told Boyd, the Parkersburg reporter:[35]

   · Ever since Morgan was sentenced the strain has continued until I doubt not I was more rattled than Morgan when on the scaffold. There has been so much to attend to and the escape two weeks ago increased the worry… I hope I shall never have to perform the same kind of duty again but there is one thing I want to say and that is I do not want to ever see another public hanging.

   The sheriff had not taken his responsibilities lightly, and he had begun his preparations as soon as the verdict was read. Owen Shinn was a careful, deliberate man and he had walked himself through the steps he needed to take on the scaffold. Just that morning the New York reporter had found him upstairs in the courthouse practicing the placement of the knotted noose on his brother Reuben— placing the noose around his "victim's" neck, adjusting it just so, then removing it and starting over—each repetition helping to allay his anxiety.[36]

   The enormity of this task had weighed heavily, yet despite the strain of the past several weeks Shinn had stoically endured, remaining unfailingly polite and reassuring when dealing with a demanding, frightened public. He had been stalwart in the face of angry lynch mobs and fellow-lawmen, and staunchly supportive of his many helpers, even when they made grave errors of judgment, as had happened during Morgan's escape. He had demonstrated infinite patience when dealing with the swarm of newspaper men and was, *"universally voted as courteous in his treatment of ...the press in their efforts to obtain the news..."* [37]

The lawman's bill for expenses associated with hanging John Morgan amounted to less than $200, [38] but there was no reckoning the emotional price paid by the exhausted sheriff, and things weren't over yet. He watched as Morgan's body was placed into the simple pine coffin and loaded onto the wagon. Major Progler's men were already starting to dismantle the gallows. It wouldn't do to leave it standing any longer than necessary or the crowd would whittle it down to nothing for souvenirs. Shinn had already decided to store it in the upper story of the courthouse along with the rope, which would eventually be cut into pieces and distributed as keepsakes. [39] Then he accompanied the coffin back into town, making sure it was safely housed in Morgan's old cell overnight as a deterrent to thieves and vandals.

Before they'd left the jail that morning, Morgan had turned to him and said, *"We have always been neighbors. Be a friend to my wife and help her bring the other guilty man to justice."* [40] He was referring of course to Ben Anderson. Shinn had harbored a strong sense of foreboding even before Morgan made that final confession, and it was not alleviated by Morgan's desperate words just before the noose was placed around his neck. One last time he implored Shinn to see justice done, *"For,"* he said, *"he is as guilty as I am."* [41]

Morgan had been a complete mystery. The sheriff had found himself charmed by Morgan's teasing banter and self-deprecating humor on more than one occasion, only to experience the strong desire to strangle him without benefit of the noose the next. He still had nightmares of the carnage Morgan had wrought at the Pfost-Greene farm, yet he had also witnessed his deep and abiding affection for Rebekah and Albert. He had been dismayed by Morgan's downward spiral and collapse in the hours before the hanging, then marveled as John sturdily marched up the gallows steps, faced the crowds and said his piece.

Most people left the hanging ground content that justice had been served. No one could be blamed for wanting to close the book and move on with their lives. Later that evening, the gentlemen of the press put the finishing touches on their descriptions of the hanging for the next day's editions. They too were wondering what would come next, now that their coverage of Morgan's exploits was complete. The Parkersburg editor was contemplative as he wrote: [42]

The curtain has fallen on the last act of one of the darkest tragedies that ever stained the fair name of West Virginia. The final chapter in the history of that most notorious criminal, John Morgan, has been concluded.

Relentless justice has accomplished its end and fate has cut the thread of a life which has spread over the lives of others a pall of deepest gloom.

Where two months ago quiet, peace and contentment reigned, today only the dregs of bitter recollections like some horrid nightmare, remains. Two families have been broken up and a story that probably can never be entirely effaced has touched them with an icy finger.

In truth, an entire community was left dazed and shivering in the aftermath, but for a few there was no surcease. Owen Shinn lay awake long past the witching hour listening to the whispers of the dead man standing in the shadows of his room. There was still work to be done.

And just a few miles away as the crow flies another man tossed and turned through the night, feverishly ill and sweating, and in mortal terror of what might come.

End Notes

[1] *Wheeling Register,* Wheeling, WV, 17 December, 1897.

[2] *Ibid.*

[3] *Baltimore Sun,* Baltimore, MD, 17 December, 1897.

[4] *Cincinnati Enquirer,* 17 December, 1897.

[5] *Parkersburg Sentinel,* Parkersburg, WV, 17 December, 1897.

[6] *New York Sun,* 19 December, 1897.

[7] *Ibid.*

[8] *Ibid.*

[9] *Wheeling Register.*

[10] *Cincinnati Post,* Cincinnati, OH, 17 December, 1897.

[11] "The Last Public Hanging," *Goldenseal Magazine,* Spring 1990

[12] *Clarksburg Telegram,* 24 December, 1897.

[13] *Jackson Herald,* Ripley, WV, 17 December, 1897.

[14] *Ibid.*

[15] *Ibid.*

[16] *New York Sun.*

[17] *Cincinnati Enquirer,* 17 December, 1897..

[18] *Morgantown Post.*

[19] *Clarksburg Telegram*, 24 December, 1897.

[20] *Ibid.*

[21] *Ibid.*

[22] *Ibid.*

[23] *Cincinnati Enquirer, 17 December, 1897.*

[24] *Clarksburg Telegram*, 24 December, 1897.

[25] *"The Last Public Hanging"*

[26] *Ibid.*

[27] Clipping from the *Charleston Gazette* (undated).

[28] *New York Sun,* 19 December, 1897.

[29] *Parkersburg Sentinel.*

[30] *Cincinnati Enquirer, 17 December, 1897.*

[31] *Ibid.*

[32] *"The Last Public Execution in West Virginia," The West Virginia State Prison Magazine,* Moundsville, WV, July, 1926.

[33] *Cincinnati Enquirer, 17 December, 1897.*

[34] *Wheeling Register.*

[35] *Parkersburg Sentinel.*

[36] *New York Sun,* 19 December, 1897.

[37] *Jackson Herald,* Ripley, WV, 17 December, 1897.

[38] *Ibid.*

[39] Author's Note: Nothing remains of the scaffold now except the large wooden frame surrounding the blown-up copy of one of Susan King's photographs of the hanging. The famous rope was also kept for many years and then cut into pieces for keepsakes; it too has been lost.

[40] *Pittsburgh Daily Post,* Pittsburgh, PA, 6 March, 1898.

[41] *Parkersburg Sentinel.*

[42] *Ibid.*

NO REST FOR THE WICKED

The next morning Shinn was back at the jail well before daybreak to oversee the loading of Morgan's coffin onto the hearse.[1] He had promised to personally deliver the body to Rebekah at her father's place out in Fairplain. He was more than eager to have this chore over and done with.

Morgan had caused him no end of trouble and it appeared his death had not put an end to it. Yesterday, after the man had been cut down and laid in his coffin for the trip back into town, some idiot started the rumor that Morgan wasn't really dead.[2] That caused a considerable stir until Shinn and the doctors managed to reassure everyone.

The distance to the Hall farm was about nine and a half miles, but Shinn expected it to take three hours or more due to the poor road conditions.[3] It had begun to rain again and the deep ruts on the Charleston Pike, heavily churned by the previous day's traffic, were soon swampier than ever. The downpour would continue throughout the day. Thanks to John Morgan, Owen Shinn once again found himself spending several frustrating hours, rain-soaked and miserable, and ruing the day he'd ever considered running for office.

Two of his faithful deputies rode with him that morning, as well as a smattering of the town's officials, a few die-hard newspaper men loath to give up John Morgan's currency in the press, and various individuals who went as a show of respect for the family. Others went along for the same reason they went to the hanging—out of a morbid sense of curiosity. But as the procession made its way through the lower end of Grasslick, a surprising number of folks were on hand to meet the little cortege, and these were joined at regular intervals by still more as they approached Poverty Ridge.[4]

There they met with disappointment. Hiram Hall refused to allow the burial. The men preparing the grave had nearly completed their work when Hall appeared and told them to fill it back in. After having thought long and hard about the future of his grandson, and recognizing that much of the boy's rearing would be left to him, he and Rebekah's brothers had come to a decision. Hiram would not allow his son-in-law to be buried on the farm after all.[5] Shinn's usual powers of diplomacy failed him in this instance. Hiram would not be moved and he ordered everyone off his property.

Rebekah's reaction to her father's intransigence can only be imagined. She had, after all, made this last promise to her husband. Hiram suggested one or two alternatives. His farm bordered land owned by the Fairview Church and so he proposed that Morgan be buried in the cemetery there, but a hasty polling of the available trustees, many of whom were on hand for the funeral, resulted in another quick refusal.[6] Next, Hiram pointed out a spot in the nearby woods, but soon after the diggers began work someone realized they were digging on Dr. Bechtel's property. Since the medical examiner wasn't around to ask his permission the work was suspended.[7]

Shinn now faced a dilemma. He had initially thought to bury Morgan on Poling's farm near the gallows, but in deference to the condemned man's request and Rebekah's acquiescence, he had agreed to bring the body to Fairplain. He considered using his own farm, but that was a fair distance away. They had arrived at the Hall farm around 9 o'clock that morning and it was now going on noon. Poor Rebekah had been waiting all morning to bury her husband and was becoming increasingly distraught. Something needed to be done and quickly.

At this point, Abe Casto spoke up and offered the use of the family cemetery at his farm on Bear Fork.[8] After all, Morgan's Casto connections on his mother's side qualified him as family, even if they weren't particularly proud of the fact. A deeply grateful Shinn took him up on the offer and before the old man could have second thoughts, the sheriff had the funeral entourage underway again. But they had gone less than two miles when they spied a rider coming to meet them. It was a member of the Casto tribe come to inform them that Abe Casto's sons had outvoted their father and would not permit Morgan to be buried on their land either.[9]

Word was now out that John Morgan was looking for a home and an exasperated Shinn had no alternative but to turn the procession back around and head for his place. It was now well into the afternoon and the beleaguered lawman was beginning to feel like Moses wandering in the wilderness. Along with everyone else in his retinue, he was cold, wet, tired, and hungry, and more than a little out of sorts. He might also have begun to wonder if perhaps there was some grain of truth in the tales of the hangman's curse.

Less than a mile later they were overtaken by yet another messenger and forced to halt once more. This time, however, the news was good. John and Ulysses "Lyss" Shinn, two of the sheriff's brothers, sent word to Owen to bring the body to their farm, located some little ways back. They had scouted out a suitable spot in a remote location on their property and had already begun preparations for the grave.[10] They turned the hearse around and headed back, relieved their journey was at last nearing an end.

The third time being charm, this grave was finished around 4 o'clock that afternoon and the hearse and the accompanying mourners arrived shortly after. Approximately 150 people had stuck it out, braving the elements and the seemingly endless meanderings, and they gathered to make their final goodbyes. They huddled beneath the bare branches of the two large oaks that marked the head and the foot of what everyone fervently hoped would be John Morgan's final resting place.[11] The Shinn brothers had chosen thoughtfully.

Those who were not present as mere on-lookers and curiosity seekers closed ranks around Rebekah's and John's family members, the cold rain dripping off hat brims and black umbrellas, and bowed their heads. The blows of the ax had rained down upon them all and so they stood together with the family and grieved for all that had been lost. The relentless rain pattered onto the thick carpet of sodden leaves beneath their feet as Reverend Rymer spoke the ageless words of comfort and overriding mercy. They raised their voices in a final hymn and offered up their own silent prayers. John Ferguson Morgan had been laid to rest.

It was almost dark by the time the short service ended at 5:15 and a weary Sheriff Shinn started for home; little did he know or care that John Morgan had snagged headlines yet again.[12]

REFUSED BURIAL SPACE
Sheriff Has a Hard Time Disposing of a Murderer's Body

Indianapolis Sun, Indianapolis, Indiana, 18 December, 1897.

—

FORBADE THE BURIAL OWNER ROUTS THE MOURNERS

Evening Bulletin, Maysville, KY, 20 December, 1897

—

THREE GRAVES STARTED BY THE DIGGERS BEFORE A RESTING PLACE WAS FOUND FOR THE BODY OF JOHN MORGAN

Cincinnati Enquirer, Cincinnati, OH, 19 December, 1897

End Notes

[1] *Cincinnati Enquirer,* Cincinnati, OH, 18 December, 1897.

[2] *Ibid.*

[3] *Ibid.*

[4] *Parkersburg Sentinel,* Parkersburg, WV, 17 December, 1897.

[5] *Ibid.*

[6] *Cincinnati Enquirer.*

[7] *Ibid.*

[8] *Ibid.*

[9] *Ibid.*

[10] *Ibid.*

[11] *Evening Bulletin,* Maysville, KY, 20 December, 1897.

[12] *Cincinnati Enquirer.*

AFTERMATH

DID BEN ANDERSON CONFESS?

A report was brought here to-night that Ben ANDERSON, THE MAN WHOM Murderer John Morgan implicated in the killing of Mrs. Chloe Green and her son and daughter, had died at his home near Ripley, and that upon his deathbed, within an hour of his soul's departure, he confessed that what Morgan had said was true.

Wheeling Register, Wheeling, WV, 18 December, 1897

Regardless of the media claims, Anderson was still very much alive. While not exactly well, he had begun to rally, and so on Sunday the 19th of December the more careful editors printed retractions. The rumor of his demise, one claimed, had been started by a *"party of traveling men,"* and another felt it only fair to add, *"no warrant has yet been served upon Anderson and … he stoutly maintains his innocence."*[1]

Opinions were still divided about how authorities should proceed in the wake of Morgan's last terrible confession implicating Anderson and Alice Pfost:[2]

…once the hanging was over, there were many who seemed content that the real murderer had been caught and justice had run its course. Others, however, seemed more determined to see things through to the bitter end.

Owen Shinn had promised John and Rebekah he would continue the investigation, and he was being hounded in this regard by David Brown, who was more determined than ever to pursue the case. Brown was interviewed in nearby Parkersburg just before the New Year and he informed reporters that Anderson was recovering rapidly and would soon be arrested. He went on to say that a preliminary hearing was in the offing and he believed a *"full confession"* was imminent.[3]

When word spread about John Morgan's final words to the sheriff as they stood on the scaffold, public opinion began to shift. Although the press noted that most people still didn't believe Alice had anything to do with the murders, they were not so sanguine about Ben Anderson. People took dying pronouncements very seriously, but since Anderson was slow to recover there wasn't much to be done about it. Nonetheless, the papers seemed determined to fan the public's interest even when there was little to report:

Mrs. Morgan believes implicitly in the dying statement of her husband and is doing a little detective work.[4]

Ben Anderson …is now able to sit up and is being closely watched, and as soon as he is sufficiently strong he will be taken into custody and placed in jail.[5]

Still hoping to cash in on Morgan's celebrity status well past his expiration date, the papers reviewed the crimes again, and dug deep for any *"DETAILS NOT BEFORE PUBLISHED,"* while praying for Anderson to rally.[6]

Now seemed as good a time as any to revive conveniently recalled or confabulated stories of Morgan's childhood and past deeds, and readers shuddered as they pored over his early attempts to slaughter innocent babies and grown-up propensities to brutally mistreat livestock.[7]

Two weeks later, on January 17th, a very nervous Ben Anderson rode into Ripley and surrendered to authorities. Now the legal arguments could begin again. Even though Anderson had been making steady progress in regaining his health, Shinn had for some reason held off serving the warrant. The *Cincinnati Post* claimed the warrant was originally sworn out by Rebekah Morgan following her husband's execution, and that by the time Ben Anderson finally appeared the evidence against him had been *"thoroughly investigated"* and found to be insufficient to hold him in jail.[8] That didn't mean, however, that the law was done with him. The State, this time with Attorney David Brown acting as prosecutor, planned to bring him to trial. Still, he was permitted to go home with instructions to return for his hearing on January 27th.[9] Anderson engaged Attorney Elmer L. Stone, the sheriff's cousin, to represent him.[10]

The only records in existence of the hearing are a few scant lines to be found here and there in newspaper reports. The *Pittsburgh Post-Gazette* and the *Cincinnati Post* provided the only surviving documentation of Anderson's legal proceedings and reported that fourteen witnesses were called, four more than were used in Morgan's trial, but there is little indication of who they were. The *Cincinnati Post* offers the name of only one of them—Mrs. John Morgan. Rebekah is mentioned because, along with two other material witnesses, she did not show up for the proceedings.[11] This seems at odds with earlier reports of her pressuring the authorities for Anderson's arrest and prosecution.

Anderson assured the newspaper correspondents that he had no fears about his abilities to clear himself of all charges, but one of the man's neighbors doubted that Anderson could *"satisfactorily prove his whereabouts at the time, and that his prospects for complete vindication of the charges against him were not very bright."*[12] Brown requested a continuance since his most important witnesses were absent and *created a sensation by stating that he had evidence implicating a third party in the crime."*[13] Anderson's attorney, E. L. Stone, put up a vigorous fight to have the case proceed there and then, but Justice Parsons, who was presiding, agreed to adjourn court until the following Thursday, February 3rd. This time, Ben Anderson was kept in jail without bond.[14]

The mysterious *"third party"* is never named in the surviving newspaper accounts, and so it is impossible to know whether in the end Brown accused Alice Pfost of being the third accomplice. If so, the *"sensation"* mentioned by the reporters would have been an understatement. Did David Brown jump off that bridge at the final hearing, risking political suicide in the process, and accuse the victimized Alice Pfost of having been involved in the murders of her siblings and her mother? If he did, it was all for nothing.

NO EVIDENCE
To Connect Anderson with the Jackson County Crime

Ben Anderson, who was arrested and jailed recently, charged with having been an accomplice of John Morgan, the perpetrator of the Green-Pfost atrocities at Grass Lick, was given a hearing by Justice Parsons and discharged, as there was not sufficient evidence to sustain the statements made by Morgan in his dying confession, implicating Anderson. Anderson, his family and friends are overjoyed at the outcome.

From the Parkersburg Sentinel, 6 February, 1898

The papers reported very succinctly that Ben Anderson's final hearing was held on February 3rd and *"for lack of evidence he was released."*[15] Just like that it was all over and Ben Anderson walked out of the courtroom a free man. It is surprising that there was so little newspaper coverage concerning this final hearing, but perhaps that was because there was so little to say. It would appear that something or someone may have stopped David Brown from proceeding as planned and pointing the finger at Alice. The reporters would have certainly broadcasted this. But there was nothing. And Ben Anderson went on with his life, though rumors and innuendo inevitably followed him. Guilty or innocent, John Morgan's allegations, once made, could never be taken back. The damage was done.

Alice Pfost fared better and survived with her reputation intact. No doubt the trauma haunted her forever, but her family shielded her from the worst of Morgan's accusations. Alice never married. She lived to be 75, dying in 1944 of a minor injury that became infected. Though she carried the scar from the hatchet wound and suffered from headaches for the rest of her life, these were the only signs of trauma. Some might have expected her to become bitter and reclusive, but she was neither. Instead she was described as *"always cheerful,"* and as having a *"kind, sympathetic nature."* She was admired and respected by her community and beloved by her family. She overcame unimaginable horror and tragedy to attain a measure of happiness, but she never spoke of that long-ago fall and she never played the accordion again.

And what of David A. Brown who seemed so determined to prosecute according to his dead client's description of events? He would not live out the year. In June, Brown was visiting in Parkersburg when he was suddenly stricken with severe dysentery. [16] He was admitted to St. Luke's Hospital where he lingered for several days before dying at the age of forty-four, leaving behind his widow and four children. Friends and colleagues accompanied his remains to the train station where he was transported back to Jackson County for burial.

Local historian John House, writing just after the turn of the century, witnessed many of these events firsthand. He tramped the highways and by-ways of Jackson and neighboring counties gathering local history and anecdotal information. He was acquainted with just about everyone involved with the case and was one of the few contemporaries, besides O. J. Morrison, to leave a written account of the tragedy. Yet House, who wrote so prolifically about everything else, had little to say about the outcome of the Pfost-Greene murders.

What he does say is telling. He writes that John Morgan, *"...is generally supposed to have possibly, with the help of another, murdered Mrs. Chlora Green, a widow living on Grass Lick, eleven miles from Ripley, her daughter Matilda Pfost, and her son James Green."* [17]

Writing from the vantage point of a decade or more after these occurrences, one would expect a more settled perspective, but instead House seems unconvinced of the truth of the matter, and implies that others were as well. He goes on to say, "*there was little effort made to ascertain if Morgan had any accomplices or coadjutors in his crime.*"[18]

House's considerable manuscripts were compilations of the extensive notes he took during his lifetime. They have never been published, and were only recently organized by his family and made available on the county's genealogical website. He was not writing for public consumption and so did not always detail his sources or worry about the risk of giving offense. His views on the public execution were succinct:[19]

The hanging was in the presence of an immense throng, and amid scenes the most revolting and disgraceful. The people seemed to think the whole affair was a sort of picnic or "show" gotten up for their amusement.

Furthermore, House's opinion concerning the efficacy of public executions in the deterrence of crime, though couched in subtlety, is hard to miss: "*Since the Morgan execution, homicides have been common in Jackson County.*"[20]

Those who were directly involved carried emotional scars for the rest of their lives. Some, like John Chancey and others who encountered the victims that morning, and Owen Shinn, who was forced to hang his neighbor, were certainly troubled by those memories. And then there were the spectators who simply came to see an execution and were haunted by it afterwards. Thirty-five-year-old John Milhoan was one of these.

Milhoan was a law-abiding miner and slater living in Ripley who witnessed Morgan's climb to the scaffold. He subsequently developed an absolute "*horror of hanging.*"[21] In 1901, shortly after the New Year, and more than three years after Morgan's execution date, he became convinced that a posse was coming for him. He maintained a constant watch for the sheriff's men from his upstairs bedroom window.

When out of his right mind in the last few days he seemed to fear that he was going to be hanged. He kept saying that he had not done anything to be hanged for, but that they were after him.[22]

In the end, tormented by his fear of the hangman, Milhoan killed himself by cutting his own throat.

There were the inevitable ghost stories. The Pfost-Greene farmhouse was torn down, but long before its demise came tales of the "*bleeding floor*" that could not be cleansed and the screams of a young woman heard in the cornfields in the early morning hours.

And so, after a fashion the story of the hanging of John Ferguson Morgan lives on. Folks living in Jackson County and the surrounding area today believe they know the tragic story from the bits of oral history passed down to them from one generation to the next. But much has been lost, including the location of Morgan's grave.

The expenses paid by the county for John Morgan's funeral did not include a headstone and the family chose not to erect one. Many insist he is buried on the hillside near the Fairplain exit, across from the interstate highway. Some will add that his grave is in the vicinity of a large cedar tree. Cedar trees grow in abundance in Jackson County and so are always a safe bet. Still others claim he is buried close to the Fairplain Cemetery.

For years, locals declared they could easily pinpoint the location because John Morgan was so evil that no grass would grow on his grave. For several nights after his burial passers-by were startled by the sight of eerie blue flames coming from the grave. But this was easily attributed to pranksters burning sulphur.

Then too, there are some who swear that John Morgan no longer lies quietly in his grave. The story, as told by one of the Pfost descendants, is that some years ago an in-law was invited to the former home of Dr. Bechtel, which was then owned by his son. The junior Bechtel and his guest visited for some time and eventually the conversation turned to Morgan. There came a point when the host stood and invited his guest to accompany him to the basement. There he opened a closet door and stood aside to display a fully articulated human skeleton dangling from its medical stand. *"That,"* said young Bechtel, *"is John Morgan."*

As wonderfully outlandish as this tale may seem, it is thoroughly plausible that the venerable Dr. Bechtel might have decided to bring Morgan home with him, tidy him up, and put him to good use. The story is further enhanced by claims that lantern light was spotted bobbing around the site of the burial for several hours one evening.

It was common practice to use the unclaimed bodies of executed felons for the advancement of medicine, but these were not always easily obtained through legal channels. Body snatchers could still find employment selling human remains to medical colleges with no questions asked, and it was not unheard of for well-regarded physicians, teaching institutions, and medical students to be directly involved in so-called *resurrectionist* activities.

Just the month before Morgan's hanging, Dr. P. K Drummond, a distinguished young Ohio State physician, was arrested, along with his medical students, for grave robbing.[23] They set out to steal the body of Samuel Jones, who'd died, interestingly enough, from an overdose of peppermint. They had reason to believe Mr. Jones would not be missed. Unfortunately, they dug up Carlon W. Kelly instead and his relatives were not the careless sort. Dr. Drummond was still languishing in an Ohio jail awaiting trial when Morgan's body was ostensibly removed. An even more famous incident occurred in Chillicothe some years prior. The body of a hanged murderer had been dragged from his grave by a group of medical students, dressed in a nice suit of clothes, and driven upright in an open buggy through the middle of town to a local hotel for a dissecting party. No one was arrested, *"for though everyone knew the body was stolen, and it was a matter of common knowledge who the body snatchers were, no one cared enough about the case to initiate a prosecution."*[24] The next morning the grave was visited by hundreds of locals who carved up the empty coffin and carried away souvenirs.

Separating fact from fiction at this stage has been no easy task. So much of what is true seems far stranger than what could be imagined. If there is anything to be learned from Morgan's story it is that history is not a single truth or even a collection of facts. It is far more complex— an interwoven multi-layering of individual experiences and perspectives *believed* to be true. As the years have passed those who lived through the fall of 1897 and their descendants have refashioned their separate pieces of the historical fabric for a better fit.

No one really knew why John Morgan murdered the Pfost-Greene family. They had no way of making sense of these events short of creating their own mythology. And to that end, John Morgan was transformed into a *"wood's colt,"* a murdering illegitimate son who killed his foster family to pay a $35 lien on his horses. The rest of the mystery, if there ever was any, was never solved, and so it was all but forgotten.

This legacy from the past, along with Morrison's manuscript and myriad newspaper articles, has been collected in these pages. Newspaper coverage did not end with Morgan's execution. The shock waves that tore through Jackson County in 1897 continued to reverberate into the next century as the *"Last Public Hanging in West Virginia"* was revisited on subsequent anniversaries, and aging eye witnesses were rounded up to share their experiences yet again.

It was one such revival—Jim Comstock's series in the *West Virginia Hillbilly*—that inspired Tom T. Hall to write the murder ballad, *"The Last Public Hanging in West Virginia,"* made famous in the late 1960s by those Foggy Mountain Boys, Lester Flatt and Earl Scruggs. Thanks to these men, John Morgan joined ranks with *Frankie and Johnny*, *Tom Dooley* and *Stagger Lee* in popular folk culture.

Such murder ballads were simply another kind of journalism, a grassroots approach to telling the story, and they usually made their appearance right after the murderer was caught or executed. Morgan's first ballad began making the rounds shortly after his death.[23]

> *On the 16th of December*
> *Just at the hour of noon*
> *In Ripley, Jackson County*
> *John Morgan met his doom.*

The most recent retelling of the dead man's tale is a haunting bluegrass ballad by the Grass Stains, which adds its own doleful refrain.[24]

> *There's nowhere to hide*
> *with the hounds on your trail*
> *Lawman's gonna ride*
> *Better say your farewells*
> *The gallows are high*
> *and the road there is long*
> *The end's drawing nigh*
> *Hear the hanging man's song.*

End Notes

[1] *Wheeling Register*, Wheeling, WV, 19 December, 1897.

[2] *Cincinnati Enquirer*, Cincinnati, OH, 16 December, 1897.

[3] *Pittsburgh Post-Gazette*, Pittsburgh, PA, 31 December, 1897.

[4] *The Evening Bulletin*, Maysville, KY, 18 December, 1897.

[5] *Wheeling Register*, 22 December, 1897.

[6] *Parkersburg Sentinel*, Parkersburg, WV, 17 December, 1897.

[7] *The Evening Bulletin*.

[8] *Cincinnati Post*, Cincinnati, OH, 18 January, 1897.

[9] *Pittsburgh Post-Gazette*, Pittsburgh, PA, 18 January, 1897.

[10] *Cincinnati Post*.

[11] *Pittsburgh Post-Gazette,* 29 January, 1897.

[12] *Ibid.*

[13] *Pittsburgh Post-Gazette,* 05 February, 1898.

[14] *Pittsburgh Daily Post,* 05, February, 1898.

[15] *Pittsburgh Post-Gazette,* 05 February, 1898.

[16] *Parkersburg Sentinel,* 21 June, 1898.

[17] House, John A., ***Pioneers of Jackson County,*** an unpublished collection of historical notes donated by his family to the Jackson County Library. Found on www.wvgenweb.org/jackson/jh_jackson.index.html

[18] *Ibid.*

[19] *Ibid.*

[20] *Ibid.*

[21] *Jackson Herald,* Ripley, WV, 25 January, 1901.

[22] *Ibid.*

[23] *Evening Bulletin,* Maysville, KY, 13 November, 1897.

[24] *Cincinnati Enquirer,* 21 November, 1897.

[25] Author's Note: These lyrics are recalled by Sue Allen Nichols of Glenville as sung by her grandmother Beulah Burch Carpenter, whose husband Charles Burch attended the hanging. The words were printed in the *Jackson Star News,* 19 December, 1992. Jesse Adams Garnes from Looneyville, WV claimed authorship and sold his own copies of *The Legend of John Morgan,* with slightly altered wording, for $5 a page. A copy of one of these sheets was later donated to the Jackson County Historical Society.

[26] Lyrics from *The Ballad of John Morgan* are used here with the permission of Matt Poth and the Grass Stains.

BREAKING WITH THE PAST

The New York *Sun* sent a special correspondent to cover the story of John Morgan's execution, and the article produced by this anonymous reporter is by far the most famous coverage of that event. It ran as a human-interest story and took up nearly a full page in the *Sun's* Sunday edition on December 19, 1897. The journalist relentlessly dragged his readers along for the ride as he chronicled the day's events with his rollicking you-are-there style. Local editor Henry Deem later described it as "*an extremely extravagant exaggeration of weird wonders* [which] *left out none of the details.*" One year later, on the anniversary of Morgan's execution, Deem published his colleague's article in the *Jackson Herald*, prefaced by this caveat:[1]

Alleged Report Made Up of a Skillful Blending of Some Unpleasant Facts and MUCH LIBELOUS FICTION After the New York reporter's Imagination Had Been Quickened and His Conscience Deadened by Frequent Potations from the 2-Gallon Jug and the 10-Gallon Keg

An envelope in the state archives, labeled "*November Term, 1897 State of West Virginia,*" contains John Morgan's indictment, his death warrant, and a copy of the *Sun* article which is noted as a "*sensational and an exaggerated account of the execution, in the above styled case.*" While the transcripts of the trial were apparently not considered important enough to be preserved, this marvelous, over-blown narrative was.

The article was written at the end of 1897, a year that changed the appearance and content of American newspapers forever. From its inception, the *Sun* was in the vanguard of progressive journalism during the epic battle over what should be called "*news.*"[2] It was the first newspaper to recognize the growing literacy of the working class and understand that there was profit to be made from writing stories about ordinary people. It catered to the voracious appetite of its readers for the sensational, and was the first paper to cover the seedier side of life—crimes, suicides, divorces, and other scandals. The *Sun* was also the first newspaper to send its reporters out into the field to collect news rather than waiting for someone to bring it to them.

By the second half of 19th century the *Sun* had matured into "*the newspaperman's newspaper,"* its focus on thought-provoking editorials, society pages and lengthy human-interest stories as literary art.₃ And while the account of John Morgan's hanging has enjoyed a little notoriety on the internet under the heading of *"The Last Public Hanging in West Virginia,"* an editorial written a few weeks earlier is known to readers everywhere:

Dear Editor:
I am 8 years old. Some of my little friends say there is no Santa Claus. Papa says, "If you see it in the Sun it's so". Please tell me the truth; is there a Santa Claus?

Virginia O'Hanlon
115 West Ninety-Fifth Street

On the 21ˢᵗ of September 1897, the *Sun's* veteran journalist, Francis Pharcellus Church, famously penned, *"Yes, Virginia, there is a Santa Claus."* It became an overnight sensation and was reprinted every year until the *Sun* closed its doors in 1949. Less than three months after its debut, in the week before Christmas, headlines in the Sunday edition read: *HANGED BEFORE 5000, Ripley Took a Holiday to See John F Morgan Die.*

The *Sun* had already provided detailed coverage of John Morgan's crimes, trial, escape and a factual account of the hanging the day after it took place. *The Shetting Out of John Morgan,* as the lengthier piece came to be called, was something very different. It is a remarkable example of the sensational journalistic color style. At the time, it stood out as an exceptional journalistic *tour de force,* and created its own news. The editor of the *Daily Argus* out of New York remarked that it was, *"one of the best newspaper stories which has appeared in any paper in many a day."*₄

"W-e-l-, w-e-l-l-, the world is shet of John F. Morgan, I reckon"
That's the way they say it in Jackson County. W.Va...
Jackson County, in West Virginia, is not a county where great events happen frequently. Her people are ordinarily law abiding, save, perhaps, in the matter of distilling moonshine, and as anybody down there will admit, it's "no harm to beat the Government out'n a bit of revenue" now and then. Once a year in the town of Ripley, or Jackson Court House, there is a county fair. This fair is the only event that ever draws a crowd to the county seat - hence the event of Thursday, when John F. Morgan was "shet out" was compared in every man's mind with the fair, and every man said:
"Well, now, I reckon, they ain't no two county fairs has ever drawed like this here hangin.'"

To fully appreciate coverage of this nature, it is essential to understand the context in which it was written and the meaning it held for its readers. As amusing as it was meant to be, and indeed, despite its politically incorrectness, it is a pleasure to read even today, the fact remains that it was written with a cavalier superiority that would resonate with northern readers.

From the beginning, a perverse duality dogged those rugged individuals who settled in the western reaches of the Appalachians, and it eventually evolved into the *hillbilly* stereotype. The heroic figure of the courageous and noble mountaineer who, like Morgan's ancestor Jesse Hughes, overcame all odds to tame a wilderness frontier, cast a dark shadow of primitive ignorance, poverty, and violent barbarism. All of this was shamelessly exploited by the press during the decades leading up to the twentieth century. Turn-of-the-century newspapers were filled with tales from what one journalist referred to as *"Murderland,"* where *"surly mountaineers"* engaged in wholesale slaughter—running gun battles among feuding clans, shootouts between revenuers and moonshiners, and fearful uprisings in southern coal fields.[5]

Appalachia was discovered, as far as the reading public was concerned, in the latter half of the 1800s, and was described purely for entertainment purposes as a primitive, somewhat exotic locale—a fascinating place to read about even though no sensible person would want to go there. It was a place apart—*"A Strange Land and Peculiar People"* as one color writer labeled it—with a lifestyle, language, and customs of its own, sometimes charming and picturesque in the extreme, but with a serious undercurrent of danger.[6] Though adjoined to the rest of the United States, inside its boundaries there resided a powerful sense of *"otherness"* that set it apart.[7]

This was the tenor of the times in which the last public hanging in West Virginia took place. The northern press went out of its way to refer to West Virginians as *"mountaineers,"* a term that while not necessarily pejorative, was certainly the antecedent of *hillbilly,* a word that did not appear in print until 1904.[8] The use of the term *mountaineer* conjured up all the necessary elements. When the *Sun's* special correspondent arrived from New York City on a mission to provide his readers back home with entertaining coverage of backwoods justice, he came prepared to put all those images into play. *"It was a scene as strange as any ever witnessed,"* he began, and while there was no barbed malice intended, he went to great lengths to include every caricature of this exotic culture that his readers had come to expect.

At the heart of this archetypal approach is a murderer that is portrayed as "*shiftless...shiftless as well as harmless,*" and other local character descriptions that border on buffoonery. The sheriff's speech, as is his deputies', is that of a rough-hewn backwoods lawman whose quotes are liberally sprinkled with "*aint's*" and "*hear tell's*," when in fact Shinn was a well-educated, well-spoken, contemplative man whose direct quotes in other publications read nothing like this. The entire scene is described in terms of wild carnival misrule whose revelers are careless and indifferent regarding the plight of the condemned:

When morning came Ripley had a "head on"... As the morning wore on the hilarity increased...

"Oh, he's singin' for his precious soul," bawled the Negro once..."he's a-singin' for his precious soul, but I tell you, child he'd better make his peace with Satan, 'cause he's goin' to meet him in jus' about one minute - oh, Eliza Jane, what make you look so plain," and the crowd would shout and roar with laughter and again throw their money at him, forgetting temporarily the miserable wretch in his cell.

The crowd was greater. A wild rumor got around that the Governor had decided to respite Morgan. Then there was real excitement. Men gathered together in groups. They looked ugly and they talked ugly. The women joined them, and they were ugly, too...

It was a scene as strange as any every witnessed. The attention of the crowd was divided between the jail and the fakirs. When the voices of those on the inside were in the ascendant, the crowd would sway toward the jail and listen. When the voices of those on the outside were in the ascendant, the crowd would sway back to them.

The New York reporter rode in one of the wagons with a couple dozen other newspaper men, jotting down all the details and adding embellishments as he went along:

Out into the country the procession spread; the confusion now great and now little, with occasional silence save for the rumbling of the wagons and the hopping up and down of the coffin as the mud holes were struck. Now and again singing was heard, now and again cursing as this horse or that horse slipped, or this rider was crushed against the sides of the wagons. The road to the gallows from the town winds around a bluff, and the gallows became visible about one-quarter of a mile away. As the Sheriff's wagon wheeled around Morgan sang:

The mistakes of my life have been many,
The sins of my heart have been more,
And I scarce can see for weeping,
But I'll knock at the open door.

Arriving on the scene, he began collecting paragraph after paragraph to help describe the chaotic atmosphere around the gallows;

"Last and only true confession of John F. Morgan, the murderer. Here ye are." Or, "Fresh roasted peanuts, five cent a quart."
The gamblers cried: It's all right, good people. It'll be half an hour before they "shet him off" yet. Here's your fortune right here. Don't mind till you get him up there, and the like.

He too was surprised when Mrs. McVay made her ascent up the gallows steps and wrote: *"She walked up the gallows steps and seated herself at the top to watch the proceedings, and cast on her were the envious eyes of every woman in the crowd."*

Regarding the actual moment of execution, however, he had very little to say:

The crowd lingered. Those who could drank rum, and it was not until dark that those who had remained started on their long journey home, satisfied that the world was "shet" of John F. Morgan. The celebration was over.

Considering the bad press West Virginia had already received, and the damning out-of-state coverage that followed the execution, the *Sun's* article seems relatively benign. Yet it carried considerable weight and came to symbolize outside opinion. The scales had reached the tipping point. Once again, West Virginia editors spearheaded the crusade:[9]

If anything were needed to convince the law-makers of West Virginia of the necessity of abolishing public hangings they would but have to read the accounts of the hanging of John Morgan that were telegraphed to the metropolitan papers…

West Virginians had already been deeply shocked a few months before when, in response to Fayetteville's preparations for a triple hanging, the *Pittsburgh Times* let loose the following barrage on the state's *"Bloody Civilization:"*[10]

West Virginia's love of amusement has in it some things which recall the days of Rome, when the gladiators, fighting in the arena, brought crowds of delighted spectators to witness the exhilarating sight of men butchering each other to make a holiday…West Virginia has a fondness for dabbling in warm blood.

And the editor had gone further, commenting on the infamous Hatfield and McCoy feuds, and noting that murder inspired by passionate hatred was far more understandable than the curiosity which inspired West Virginians to gather for a hanging. Then came this parting shot:

West Virginians will go to the Fayetteville hangings just as the country boy will travel miles to the village on circus day to get a glimpse of the elephant and the clown. It is a queer manifestation of curiosity. But it must be borne in mind that life is cheap in that section of the state, and that they kill very easy there.

West Virginia editors were incensed and for a while border warfare was waged in black and white newsprint. Trading tit for tat, the diatribes continued until it became clear in early November that West Virginia was getting ready to conduct its fourth hanging in less than a year.

The state's editors fell glumly silent until descriptions of John Morgan's hanging hit the streets, and then turned their ire on their own politicians, railing against their lack of progress in prohibiting public executions:[11]

It is not conducive to our advancement to have it said that West Virginia, which has made such wonderful strides in her industrial development, and is making her way to her standing among the greatest of her sisters in enlightenment, wealth and general progressiveness, is deficient in this one particular.

West Virginians had no one to blame for bad publicity, they announced, but themselves. It was time for a change and *"men of intelligence"* were expected to lead the way—men like the politically astute James Owen Shinn, who weighed in on the matter shortly after he pulled the lever:[12]

I sincerely hope that the legislature will provide that hangings shall take place in the penitentiary and be witnessed by as few persons as possible. While I believe in capital punishment I do not believe in making a spectacle of it, as was witnessed today.

Although the news coverage following Morgan's execution may have influenced state legislators, several well-intentioned men already believed it was past time for a change. Standing in the barbed-wire enclosure on

the day Morgan was hanged was the
Honorable John Sherman Darst, a
37-year-old miller who had just been
elected to his first term in the House of
Delegates.[13] Darst was deeply disturbed
by the experience, and joining ranks
with like-minded individuals, including
Senator Commodore Dotson from
nearby Wood County, who also attended
the hanging, he was determined to do
something about it. A little over a year
later Darst introduced a bill to ban public
hangings in West Virginia:[14]

Such punishment shall be executed   *The Honorable John Sherman*
within the walls of the West Virginia   *Darst*
penitentiary…and within an enclosure to be prepared for that purpose…so
constructed as to exclude public view…

Governor George Atkinson signed the bill into law on February 18,
1899, and shortly afterwards construction began on a new execution
building at the Moundsville Penitentiary at a cost of $6,000.[15] Former
Fayetteville sheriff's deputy and master scaffold builder Milton Koontz
was called in to design and build a state-of-the-art oak gallows. Koontz
filed a patent for his design, but was too late to reap any sizable rewards.
Hangmen, along with noose and scaffold, were rapidly becoming obsolete.

Between 1899 and 1949, a total of 85 men were hanged in the
Moundsville Penitentiary, beginning with Shep Caldwell, the first man to
be privately hanged at the hands of the state on its new gallows.[16]

The most famous criminal to be hanged in Moundsville was a near-
sighted, pudgy little vacuum salesman with an implausible talent for
romancing the ladies. A West Virginia serial killer named Harry Powers,
styled *"The Killer of Quiet Dell,"* fed the national appetite for sensational
crime stories, easily eclipsing John Morgan's brief notoriety. Along with
news of the crimes came blistering commentary about West Virginia's
"Circus of Justice."[17]

Public hangings continued in other hold-out states until 1936, when
a 22-year-old African-American named Rainey Bethea was hanged for
rape and murder in Owensboro, Kentucky. Hundreds of reporters and

photographers arrived from all over the country to cover what had become a rare occasion, and ended up blasting *"the carnival in Owensboro."*[18] This coverage pushed federal lawmakers into banning *all* public executions in the U. S.[19]

Slowly but surely, death by hanging, whether public or not, was becoming an anachronism. On February 10, 1949, West Virginia became the last state to adopt the electric chair as its only means for carrying out the death penalty.

The penitentiary at Moundsville closed its doors in 1995 after a turbulent history as one of the top ten most violent correctional facilities in the country, known for its appalling conditions, frequent rioting, and prison breaks. Ninety-four

Photograph of Harry Powers, "The Killer of Quiet Dell", also known as Cornelius Pierson, Joe Gildaw and Herman Drenth.

men had been put to death within those walls, all of them hanged except for the nine who were electrocuted following the introduction of the electric chair.[20]

In 1965 West Virginia abolished the death penalty altogether.

End Notes

[1] Reprinted in *The Jackson Herald,* Ripley, WVa, 16 December, 1897; originally ran in the *New York Sun,* New York, NY, 19 November, 1897.

[2] The Library of Congress' Chronicling America essay on the New York Sun retrieved from the world wide web 08-25-2015 http://chroniclingamerica.loc.gov/essays/5/

[3] *Ibid.*

[4] *Middletown Daily Argus,* Middletown, NY, 20 December, 1897.

[5] Anthony Harkins, *Hillbilly: A Cultural History of an American Icon* (Oxford: Oxford University Press, 2004), pp. 7-12.

[6] Will Wallace Harney, "A Strange Land and a Peculiar People," *Appalachian Images in Folk and Popular Culture,* ed. W.K. McNeil (Ann Arbor, MI: UMI Research Press, 1989).

[7] *Ibid.*

[8] Harkins, p. 4.

[9] *Wheeling Daily Intelligencer,* Wheeling, WV, 18 December, 1897.

[10] *Wheeling Intelligencer*, 27 June, 1897

[11] Wheeling Daily Intelligencer, 18 December, 1897.

[12] *Parkersburg Sentinel,* Parkersburg, WV, 17 December, 1897.

[13] *House, John A.*, **Pioneers of Jackson County,** *an unpublished collection of historical notes donated by his family to the Jackson County Library. Found on www.wvgenweb. org/jackson/jh_jackson.index.html*

[14] *Acts of the Legislature of West Virginia 1899*, Charleston: Press Butler Printing, 1899, 12.

[15] Bumgardner, Stan and Kreiser, Christine, "Thy Brother's Blood: Capitol Punishment in West Virginia," *West Virginia Historical Society Quarterly, Vol IX No.4 & Vol X, No.1,* March 1996.

[16] *List of Executed Prisoners Within West Virginia Penitentiary,* Office of Parole & Record Clerk, WV Archives and History, Retrieved from the World Wide Web 08-22-2015, http://www.wvculture.org/history/crime/executions.html

[17] *Cleveland Plain Dealer*, Cleveland, OH, 11 December, 1931.

[18] Ryan, Perry T. *The Last Public Execution in America,* self-published, 1992.

[19] *Ibid.*

[20] Bumgardner, Stan and Kreiser, Christine, "Thy Brother's Blood: Capitol Punishment in West Virginia."

POSTSCRIPT

A few months after John Milhoan committed suicide in 1901 to avoid what he believed to be an inevitable hanging, a recently bereaved local blacksmith began courting a handsome 35-year-old widow. Rebekah Hall Morgan and James Madison Eskew were wed on Wednesday, December 18, 1901, just two days after the 4th anniversary of John's execution. But once again there would be no happily ever after for Rebekah. The two would remain together for less than a year.

On the 14th of November 1902—a month before their first anniversary—Rebekah announced that she was leaving. Trouble had been brewing for some time. Eskew complained that *"Becky"* was *"sullen, morose, and ill-natured"* long before she left him, and that *"for a long time prior"* she had *"refused to cohabit…although she was in good health and had no reason therefore."*[1] Or at least none that Eskew cared to mention when he sued for divorce. Instead, he blamed all their marital discord on John Morgan's son.

Albert Thorn Morgan was only 5 ½ years old when he started school that fall. It had proved to be a very difficult adjustment and word of his infractions had been sent home. Albert, insisted his step-father, who consistently referred to him as *"it"* or *"the child,"* *"had been a very bad boy, and she* [Rebekah] *failed to correct it."* Jim and Rebekah were arguing about the recent incident at school, and he threatened to discipline Albert. *"It had gotten to the point,"* he later explained, *"that the child had to be corrected in order to live with it."*

Rebecca was furious. No man had the right to punish her child! The argument occurred on a Friday just as their neighbor, Rebekah's brother-in-law, Jim Barnett, dropped by for a visit. Rebekah met him at the door and ordered him to load up her household goods. Eskew begged her not to leave him, saying, *"such a thing would be a disgrace."*

I told her that was her home…I did not want her to leave…I gave her no cause to leave. I never in my life mistreated her. I never laid the weight of my hand on her in an angry way.

But Rebekah was in no mood for further discussion or negotiation. *"[S]he said that she would not live with me if I were the last man in the*

Most of the photos taken of Rebekah in later life show her with her
grandchildren and great- grandchildren

world." And then she was gone, back to her parents' home on Poverty
Ridge.

A full divorce was difficult to obtain in West Virginia in those days
and Rebekah had no intention of attempting it. The most common form
of divorce was the so-called *bed and board*—what today might be called a
legal separation.₂ It prevented remarriage, and in theory at least, preserved
the family even though the parties elected to remain apart.

The traditional values of late Victorian society were even less
accommodating than the law itself. Eskew was clearly worried about what
people were going to say. Rebekah on the other hand, having lived four
years as the widow of a hanged triple murderer, may have felt she could
suffer no worse.

After waiting the requisite three years required by law, Eskew applied
for a full divorce based upon Rebecca's desertion. Reuben Shinn was the
county sheriff at the time and his brother served as his deputy. It was in
this capacity that Owen Shinn served the divorce summons on Rebecca
Morgan Eskew.

Rebekah never remarried. After her parents died she remained on
the farm on Poverty Ridge with her brother John. Both mother and son
changed their last names back to Hall.

In 1917, 20-year-old Albert Hall married Pearl White Childress, who

Photo of Albert and Pearl Hall courtesy of the family.

was several years his senior. They set up house keeping in South Charleston and brought Rebekah to live with them.

The following year Albert registered for the draft just as the war was ending. He never served, but his draft card describes him as having dark hair and grey eyes.

Things began well for the new couple, but there would be heartache to come. Albert found steady construction work at the Rollins Chemical Plant and the couple celebrated the births of two children. Sometime during the mid-1930s, things began to go wrong. Perhaps Albert just seemed a bit clumsy—dropping things, stumbling. He might have been moodier than usual, prone to outbursts of temper or fits of depression. But it would not be long before nagging doubts about mood swings and peculiar behaviors gave way to more pressing concerns. And then came the accident.

Albert was part of a paint crew working on the dome of the state capitol when he stumbled and fell from the scaffolding. Fortunately, he didn't fall far, but although he survived, he was unable to return to construction work. This was only the beginning of a downward health spiral and it wasn't long before he was diagnosed with what was then called *Huntington's chorea.* Albert Hall, nee Morgan, had just been given his own death sentence.

At first the family tried to care for him at home, but he eventually had to be hospitalized at the State Hospital for the Insane in Spencer. Albert spent the last year and a half of his life in the asylum where ironically, some 40-odd years before, Dr. Lewis Guthrie had been working when he was called upon to examine John Morgan for signs of insanity.

Albert died in 1942 at the age of 45. Rebekah died three years later at the age of 74. The two are buried side by side in the Fairview Cemetery near the place of Rebekah's birth. Their last names are engraved as *"Morgan-Hall."*

Owen Shinn chose not to run for a second term. The two brothers' farming interests grew and prospered, and two years after the murders they bought nearly half of the Pfost-Greene farm to add to their own acreage. Reuben served two terms as sheriff before handing the reins over to their younger brother John. In 1908 Owen was elected to the West Virginia Senate and it was shortly after this that he and Reuben found themselves at odds over perceived imbalances in their shared office holdings. The rift became so great they could not continue to live and work together.

Late in 1909 Reuben bought out Owen's interest in their farm, and they split the proceeds of their office terms. Owen and his wife Mary bought a 500-acre farm near Point Pleasant, West Virginia, and left Jackson County. The two men who had supported one another so steadfastly over the years began a series of protracted court battles that lasted eight years.

In the meantime, Reuben became president of the Valley Bank, which changed its name to the First National Bank of Ripley, and was a major stockholder in O. J. Morrison's new stores in Charleston and Clarksburg. He ran for the West Virginia Senate in 1920 and later died in his senate office in Charleston.

John Chancey never forgot what happened in the pre-dawn hours of November 3, 1897, but the land healed and so did the resilient Chancey family. They welcomed a new arrival two years later; little Lucy was born when Emily was 48 and John was 55. John began keeping store in a little building across the lane from his house, and in 1914 at the age of 70, he opened the doors to his newly-built premises. It was the perfect retirement plan for this sociable old man. Mary said of her father that, *"he was a man who welcomed everyone:"*

He enjoyed the store more than anything he ever owned because he liked people, and there was always a crowd here to mix with." [3]

The store sold everything from wood-burning stoves to Navy Sweet Snuff and Doctor LeGear's Spavin Remedy. One after another, John's daughters took turns managing the business end of things while he sat on the front porch or by the pot-bellied Burnside stove enjoying his customers. Mary took over the store in 1924, also serving as the community post-mistress. Her father died in 1932, and although the post office officially closed three years later, Mary kept her "*Poppy's*" store open for business until she was 94, long after her trade had gone into serious decline. She never married, claiming that, it *"seemed like I was always needed at home...seemed like everyone was spoken for except me...and pretty soon I was the only one left."* [4]

John Chancey sits in the doorway of his county store in Plum Orchard. Photo courtesy of Bobbi Chancey.

Mary lived to be 103 years old, dying in 1991 in a nursing home in Ravenswood. Her brother-in-law, Charlie Southall, had already set the record as the oldest living resident in Jackson County, although he preceded her in death at the age of 105.

Judge Reese Blizzard served two terms as a United States attorney for the northern district of West Virginia. His reputation for never backing down from a fight made for good copy, and his name had staying power with a press that

Mary Chancey and her brother Billy. Photo courtesy of Bobbi Chancey.

liked to remind readers how the former judge first gained prominence for
facing down not one, but two lynch mobs prior to whatever latest political
coup was being reported.

He wielded considerable weight in resurgent Republican politics
and gained further notoriety one hot summer day during the 1904 State
Republican Convention in Parkersburg. As two major factions fought
for mastery of the delegates, *"he was a veritable blizzard on the floor in the
roughhousing ceremonies that were necessary,"* until he was hurled from the
stage into the orchestra pit and sprained an ankle.[5]

Blizzard resigned in 1910 after eight years as a U. S. Attorney, saying
that he wanted to *"retire to private life",*[6] His purchase of the *Parkersburg
Dispatch News* at public auction began a new chapter in this man's
distinguished career and gave him a bully pulpit from which to exercise
his considerable political power. He continued his law practice a few more
years and he was once fined by a Parkersburg judge for trading punches
with the opposing attorney inside a crowded courtroom.[7]

Reece Blizzard died in 1941, less than a month before the attack on
Pearl Harbor, at the age of 77. His obituary in an Ohio newspaper read:

*Morrison's first Charleston location, circa 1910; Photo courtesy of the
Kanawha County Library*

Reese Blizzard, 77, financier, jurist, editor and harness horse breeder, died today in his home.[8]

Profits from the sale of *The Slaughter of the Pfost-Greene Family*, along with the proceeds from his store in Ripley, enabled O. J. Morrison to expand into Spencer, and in 1910 he opened a new department store in Charleston. By the time he died he owned fifteen stores in West Virginia and Ohio.

His original store in Ripley burned down when a fire swept through the town; then in 1919 and 1920 his Huntington and Charleston department stores were gutted by fire and his inventories were destroyed.[9] Each time Morrison regrouped and rebuilt bigger than ever. The construction of the new Morrison building in Charleston became one of the great wonders of the Capitol Street district as people stopped to watch the high-rise acrobatics of the iron and steel workers as they laid the beams for the new *"skyscraper."*[10]

Morrison died of a heart attack in 1952 at the age of 83. He liked to say that he had been successful after his initial investment in the little country store in Kenna, because he *"worked a little harder and had a little more energy than most people."*[11]

End Notes

[1] *Bill of Complaint of J. M. Eskew against Rebecca C. Eskew*, filed in the circuit court of Jackson County, West Virginia, 18 November, 1902.

[2] Spindel, Donna J. "Women's Legal Rights in West Virginia 1863-1984," *West Virginia History*, Vol 51, 1992, pp. 29-44.

[3] *Charleston Gazette*, Charleston, WV, May 1979.

[4] Audio taped interview with Mary Chancey conducted by Betty Jean Fourney in Jan 1986. (Mary was 97 years old).

[5] *Evening Star*, Washington, D.C., 16 July, 1905.

[6] *Baltimore American*, Baltimore, MD, 06 January, 1910.

[7] *Pittsburgh Daily Post*, Pittsburgh, PA, 11 July, 1911.

[8] *Piqua Daily Call*, Piqua, OH, 10, November, 1941.

[9] *Charleston Daily Mail*, Charleston, WV, 30 October, 1920.

[10] *Charleston Daily Mail*, Charleston, WV, 24 July, 1920.

[11] *Charleston Daily Mail*, Charleston, WV, 12 February, 1952.